DRAWING LINES™

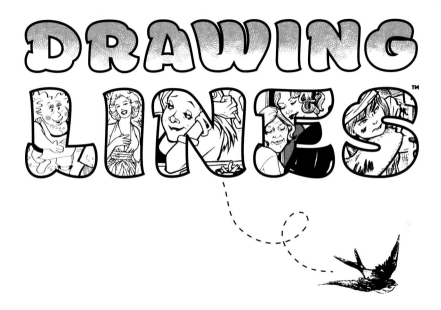

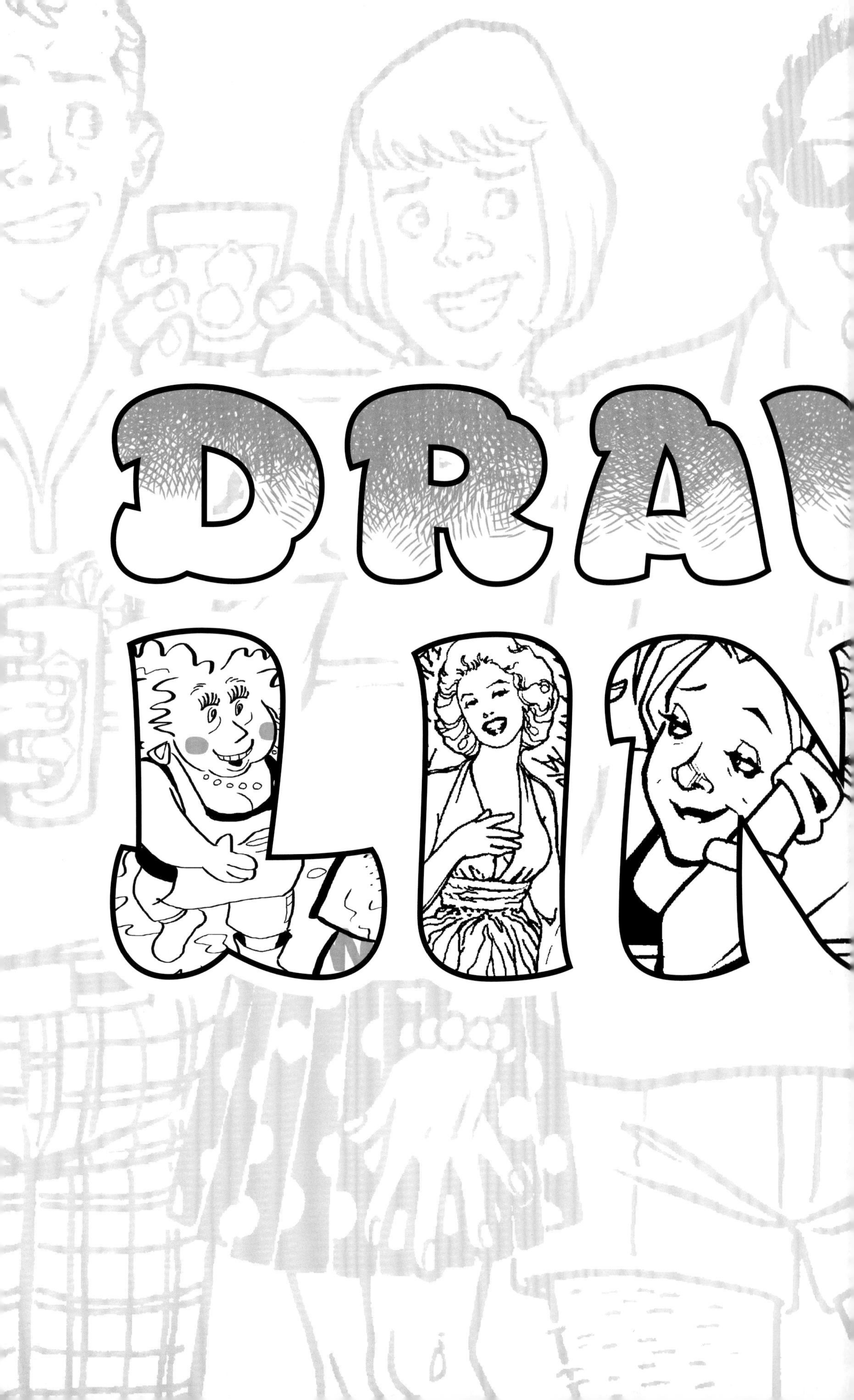

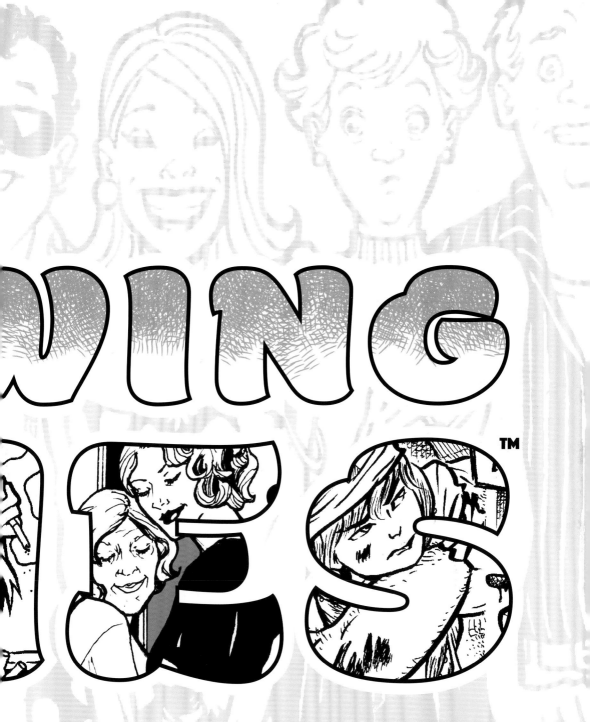

ᴡING
ᴇS ™

AN ANTHOLOGY OF
WOMEN CARTOONISTS

 Dark Horse Books

president & publisher **MIKE RICHARDSON**

original collection editor **DIANA SCHUTZ**   *second edition editor* **DANIEL CHABON**

associate editor **DAVE MARSHALL**   *assistant editors* **CHUCK HOWITT** *and* **KATIE MOODY**

designer **PATRICK SATTERFIELD**   *digital art technician* **ANN GRAY**

published by
DARK HORSE BOOKS
a division of Dark Horse Comics LLC
10956 SE Main Street
Milwaukie, OR 97222

DarkHorse.com

To find a comics shop in your area, visit
comicshoplocator.com

First hardcover edition: December 2020
Ebook ISBN: 978-1-50671-689-3
Hardcover ISBN: 978-1-50671-688-6

10 9 8 7 6 5 4 3 2 1
Printed in China

DRAWING LINES™: AN ANTHOLOGY OF WOMEN CARTOONISTS

Library of Congress Cataloging-in-Publication Data

Title: Drawing lines : an anthology of women cartoonists.
Description: First hardcover edition. | Milwaukie, OR : Dark Horse Comics, 2021. | "Originally published as Sexy Chix in 2006"
Identifiers: LCCN 2020032481 (print) | LCCN 2020032482 (ebook) | ISBN 9781506716886 (hardcover) | ISBN 9781506716893 (ebook other)
Subjects: LCSH: Women--Comic books, strips, etc. | Women cartoonists--United States. | Comic books, strips, etc.
Classification: LCC PN6714 .D74 2020 (print) | LCC PN6714 (ebook) | DDC 741.5/973--dc23
LC record available at https://lccn.loc.gov/2020032481
LC ebook record available at https://lccn.loc.gov/2020032482

CONTENTS

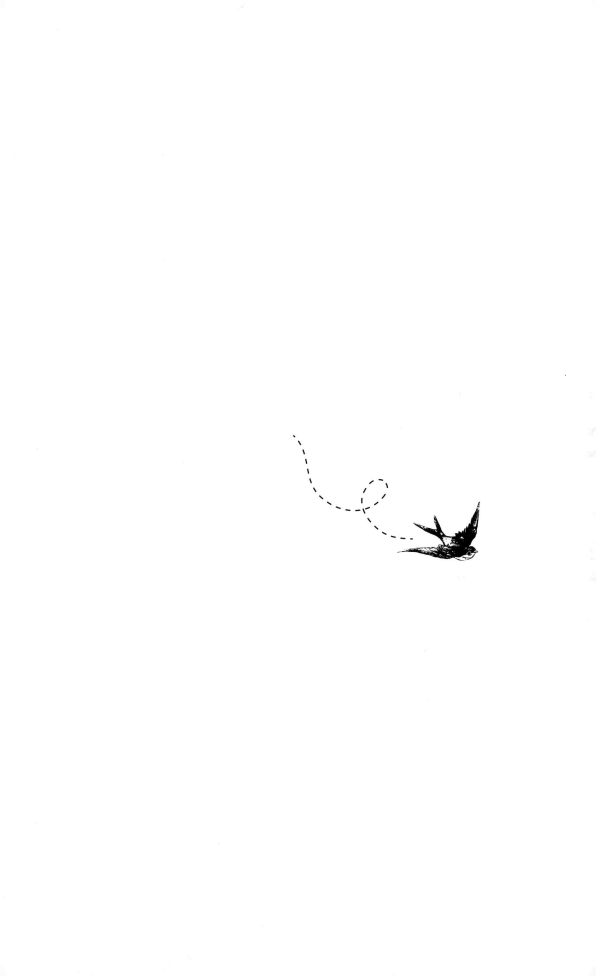

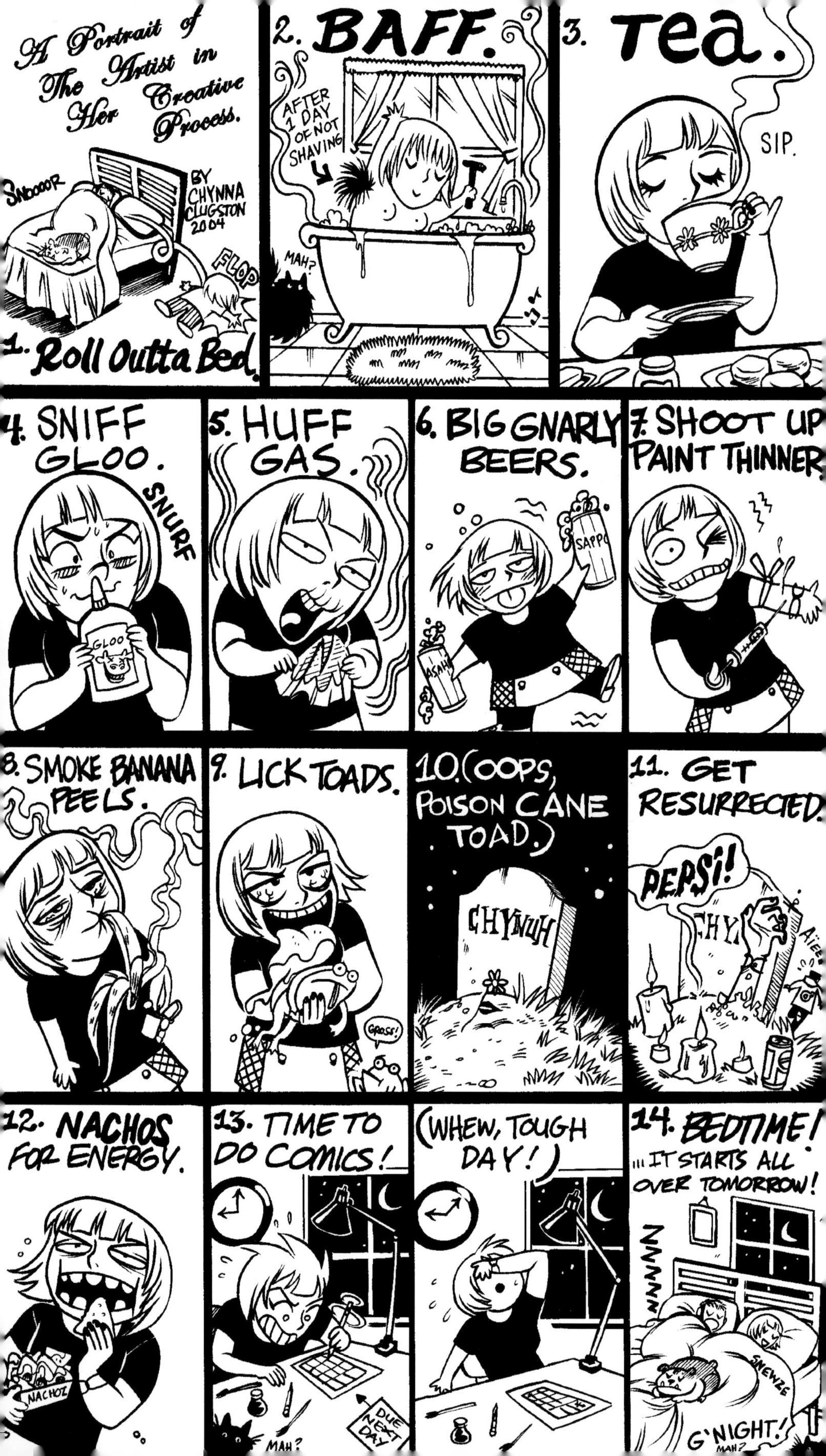
A Portrait of The Artist in Her Creative Process.
BY CHYNNA CLUGSTON 2004
SNOOOOR
FLOP
1. Roll Outta Bed.
2. BAFF.
AFTER 1 DAY OF NOT SHAVING
MAH?
3. Tea.
SIP.
4. SNIFF GLOO.
SNURF
GLOO
5. HUFF GAS.
6. BIG GNARLY BEERS.
SAPPO
ASAH
7. SHOOT UP PAINT THINNER
8. SMOKE BANANA PEELS.
9. LICK TOADS.
GROSS!
10. (OOPS, POISON CANE TOAD.)
CHYNUH
11. GET RESURRECTED.
PEPSI!
12. NACHOS FOR ENERGY.
NACHOZ
13. TIME TO DO COMICS!
DUE NEXT DAY
MAH?
(WHEW, TOUGH DAY!)
14. BEDTIME! ...IT STARTS ALL OVER TOMORROW!
NNNNN
SNEWZE
G'NIGHT!
MAH?

love triangle

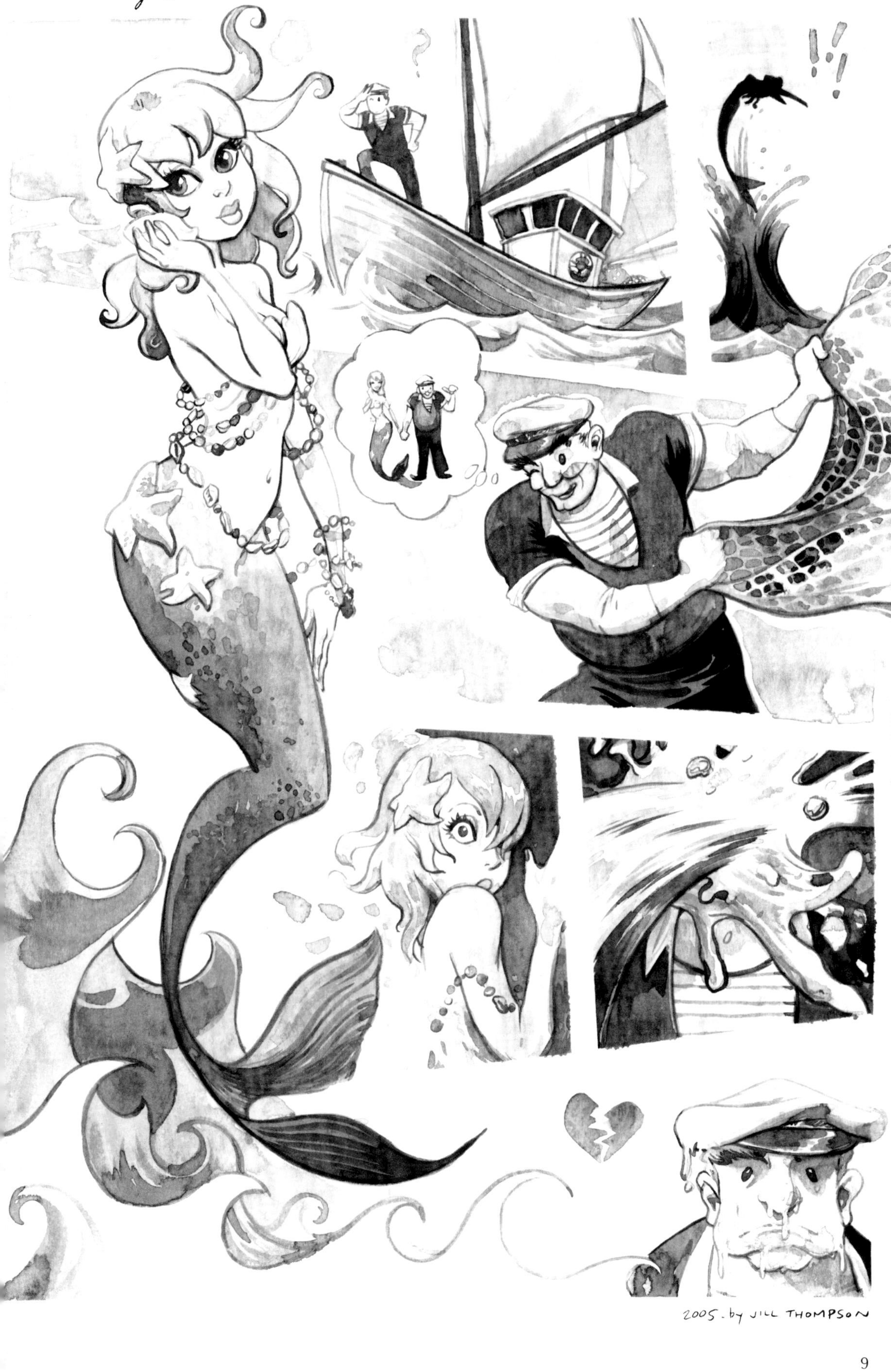
?
!!

2005. by JILL THOMPSON

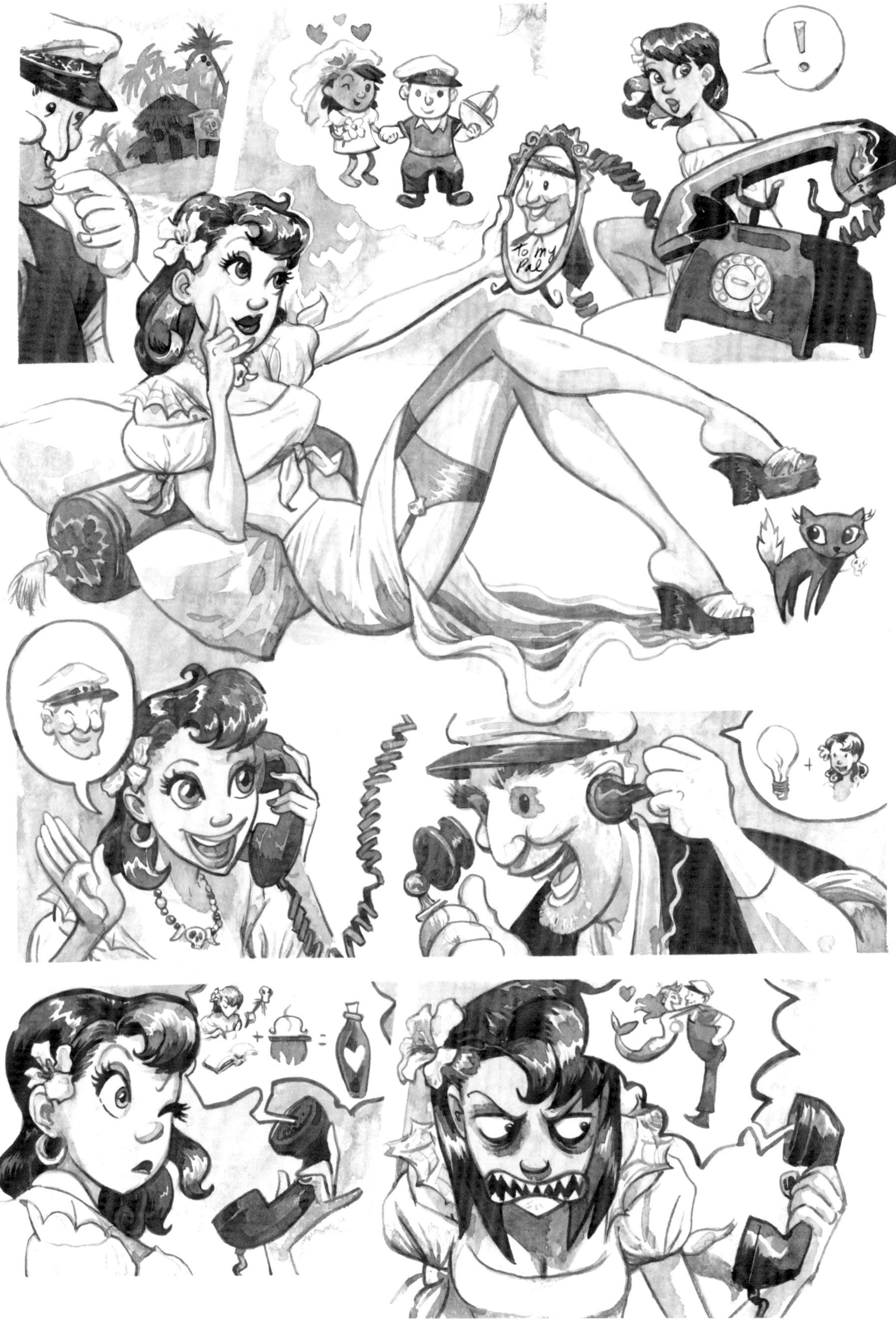
!
To my Pal

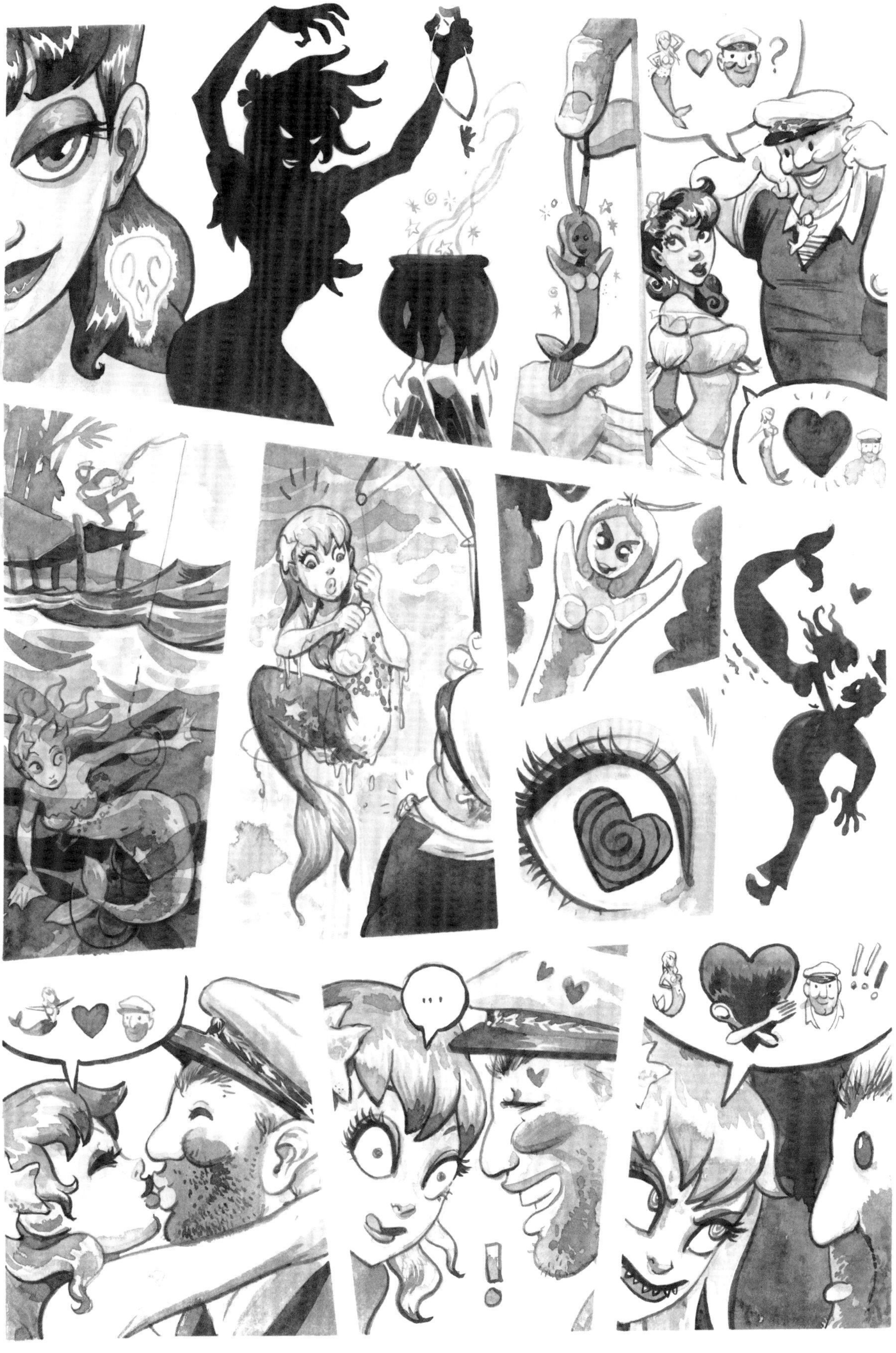
?
...
!
!!!

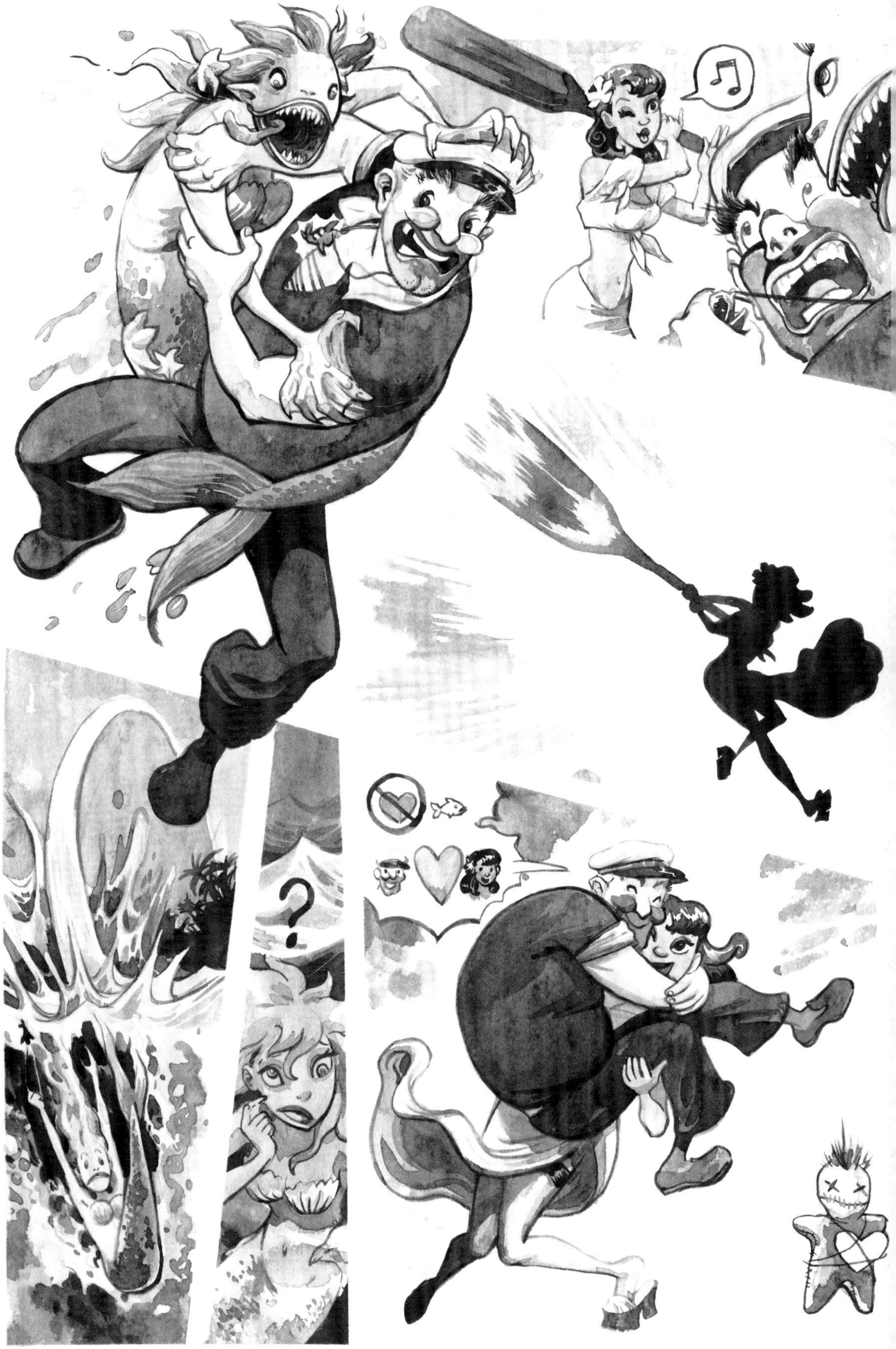

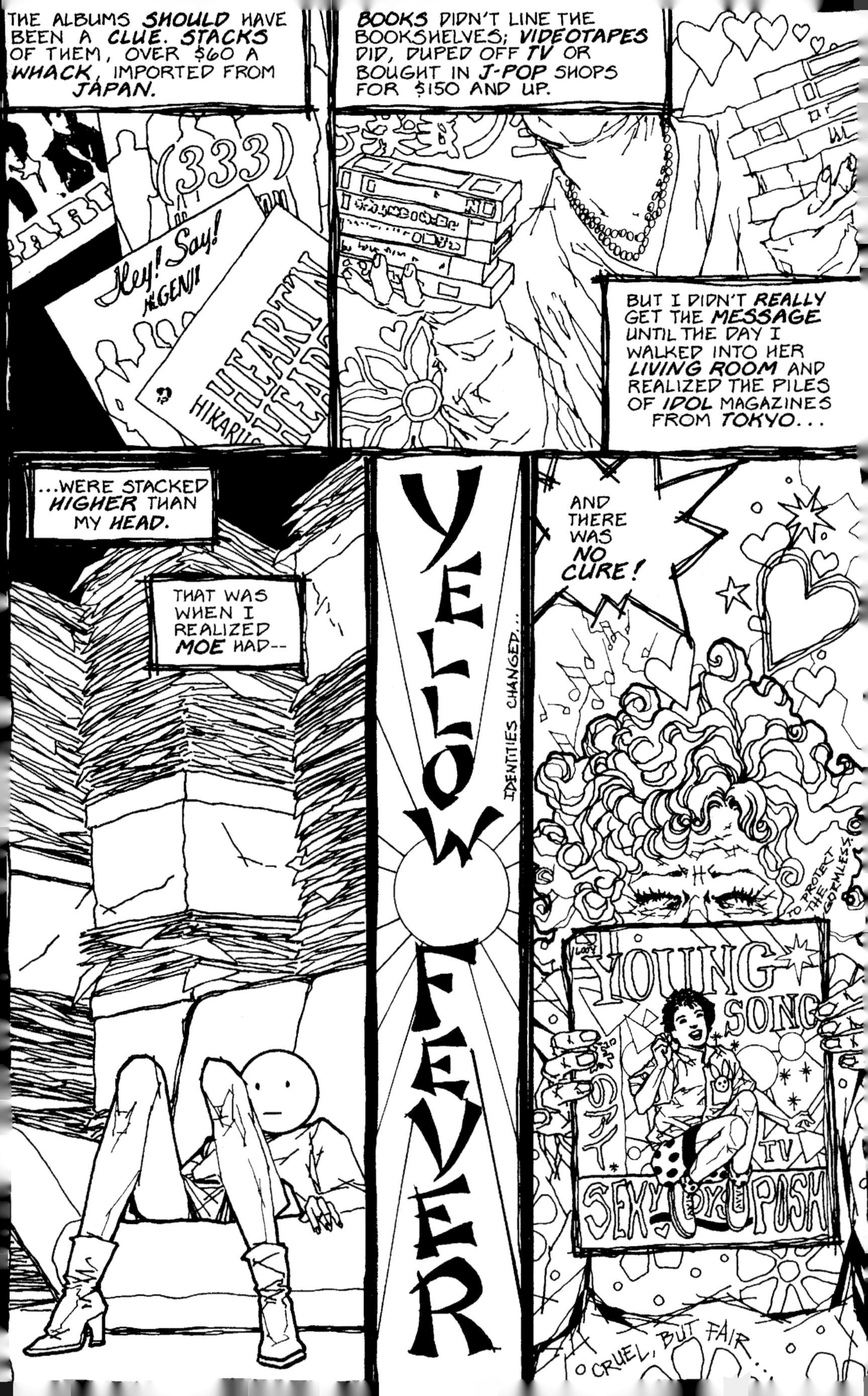
THE ALBUMS SHOULD HAVE BEEN A CLUE. STACKS OF THEM, OVER $60 A WHACK, IMPORTED FROM JAPAN.
BOOKS DIDN'T LINE THE BOOKSHELVES; VIDEOTAPES DID, DUPED OFF TV OR BOUGHT IN J-POP SHOPS FOR $150 AND UP.
BUT I DIDN'T REALLY GET THE MESSAGE UNTIL THE DAY I WALKED INTO HER LIVING ROOM AND REALIZED THE PILES OF IDOL MAGAZINES FROM TOKYO...
...WERE STACKED HIGHER THAN MY HEAD.
THAT WAS WHEN I REALIZED MOE HAD--
YELLOW FEVER
IDENTITIES CHANGED...
AND THERE WAS NO CURE!
TO PROTECT THE GORMLESS.
YOUNG SONG
SEXY BOYS POSH
TV
CRUEL, BUT FAIR...
(333)
Hey! Say!
GENJI
HEARTY HEADS
HIKARU

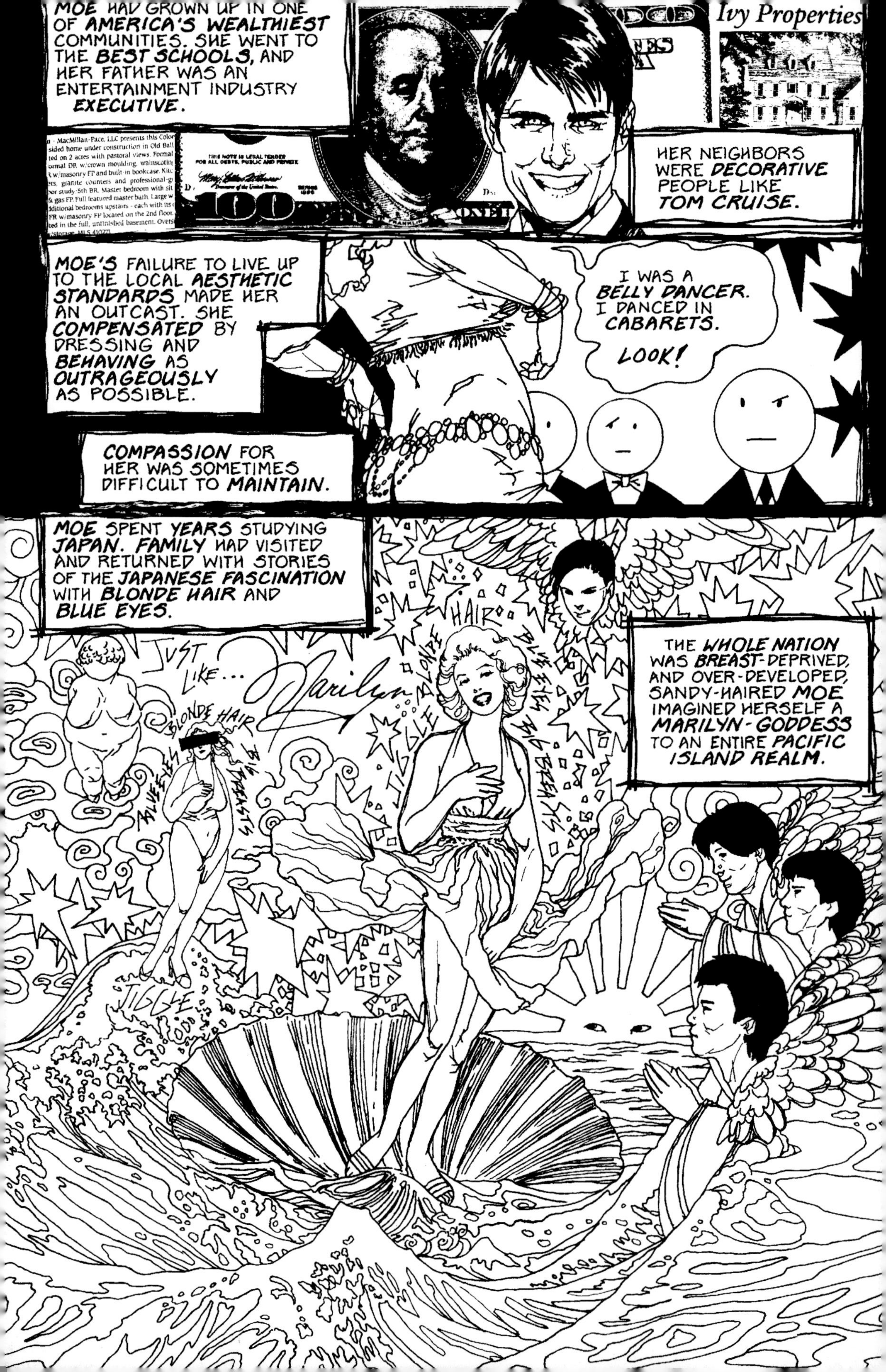

MOE HAD GROWN UP IN ONE OF AMERICA'S WEALTHIEST COMMUNITIES. SHE WENT TO THE BEST SCHOOLS, AND HER FATHER WAS AN ENTERTAINMENT INDUSTRY EXECUTIVE.
Ivy Properties
HER NEIGHBORS WERE DECORATIVE PEOPLE LIKE TOM CRUISE.
MOE'S FAILURE TO LIVE UP TO THE LOCAL AESTHETIC STANDARDS MADE HER AN OUTCAST. SHE COMPENSATED BY DRESSING AND BEHAVING AS OUTRAGEOUSLY AS POSSIBLE.
I WAS A BELLY DANCER. I DANCED IN CABARETS.
LOOK!
COMPASSION FOR HER WAS SOMETIMES DIFFICULT TO MAINTAIN.
MOE SPENT YEARS STUDYING JAPAN. FAMILY HAD VISITED AND RETURNED WITH STORIES OF THE JAPANESE FASCINATION WITH BLONDE HAIR AND BLUE EYES.
JUST LIKE...
Marilyn
BLONDE HAIR
BLUE EYES
BIG BREASTS
BLONDE HAIR
BLUE EYES
BIG BREASTS
JIGGLE
JIGGLE
THE WHOLE NATION WAS BREAST-DEPRIVED, AND OVER-DEVELOPED, SANDY-HAIRED MOE IMAGINED HERSELF A MARILYN-GODDESS TO AN ENTIRE PACIFIC ISLAND REALM.

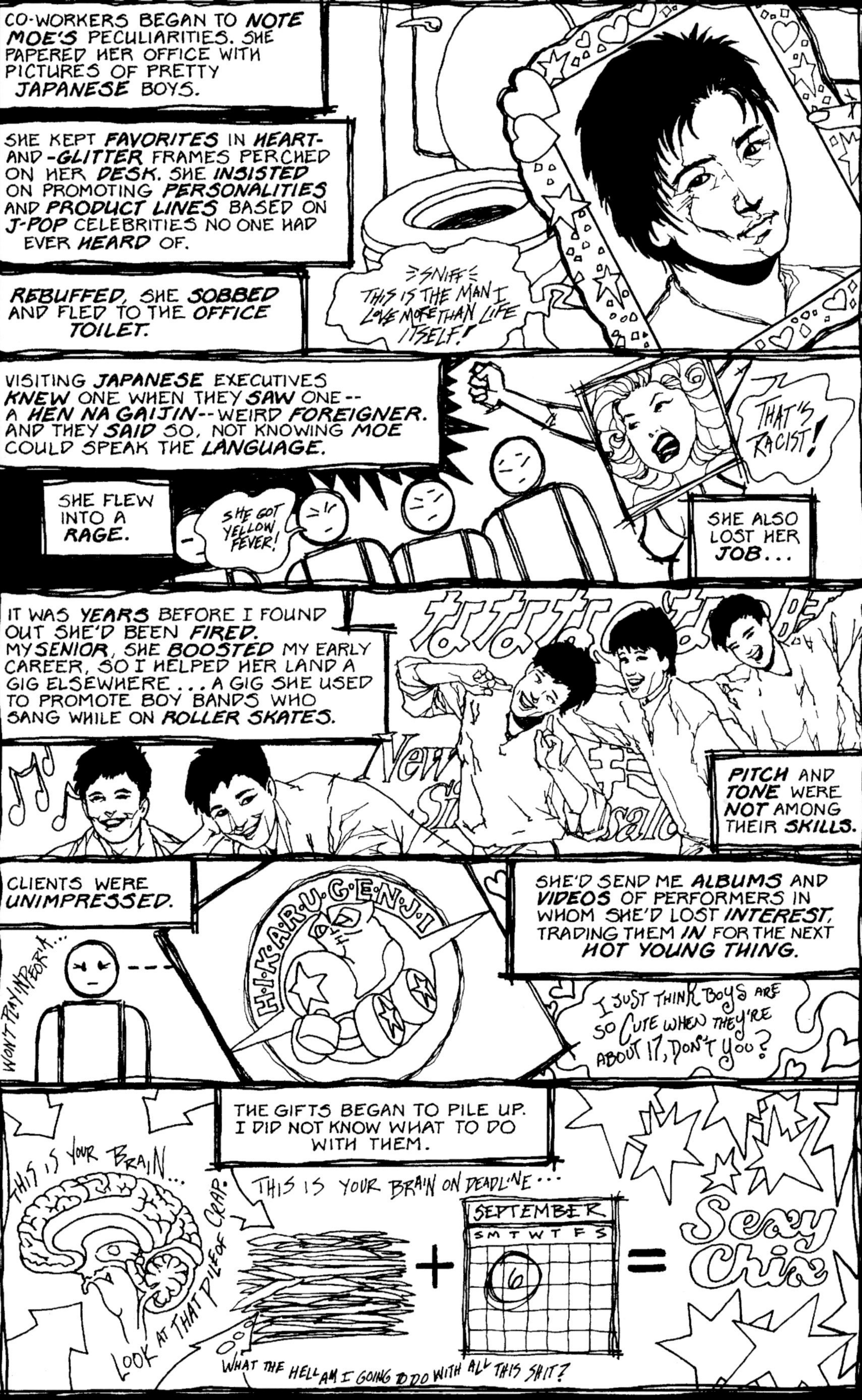

CO-WORKERS BEGAN TO NOTE MOE'S PECULIARITIES. SHE PAPERED HER OFFICE WITH PICTURES OF PRETTY JAPANESE BOYS.
SHE KEPT FAVORITES IN HEART-AND-GLITTER FRAMES PERCHED ON HER DESK. SHE INSISTED ON PROMOTING PERSONALITIES AND PRODUCT LINES BASED ON J-POP CELEBRITIES NO ONE HAD EVER HEARD OF.
REBUFFED, SHE SOBBED AND FLED TO THE OFFICE TOILET.
SNIFF
THIS IS THE MAN I LOVE MORE THAN LIFE ITSELF!
VISITING JAPANESE EXECUTIVES KNEW ONE WHEN THEY SAW ONE -- A HEN NA GAIJIN -- WEIRD FOREIGNER. AND THEY SAID SO, NOT KNOWING MOE COULD SPEAK THE LANGUAGE.
THAT'S RACIST!
SHE FLEW INTO A RAGE.
SHE GOT YELLOW FEVER!
SHE ALSO LOST HER JOB...
IT WAS YEARS BEFORE I FOUND OUT SHE'D BEEN FIRED. MY SENIOR, SHE BOOSTED MY EARLY CAREER, SO I HELPED HER LAND A GIG ELSEWHERE . . . A GIG SHE USED TO PROMOTE BOY BANDS WHO SANG WHILE ON ROLLER SKATES.
PITCH AND TONE WERE NOT AMONG THEIR SKILLS.
CLIENTS WERE UNIMPRESSED.
WON'T PLAY IN PEORIA...
H·I·K·A·R·U·G·E·N·J·I
SHE'D SEND ME ALBUMS AND VIDEOS OF PERFORMERS IN WHOM SHE'D LOST INTEREST, TRADING THEM IN FOR THE NEXT HOT YOUNG THING.
I JUST THINK BOYS ARE SO CUTE WHEN THEY'RE ABOUT 17, DON'T YOU?
THE GIFTS BEGAN TO PILE UP. I DID NOT KNOW WHAT TO DO WITH THEM.
THIS IS YOUR BRAIN...
THIS IS YOUR BRAIN ON DEADLINE...
LOOK AT THAT PILE OF CRAP.
SEPTEMBER
S M T W T F S
6
Sexy Chix
WHAT THE HELL AM I GOING TO DO WITH ALL THIS SHIT?

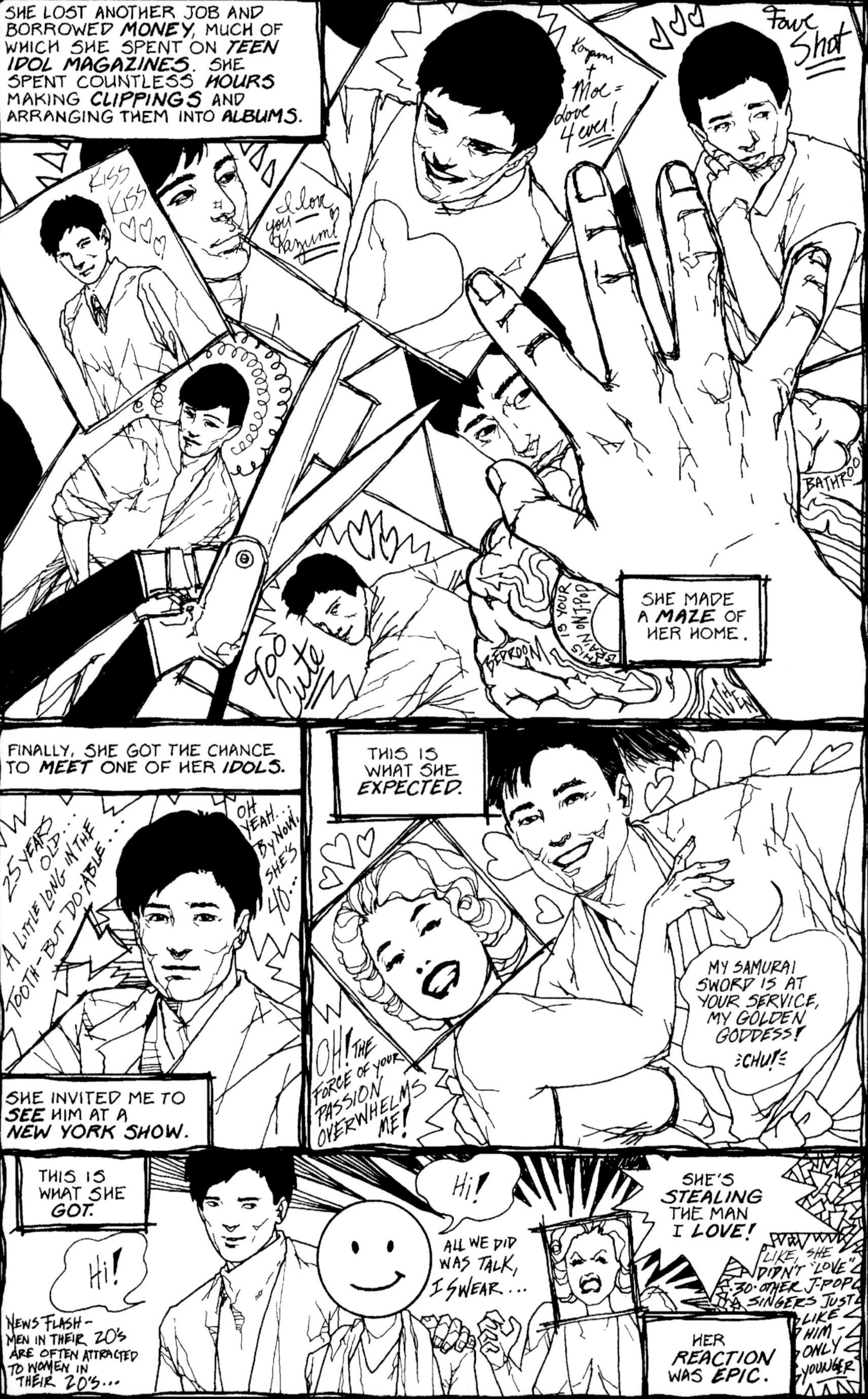

SHE LOST ANOTHER JOB AND BORROWED MONEY, MUCH OF WHICH SHE SPENT ON TEEN IDOL MAGAZINES. SHE SPENT COUNTLESS HOURS MAKING CLIPPINGS AND ARRANGING THEM INTO ALBUMS.
Kazumi + Moe = love 4 ever!
Fave Shot
KISS KISS
I love you Kazumi
Too Cute
BATHROOM
BEDROOM
IS YOUR BRAIN ON J-POP
SHE MADE A MAZE OF HER HOME.
FINALLY, SHE GOT THE CHANCE TO MEET ONE OF HER IDOLS.
25 YEARS OLD... A LITTLE LONG IN THE TOOTH - BUT DO-ABLE...
OH YEAH... BY NOW, SHE'S 40...
SHE INVITED ME TO SEE HIM AT A NEW YORK SHOW.
THIS IS WHAT SHE EXPECTED.
OH! THE FORCE OF YOUR PASSION OVERWHELMS ME!
MY SAMURAI SWORD IS AT YOUR SERVICE, MY GOLDEN GODDESS!
CHU!
THIS IS WHAT SHE GOT.
Hi!
Hi!
ALL WE DID WAS TALK, I SWEAR...
NEWS FLASH - MEN IN THEIR 20'S ARE OFTEN ATTRACTED TO WOMEN IN THEIR 20'S...
SHE'S STEALING THE MAN I LOVE!
LIKE, SHE DIDN'T "LOVE" 30 OTHER J-POP SINGERS JUST LIKE HIM - ONLY YOUNGER
HER REACTION WAS EPIC.

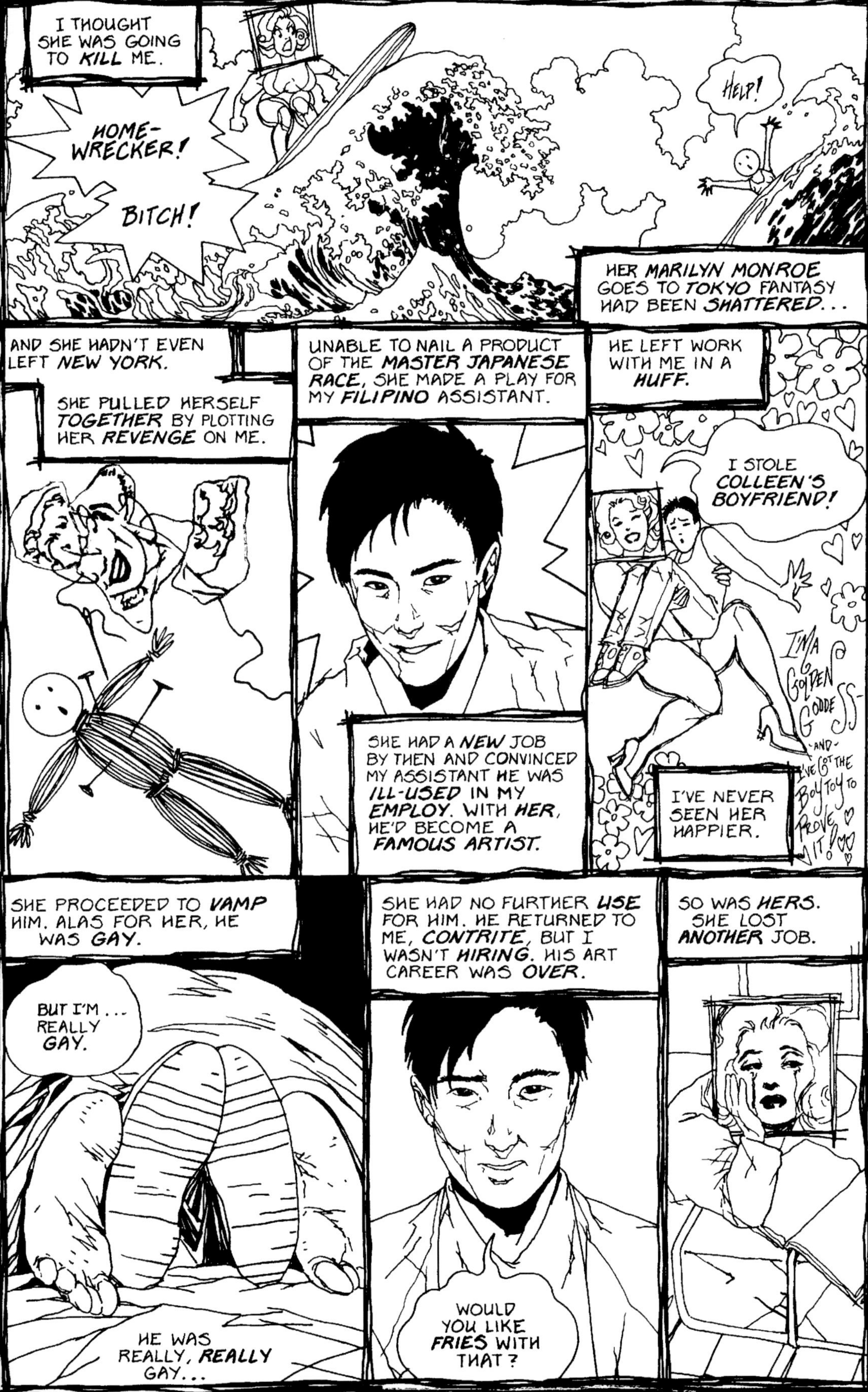

I THOUGHT SHE WAS GOING TO KILL ME.
HOME-WRECKER!
BITCH!
HELP!
HER MARILYN MONROE GOES TO TOKYO FANTASY HAD BEEN SHATTERED...
AND SHE HADN'T EVEN LEFT NEW YORK.
SHE PULLED HERSELF TOGETHER BY PLOTTING HER REVENGE ON ME.
UNABLE TO NAIL A PRODUCT OF THE MASTER JAPANESE RACE, SHE MADE A PLAY FOR MY FILIPINO ASSISTANT.
SHE HAD A NEW JOB BY THEN AND CONVINCED MY ASSISTANT HE WAS ILL-USED IN MY EMPLOY. WITH HER, HE'D BECOME A FAMOUS ARTIST.
HE LEFT WORK WITH ME IN A HUFF.
I STOLE COLLEEN'S BOYFRIEND!
I'M A GOLDEN GODDESS -AND- I'VE GOT THE BOY TOY TO PROVE IT!
I'VE NEVER SEEN HER HAPPIER.
SHE PROCEEDED TO VAMP HIM. ALAS FOR HER, HE WAS GAY.
BUT I'M... REALLY GAY.
HE WAS REALLY, REALLY GAY...
SHE HAD NO FURTHER USE FOR HIM. HE RETURNED TO ME, CONTRITE, BUT I WASN'T HIRING. HIS ART CAREER WAS OVER.
WOULD YOU LIKE FRIES WITH THAT?
SO WAS HERS. SHE LOST ANOTHER JOB.

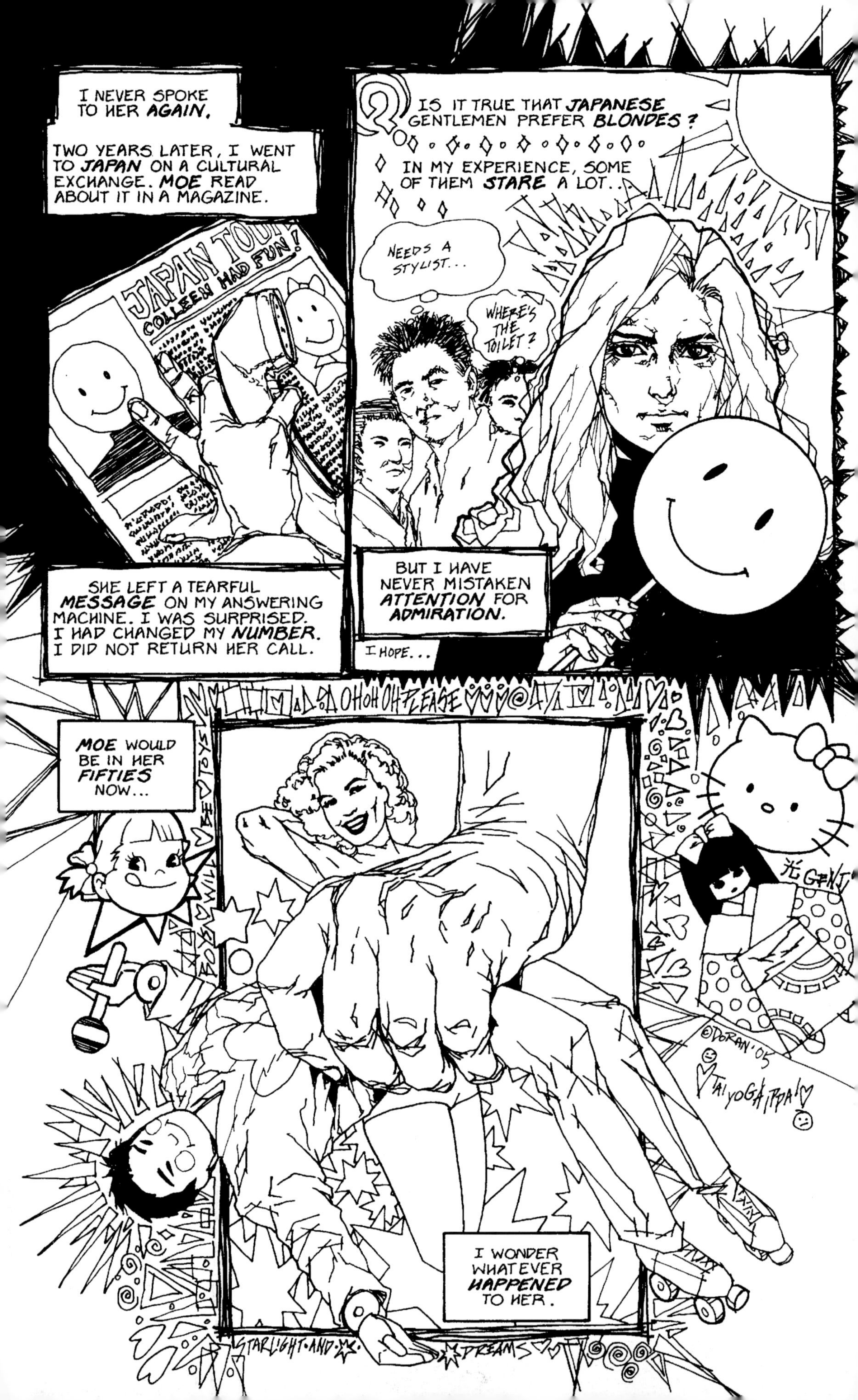
I NEVER SPOKE TO HER AGAIN.
TWO YEARS LATER, I WENT TO JAPAN ON A CULTURAL EXCHANGE. MOE READ ABOUT IT IN A MAGAZINE.
JAPAN TOUR!
COLLEEN HAD FUN!
IS IT TRUE THAT JAPANESE GENTLEMEN PREFER BLONDES?
IN MY EXPERIENCE, SOME OF THEM STARE A LOT...
NEEDS A STYLIST...
WHERE'S THE TOILET?
SHE LEFT A TEARFUL MESSAGE ON MY ANSWERING MACHINE. I WAS SURPRISED. I HAD CHANGED MY NUMBER. I DID NOT RETURN HER CALL.
BUT I HAVE NEVER MISTAKEN ATTENTION FOR ADMIRATION.
I HOPE...
OHOHOHPLEASE
MOE WOULD BE IN HER FIFTIES NOW...
I WONDER WHATEVER HAPPENED TO HER.
©DORAN '05
STARLIGHT AND DREAMS

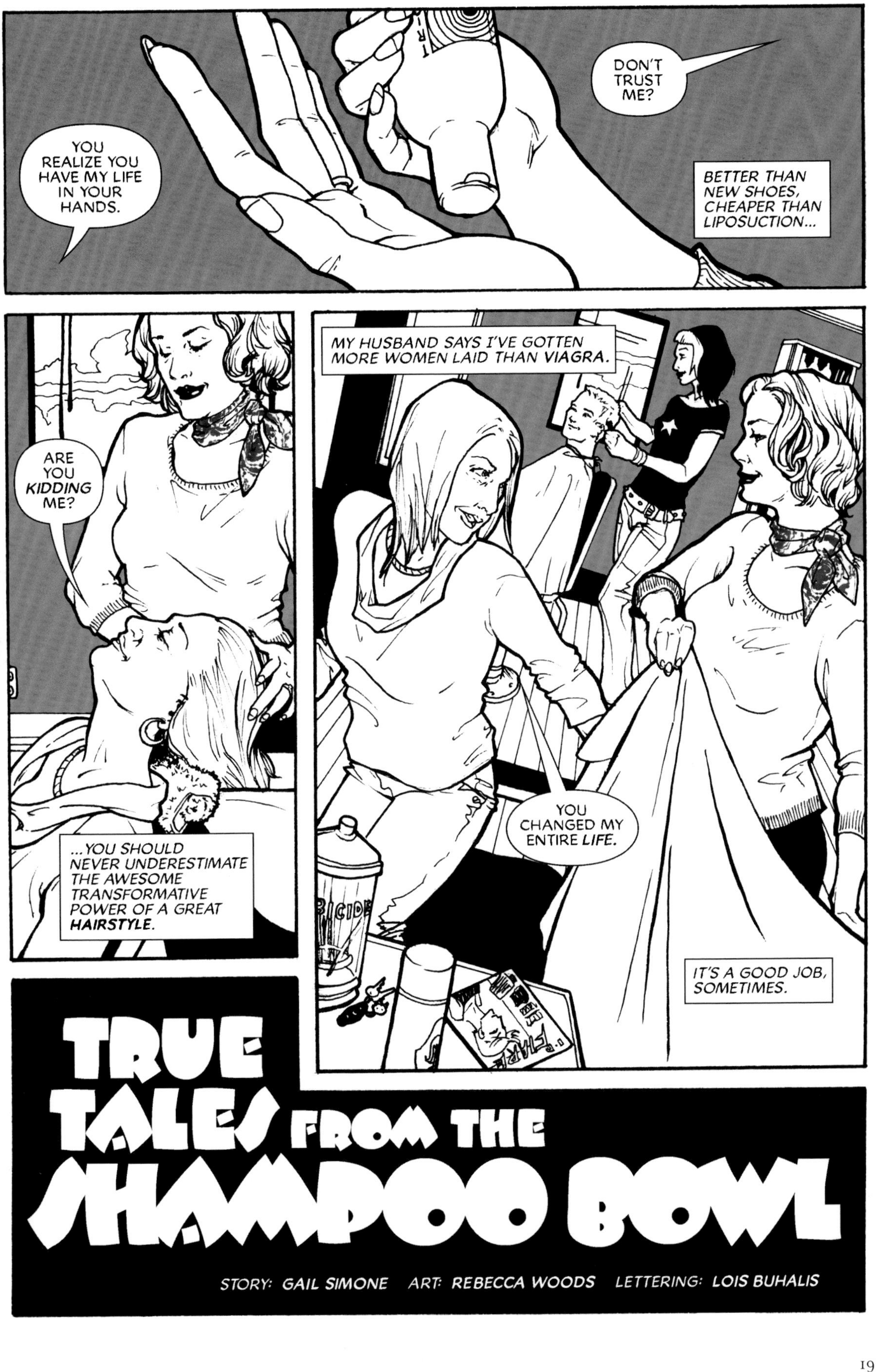
YOU REALIZE YOU HAVE MY LIFE IN YOUR HANDS.
DON'T TRUST ME?
BETTER THAN NEW SHOES, CHEAPER THAN LIPOSUCTION...
ARE YOU KIDDING ME?
...YOU SHOULD NEVER UNDERESTIMATE THE AWESOME TRANSFORMATIVE POWER OF A GREAT HAIRSTYLE.
MY HUSBAND SAYS I'VE GOTTEN MORE WOMEN LAID THAN VIAGRA.
YOU CHANGED MY ENTIRE LIFE.
IT'S A GOOD JOB, SOMETIMES.
TRUE TALES FROM THE SHAMPOO BOWL
STORY: GAIL SIMONE ART: REBECCA WOODS LETTERING: LOIS BUHALIS

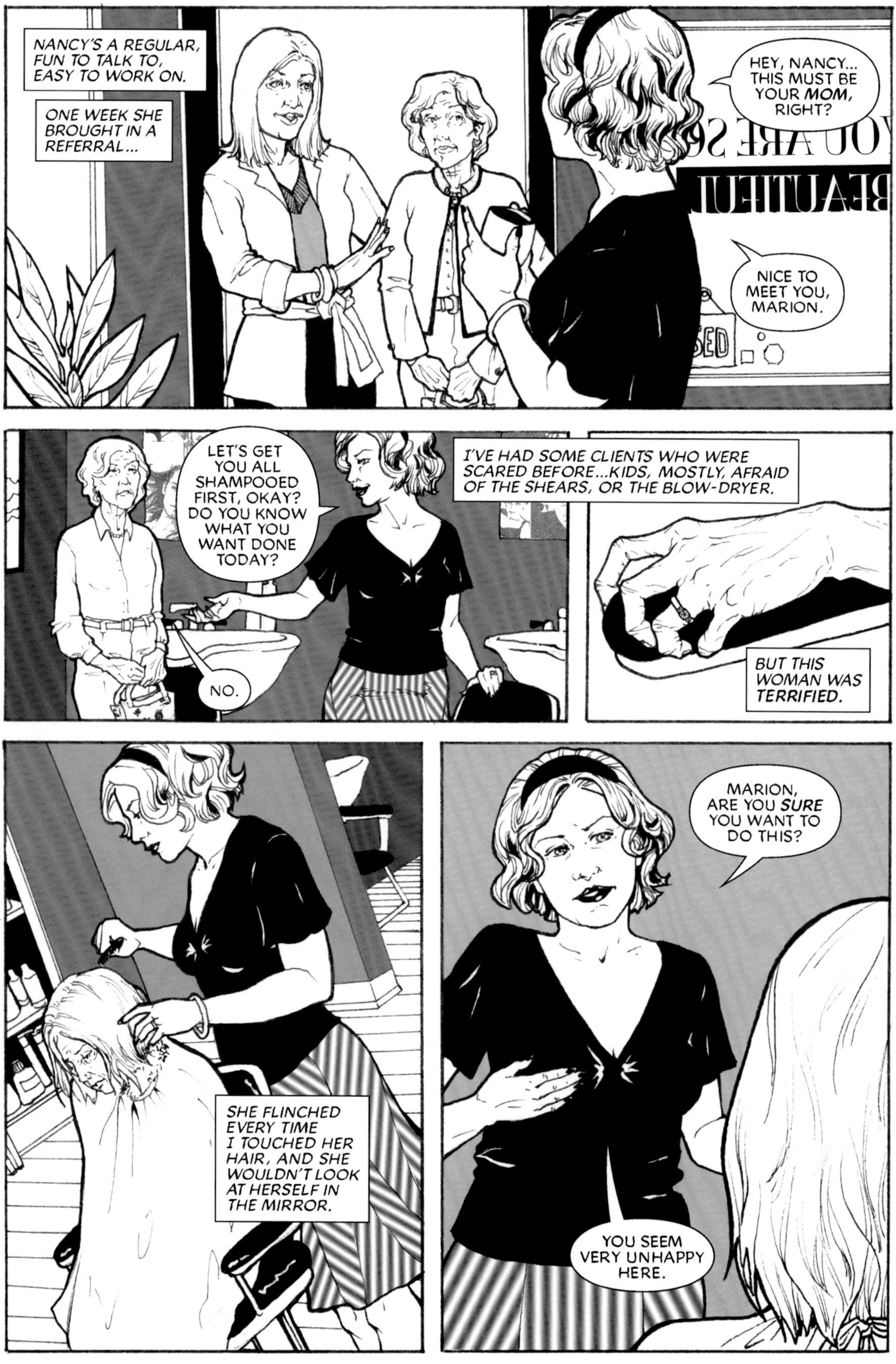
NANCY'S A REGULAR, FUN TO TALK TO, EASY TO WORK ON.
ONE WEEK SHE BROUGHT IN A REFERRAL...
HEY, NANCY... THIS MUST BE YOUR *MOM*, RIGHT?
YOU ARE SO BEAUTIFUL
NICE TO MEET YOU, MARION.
LET'S GET YOU ALL SHAMPOOED FIRST, OKAY? DO YOU KNOW WHAT YOU WANT DONE TODAY?
NO.
I'VE HAD SOME CLIENTS WHO WERE SCARED BEFORE...KIDS, MOSTLY, AFRAID OF THE SHEARS, OR THE BLOW-DRYER.
BUT THIS WOMAN WAS *TERRIFIED.*
SHE FLINCHED EVERY TIME I TOUCHED HER HAIR, AND SHE WOULDN'T LOOK AT HERSELF IN THE MIRROR.
MARION, ARE YOU *SURE* YOU WANT TO DO THIS?
YOU SEEM VERY UNHAPPY HERE.

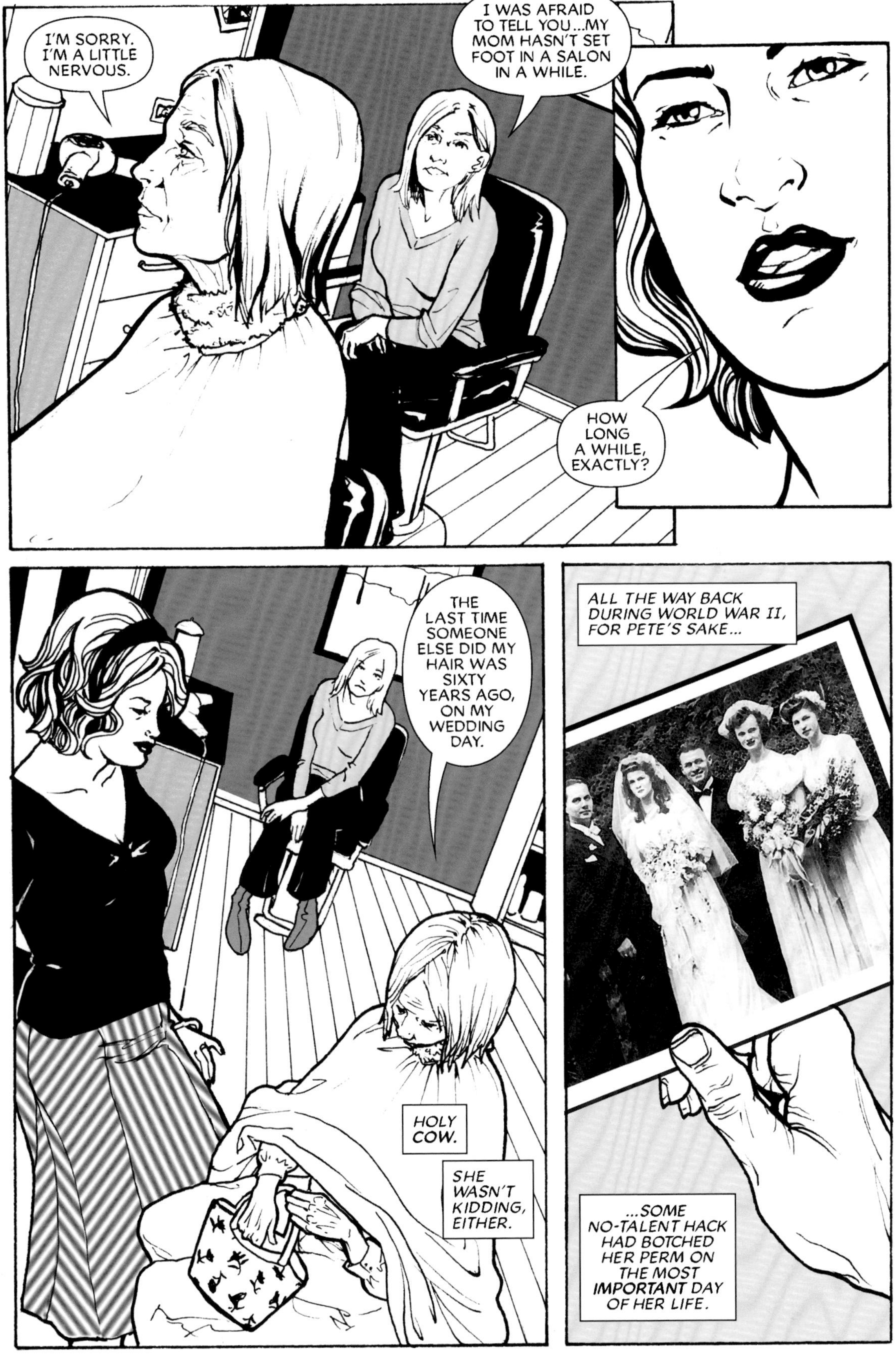
I'M SORRY. I'M A LITTLE NERVOUS.
I WAS AFRAID TO TELL YOU...MY MOM HASN'T SET FOOT IN A SALON IN A WHILE.
HOW LONG A WHILE, EXACTLY?
THE LAST TIME SOMEONE ELSE DID MY HAIR WAS SIXTY YEARS AGO, ON MY WEDDING DAY.
HOLY COW.
SHE WASN'T KIDDING, EITHER.
ALL THE WAY BACK DURING WORLD WAR II, FOR PETE'S SAKE...
...SOME NO-TALENT HACK HAD BOTCHED HER PERM ON THE MOST IMPORTANT DAY OF HER LIFE.

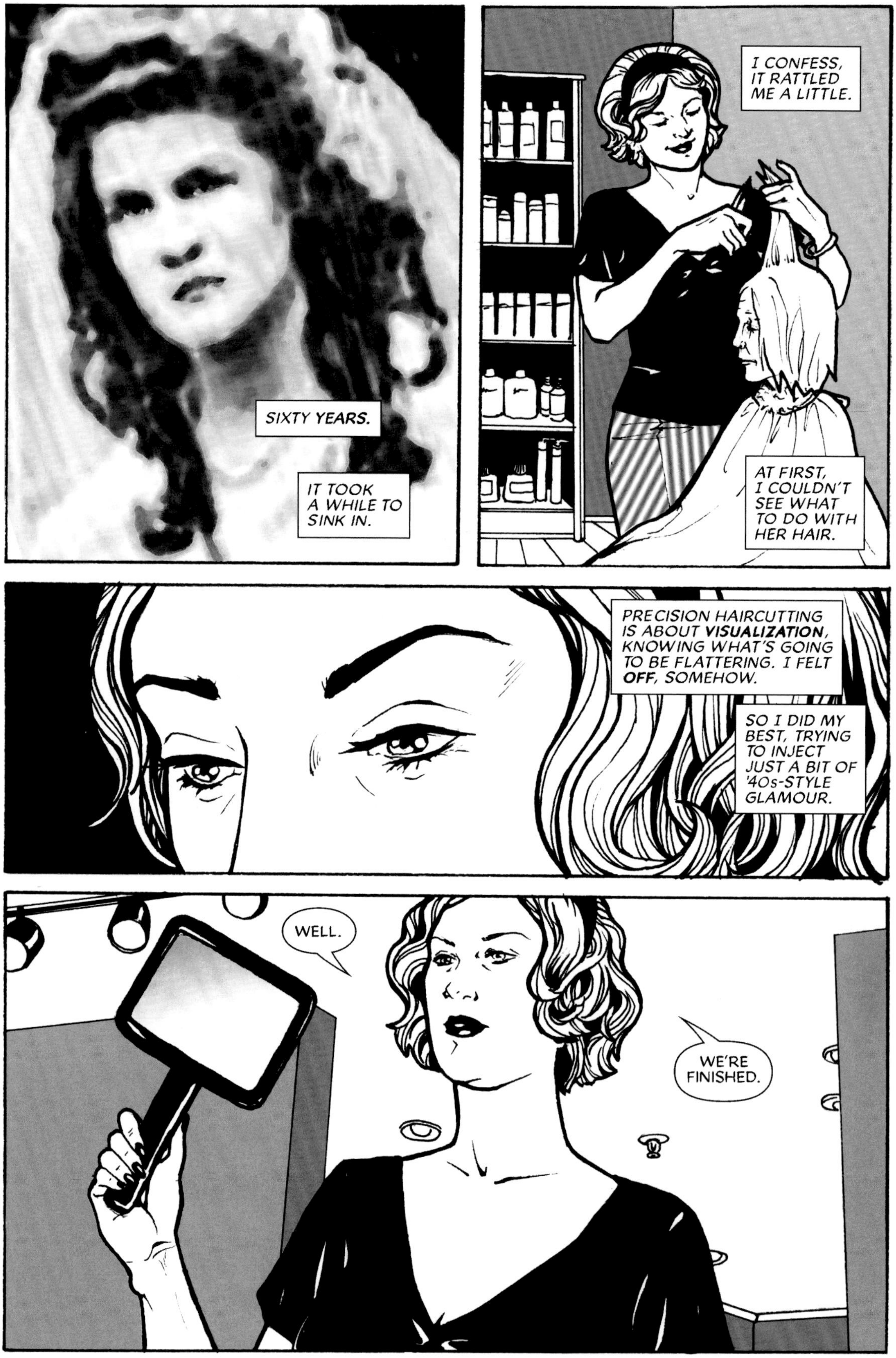
SIXTY YEARS.
IT TOOK A WHILE TO SINK IN.
I CONFESS, IT RATTLED ME A LITTLE.
AT FIRST, I COULDN'T SEE WHAT TO DO WITH HER HAIR.
PRECISION HAIRCUTTING IS ABOUT VISUALIZATION, KNOWING WHAT'S GOING TO BE FLATTERING. I FELT OFF, SOMEHOW.
SO I DID MY BEST, TRYING TO INJECT JUST A BIT OF '40s-STYLE GLAMOUR.
WELL.
WE'RE FINISHED.

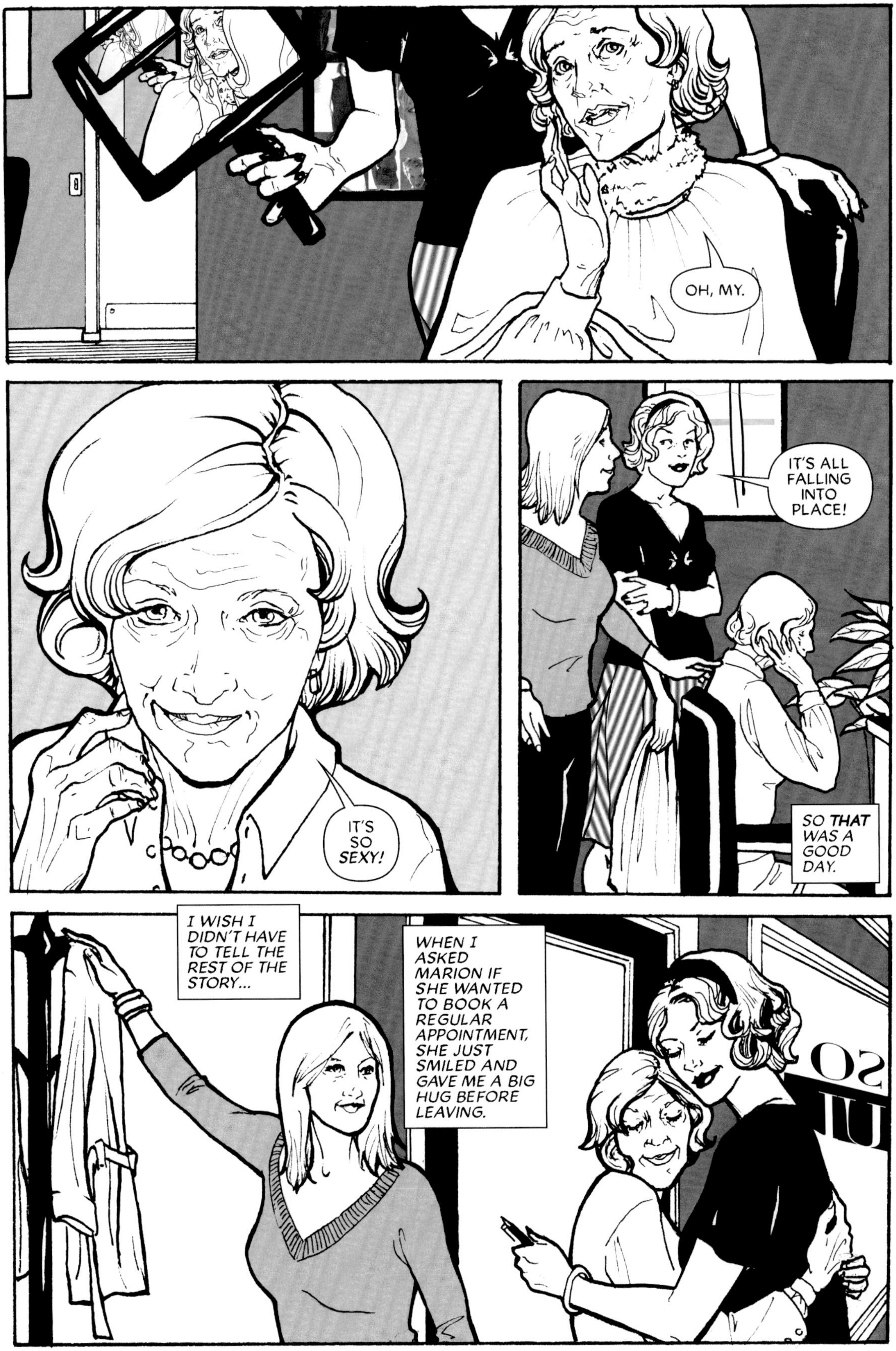
OH, MY.
IT'S SO SEXY!
IT'S ALL FALLING INTO PLACE!
SO THAT WAS A GOOD DAY.
I WISH I DIDN'T HAVE TO TELL THE REST OF THE STORY...
WHEN I ASKED MARION IF SHE WANTED TO BOOK A REGULAR APPOINTMENT, SHE JUST SMILED AND GAVE ME A BIG HUG BEFORE LEAVING.

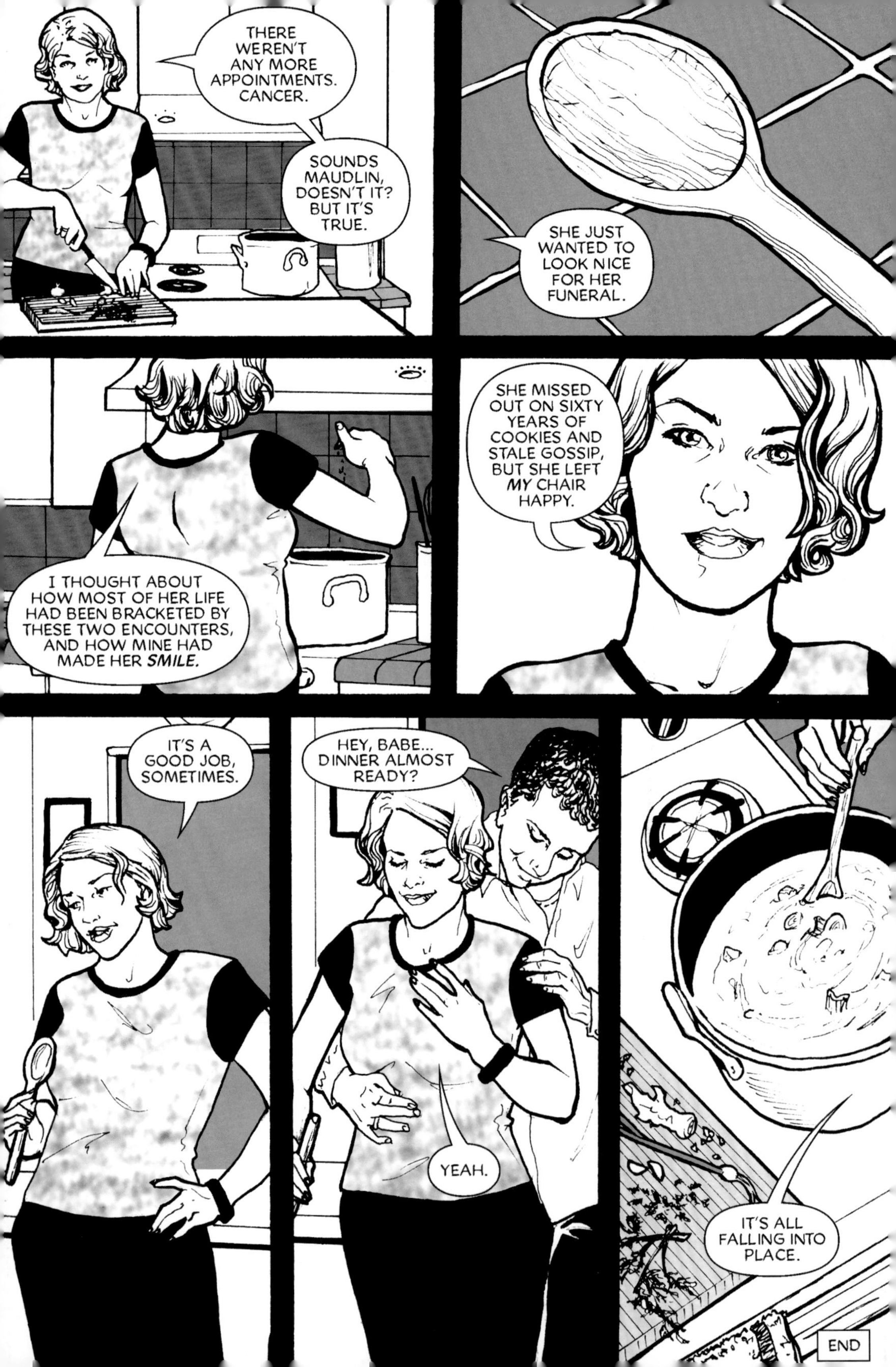
THERE WEREN'T ANY MORE APPOINTMENTS. CANCER.
SOUNDS MAUDLIN, DOESN'T IT? BUT IT'S TRUE.
SHE JUST WANTED TO LOOK NICE FOR HER FUNERAL.
I THOUGHT ABOUT HOW MOST OF HER LIFE HAD BEEN BRACKETED BY THESE TWO ENCOUNTERS, AND HOW MINE HAD MADE HER *SMILE.*
SHE MISSED OUT ON SIXTY YEARS OF COOKIES AND STALE GOSSIP, BUT SHE LEFT *MY* CHAIR HAPPY.
IT'S A GOOD JOB, SOMETIMES.
HEY, BABE... DINNER ALMOST READY?
YEAH.
IT'S ALL FALLING INTO PLACE.
END

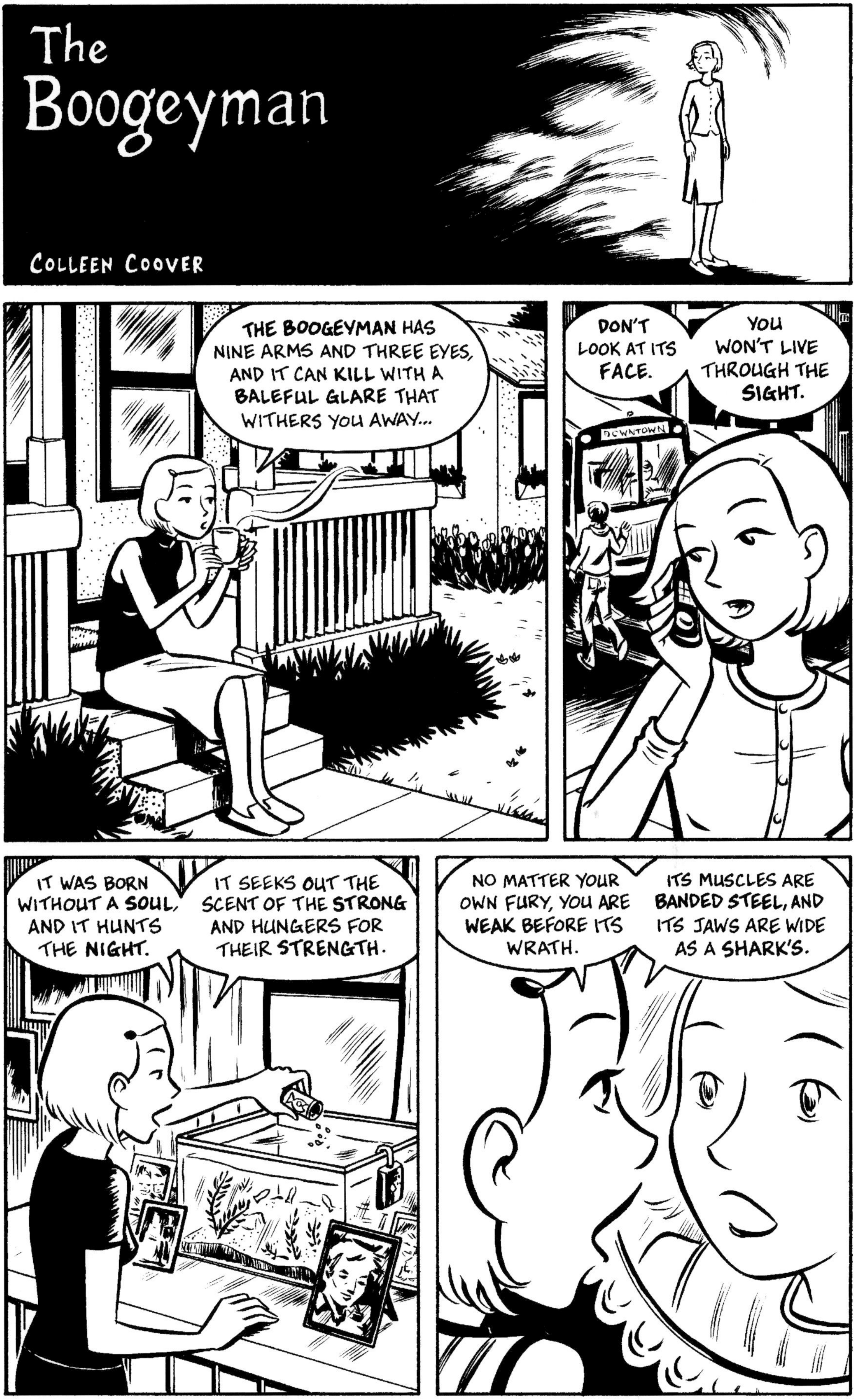
The Boogeyman
COLLEEN COOVER
THE BOOGEYMAN HAS NINE ARMS AND THREE EYES, AND IT CAN KILL WITH A BALEFUL GLARE THAT WITHERS YOU AWAY...
DON'T LOOK AT ITS FACE.
YOU WON'T LIVE THROUGH THE SIGHT.
DOWNTOWN
IT WAS BORN WITHOUT A SOUL, AND IT HUNTS THE NIGHT.
IT SEEKS OUT THE SCENT OF THE STRONG AND HUNGERS FOR THEIR STRENGTH.
NO MATTER YOUR OWN FURY, YOU ARE WEAK BEFORE ITS WRATH.
ITS MUSCLES ARE BANDED STEEL, AND ITS JAWS ARE WIDE AS A SHARK'S.

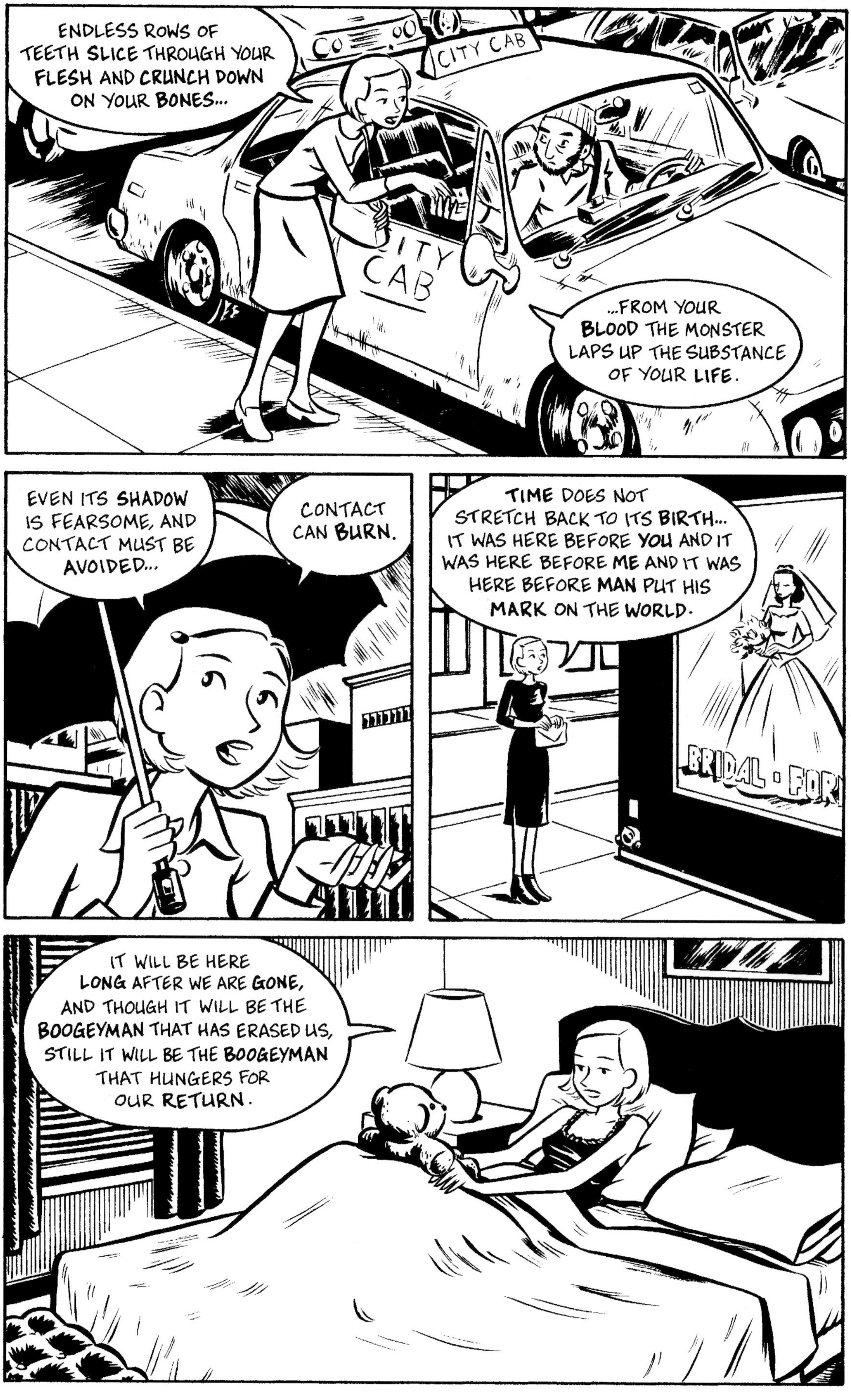
ENDLESS ROWS OF TEETH SLICE THROUGH YOUR FLESH AND CRUNCH DOWN ON YOUR BONES...
CITY CAB
...FROM YOUR BLOOD THE MONSTER LAPS UP THE SUBSTANCE OF YOUR LIFE.
EVEN ITS SHADOW IS FEARSOME, AND CONTACT MUST BE AVOIDED...
CONTACT CAN BURN.
TIME DOES NOT STRETCH BACK TO ITS BIRTH... IT WAS HERE BEFORE YOU AND IT WAS HERE BEFORE ME AND IT WAS HERE BEFORE MAN PUT HIS MARK ON THE WORLD.
BRIDAL · FOR
IT WILL BE HERE LONG AFTER WE ARE GONE, AND THOUGH IT WILL BE THE BOOGEYMAN THAT HAS ERASED US, STILL IT WILL BE THE BOOGEYMAN THAT HUNGERS FOR OUR RETURN.

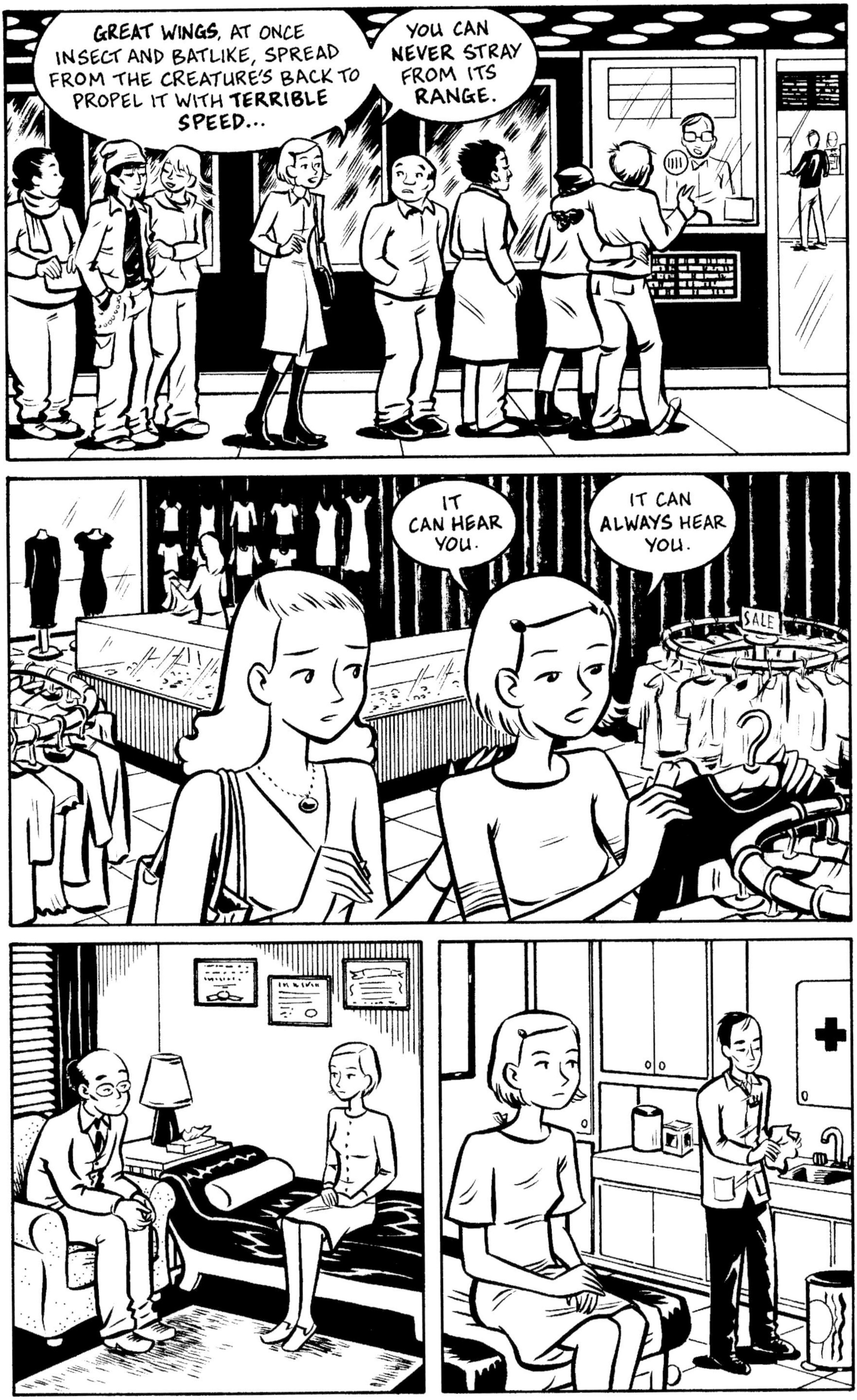
GREAT WINGS, AT ONCE INSECT AND BATLIKE, SPREAD FROM THE CREATURE'S BACK TO PROPEL IT WITH TERRIBLE SPEED...
YOU CAN NEVER STRAY FROM ITS RANGE.
IT CAN HEAR YOU.
IT CAN ALWAYS HEAR YOU.
SALE

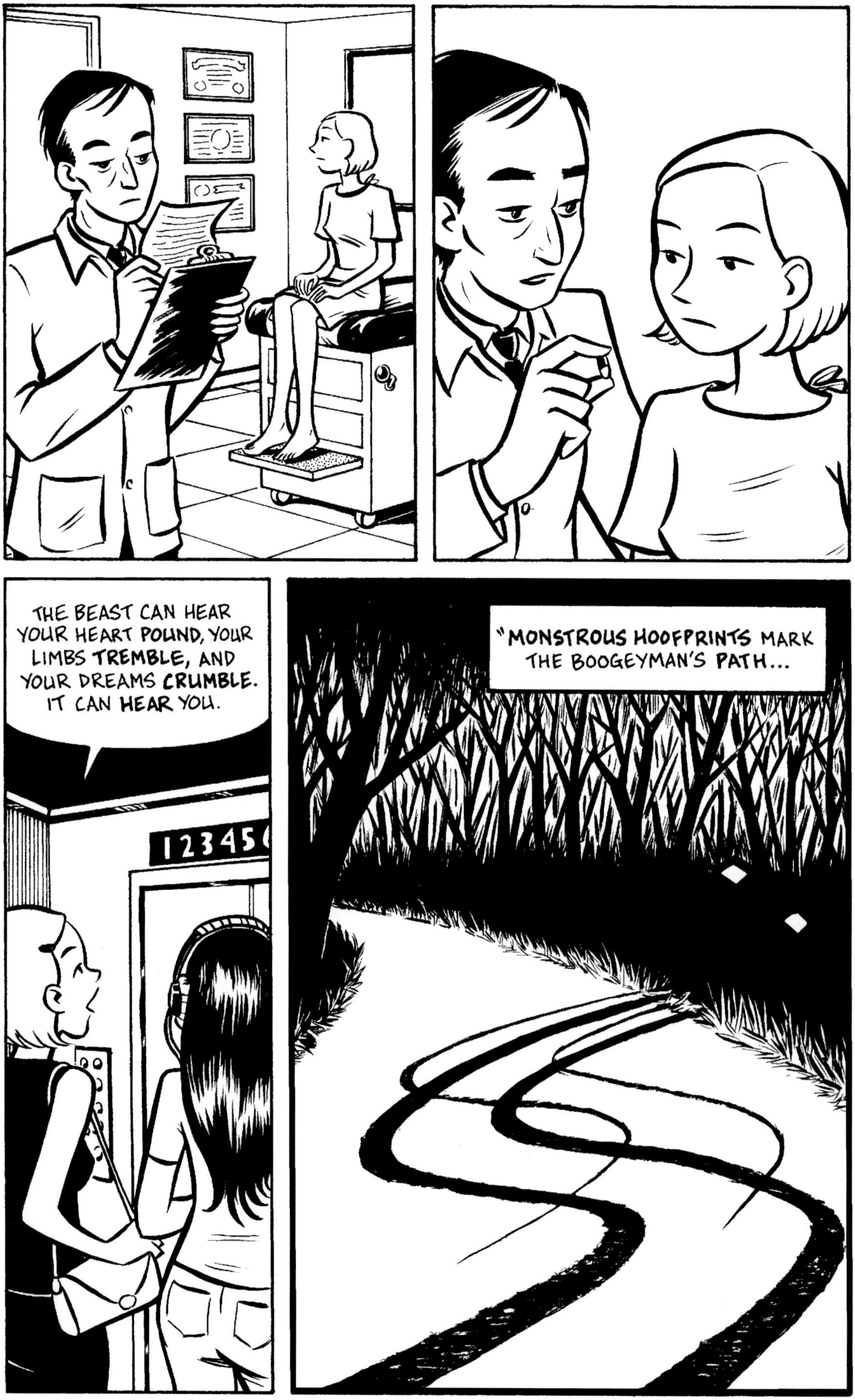
THE BEAST CAN HEAR YOUR HEART POUND, YOUR LIMBS TREMBLE, AND YOUR DREAMS CRUMBLE. IT CAN HEAR YOU.
12345
"MONSTROUS HOOFPRINTS MARK THE BOOGEYMAN'S PATH...

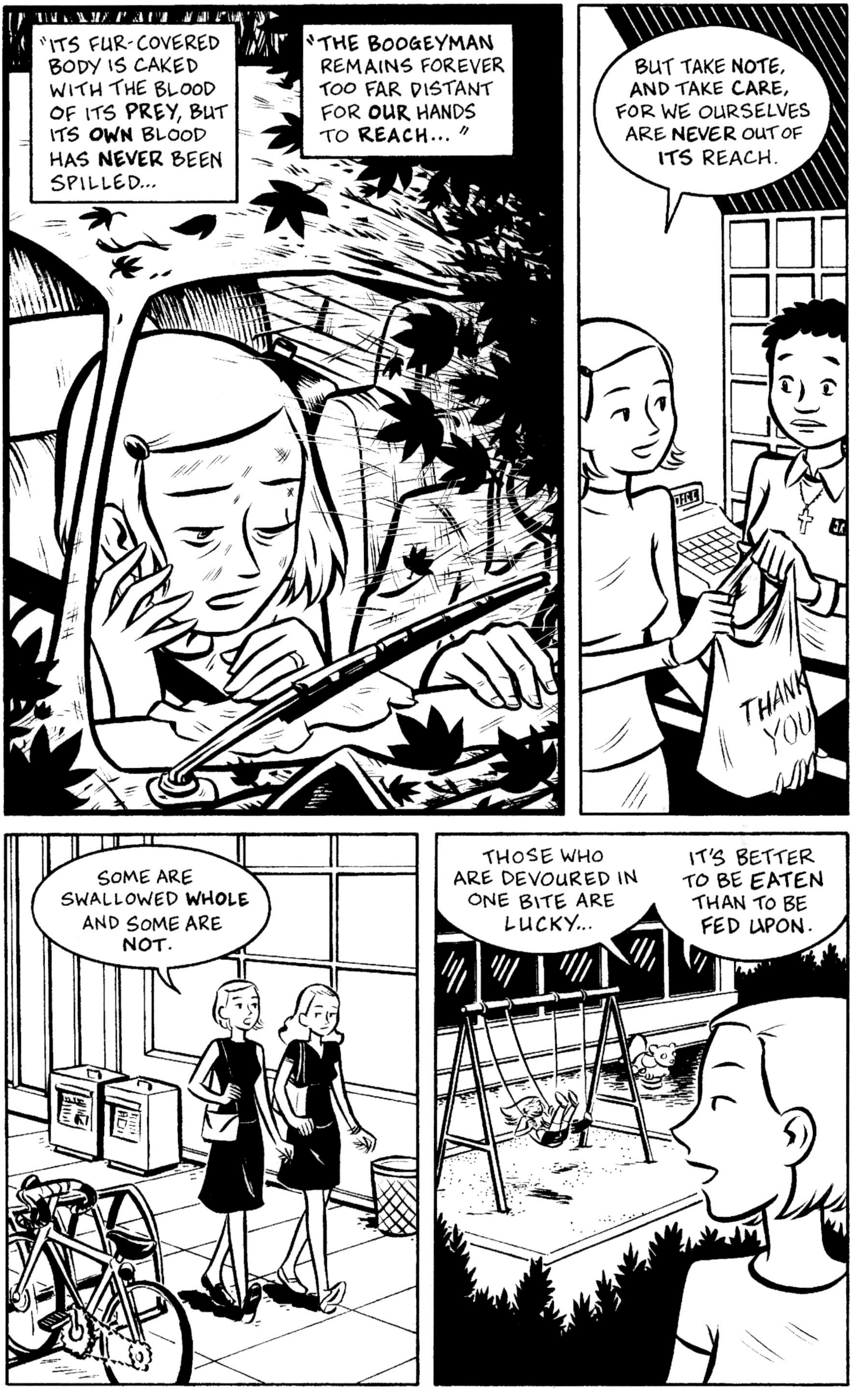
"ITS FUR-COVERED BODY IS CAKED WITH THE BLOOD OF ITS PREY, BUT ITS OWN BLOOD HAS NEVER BEEN SPILLED...
"THE BOOGEYMAN REMAINS FOREVER TOO FAR DISTANT FOR OUR HANDS TO REACH..."
BUT TAKE NOTE, AND TAKE CARE, FOR WE OURSELVES ARE NEVER OUT OF ITS REACH.
THANK YOU
SOME ARE SWALLOWED WHOLE AND SOME ARE NOT.
THOSE WHO ARE DEVOURED IN ONE BITE ARE LUCKY...
IT'S BETTER TO BE EATEN THAN TO BE FED UPON.

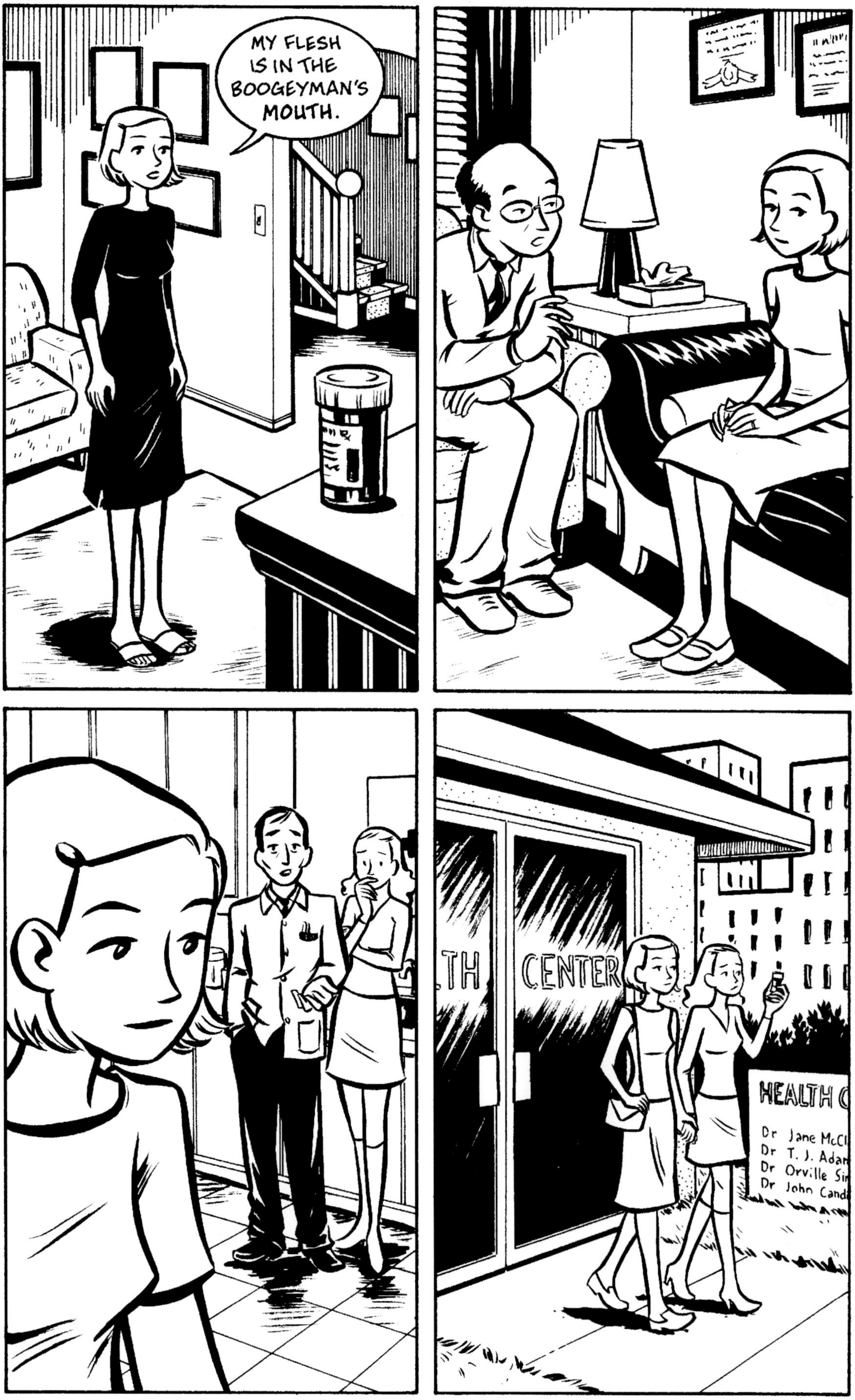
MY FLESH IS IN THE BOOGEYMAN'S MOUTH.
CENTER

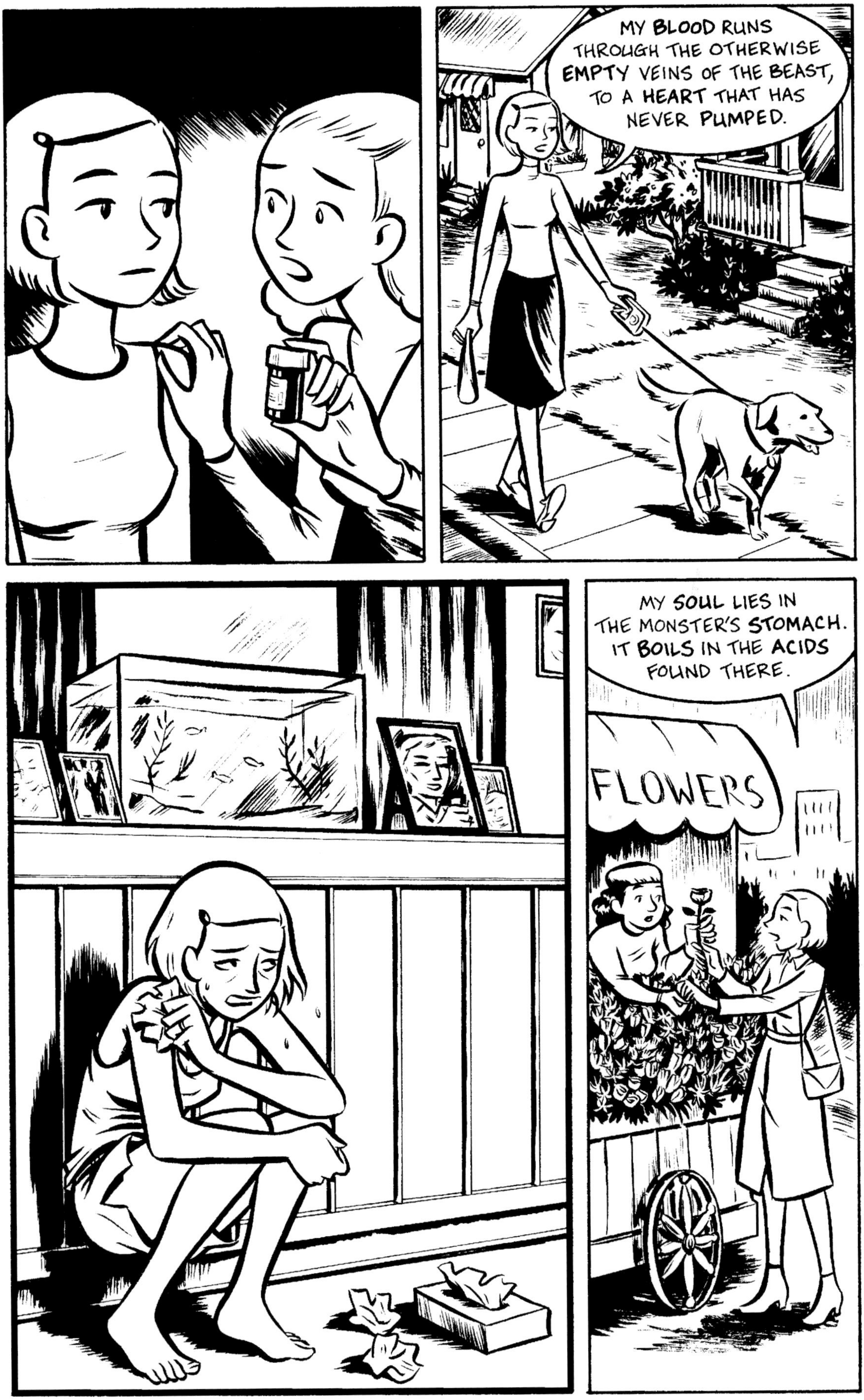
MY BLOOD RUNS THROUGH THE OTHERWISE EMPTY VEINS OF THE BEAST, TO A HEART THAT HAS NEVER PUMPED.
MY SOUL LIES IN THE MONSTER'S STOMACH. IT BOILS IN THE ACIDS FOUND THERE.
FLOWERS

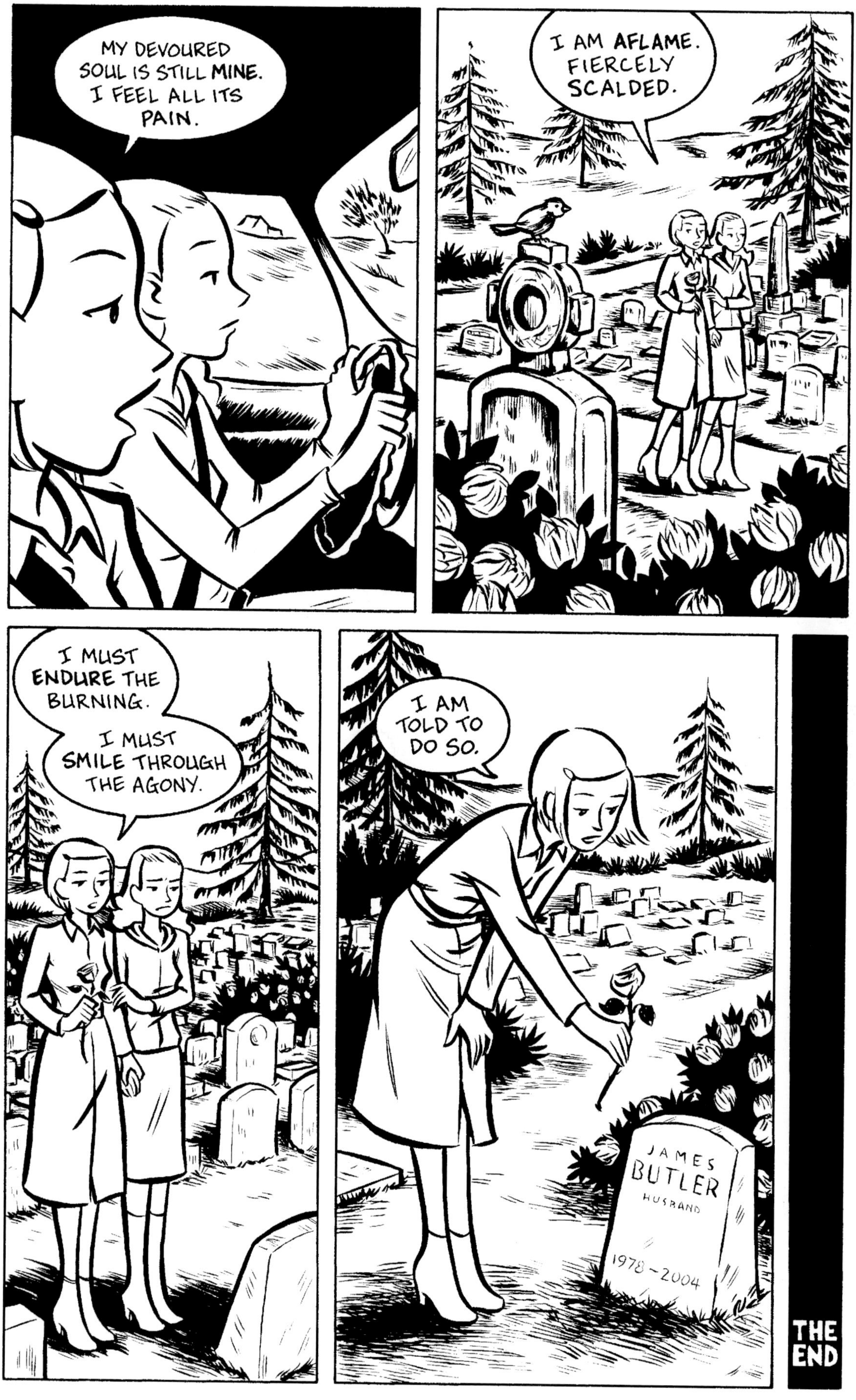
MY DEVOURED SOUL IS STILL MINE. I FEEL ALL ITS PAIN.
I AM AFLAME. FIERCELY SCALDED.
I MUST ENDURE THE BURNING.
I MUST SMILE THROUGH THE AGONY.
I AM TOLD TO DO SO.
JAMES BUTLER HUSBAND 1978 ~ 2004
THE END

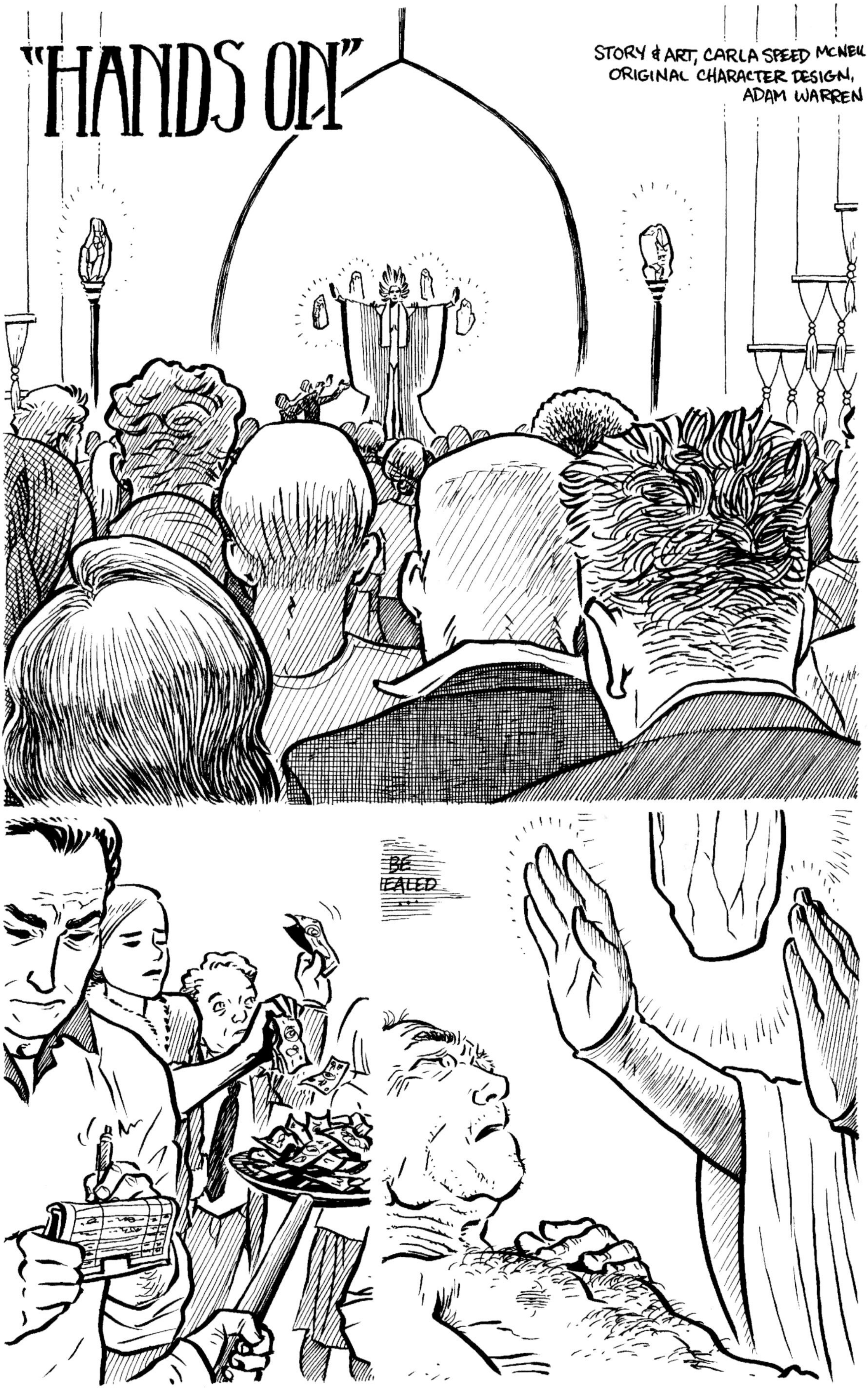
"HANDS ON"
STORY & ART, CARLA SPEED MCNEIL
ORIGINAL CHARACTER DESIGN, ADAM WARREN
BE
EALED ...

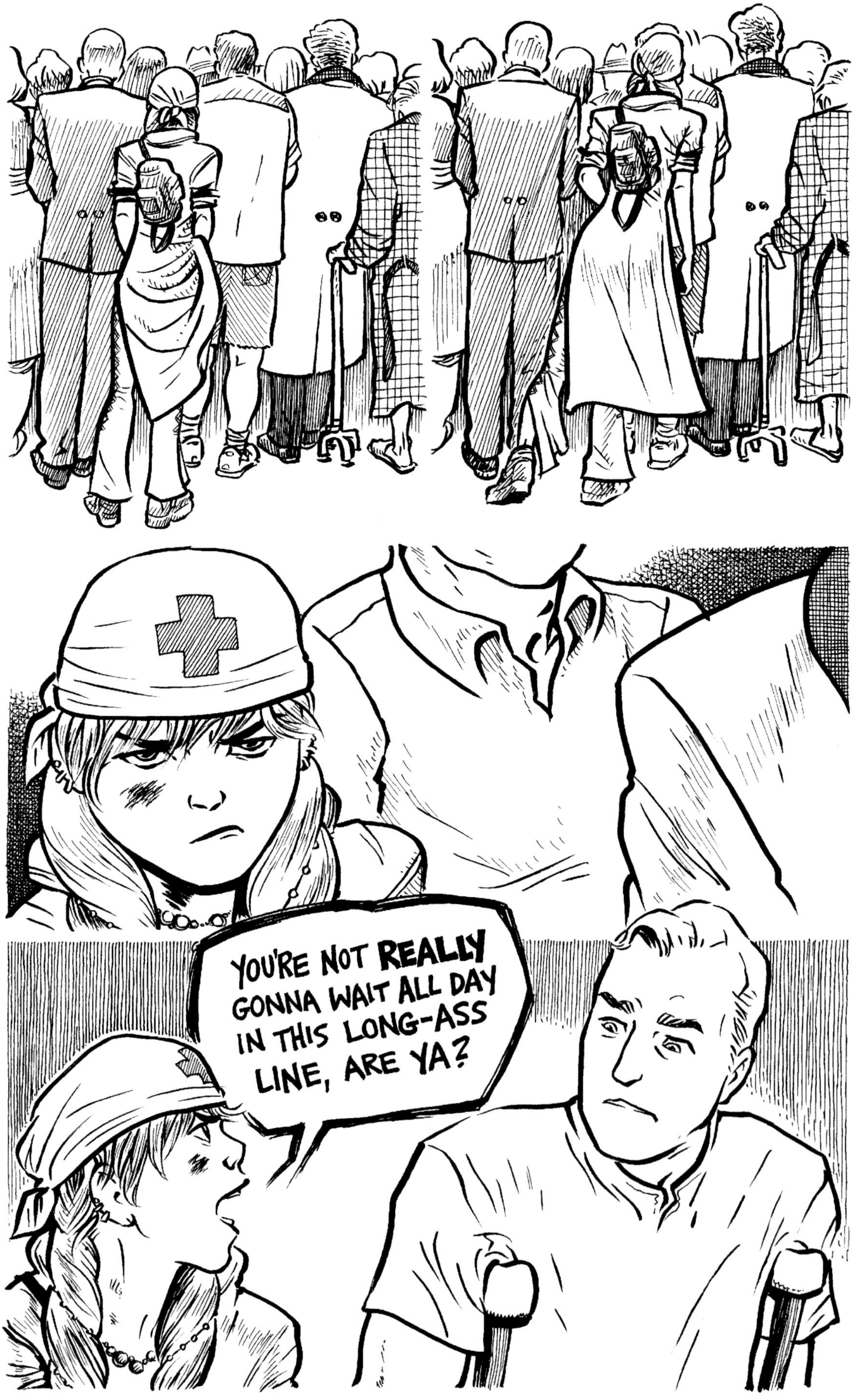
YOU'RE NOT **REALLY** GONNA WAIT ALL DAY IN THIS LONG-ASS LINE, ARE YA?

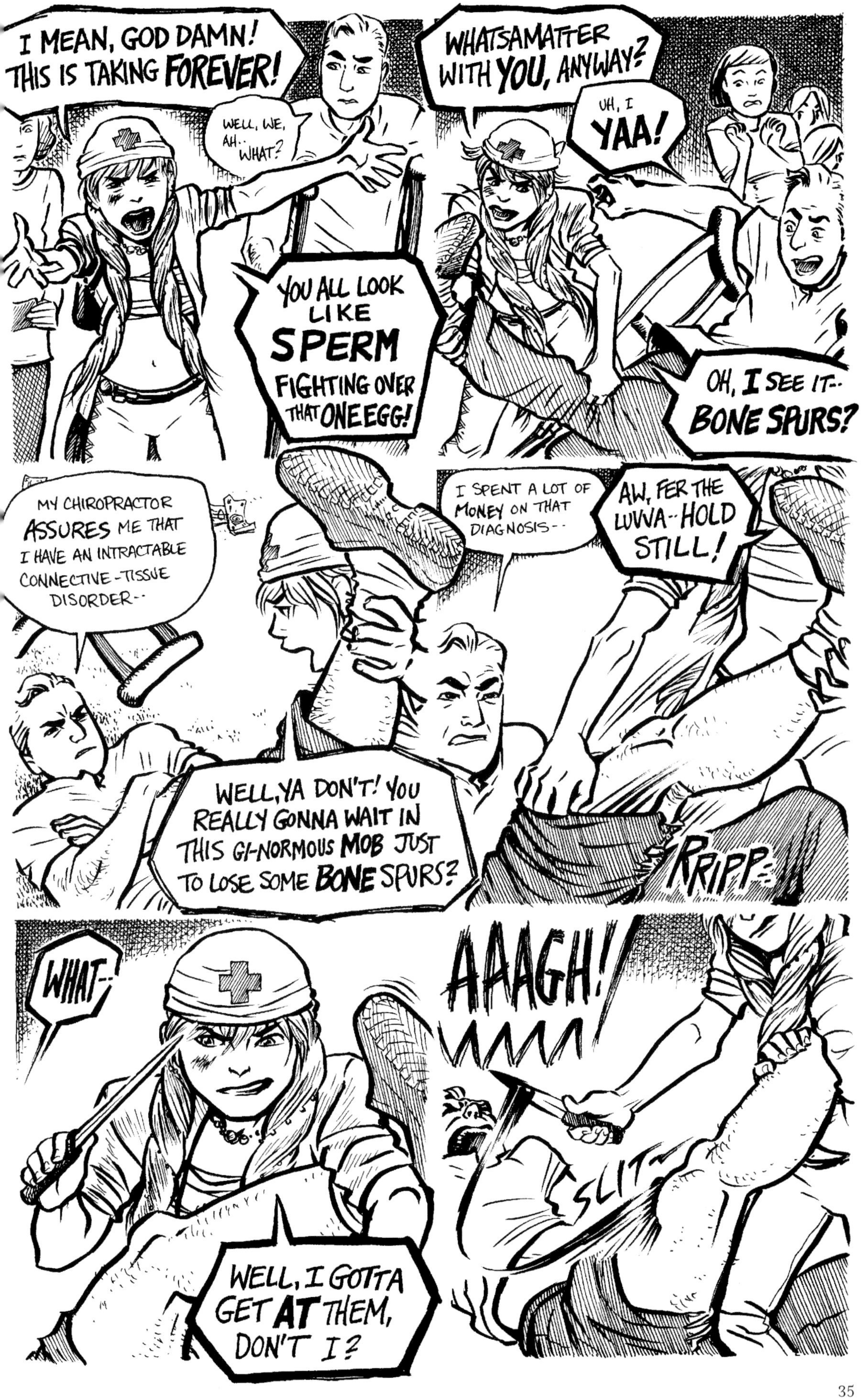
I MEAN, GOD DAMN! THIS IS TAKING FOREVER!
WELL, WE, AH.. WHAT?
YOU ALL LOOK LIKE SPERM FIGHTING OVER THAT ONE EGG!
WHATSAMATTER WITH YOU, ANYWAY?
UH, I
YAA!
OH, I SEE IT-- BONE SPURS?
MY CHIROPRACTOR ASSURES ME THAT I HAVE AN INTRACTABLE CONNECTIVE-TISSUE DISORDER--
WELL, YA DON'T! YOU REALLY GONNA WAIT IN THIS GI-NORMOUS MOB JUST TO LOSE SOME BONE SPURS?
I SPENT A LOT OF MONEY ON THAT DIAGNOSIS--
AW, FER THE LUVVA--HOLD STILL!
RRIPP
WHAT--
WELL, I GOTTA GET AT THEM, DON'T I?
AAAGH!
SLIT

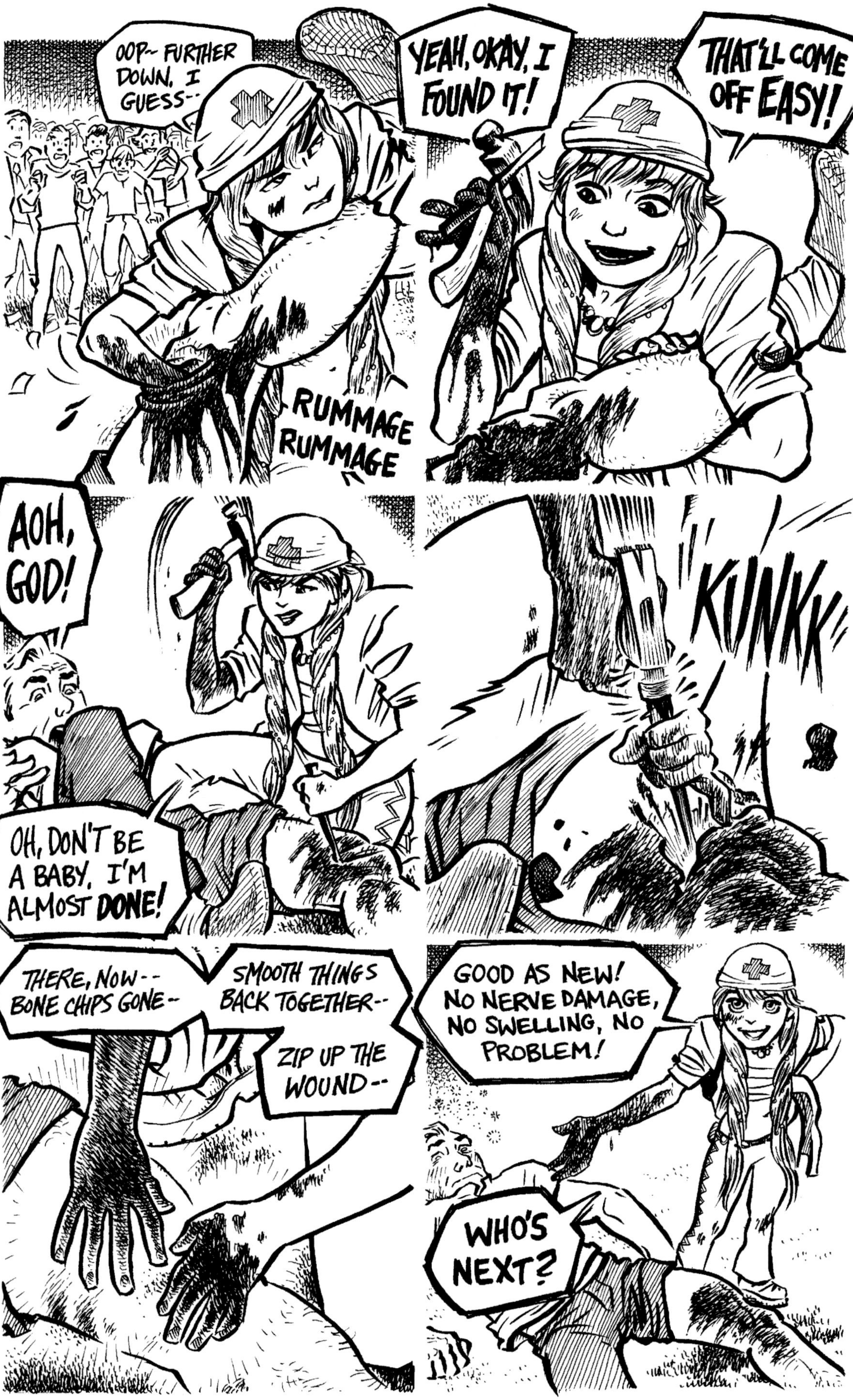
OOP-- FURTHER DOWN, I GUESS--
RUMMAGE RUMMAGE
YEAH, OKAY, I FOUND IT!
THAT'LL COME OFF EASY!
AOH, GOD!
OH, DON'T BE A BABY. I'M ALMOST DONE!
KUNKK
THERE, NOW-- BONE CHIPS GONE--
SMOOTH THINGS BACK TOGETHER--
ZIP UP THE WOUND--
GOOD AS NEW! NO NERVE DAMAGE, NO SWELLING, NO PROBLEM!
WHO'S NEXT?

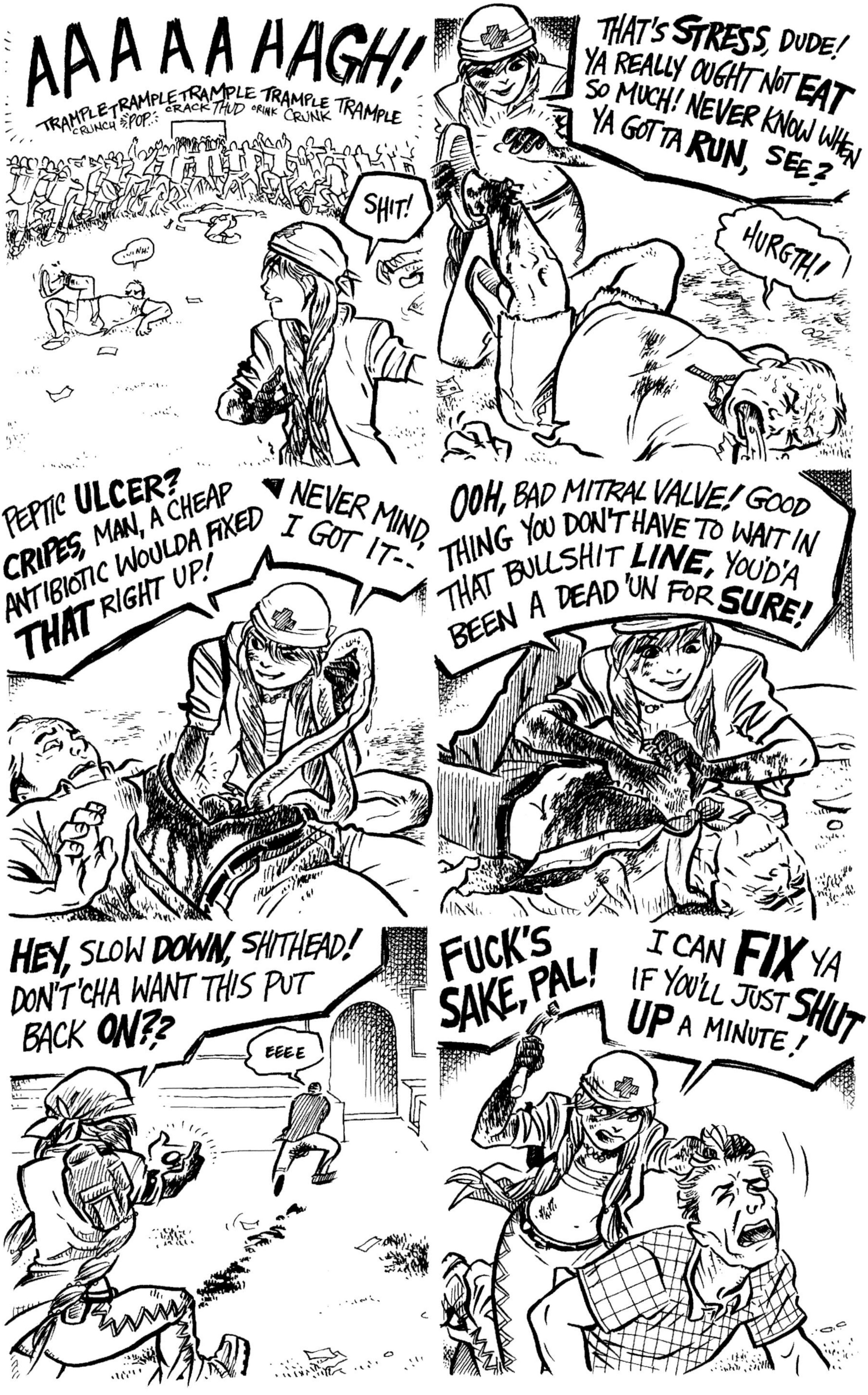
AAAAAAAGH!
TRAMPLE TRAMPLE TRAMPLE TRAMPLE TRAMPLE
CRUNCH POP CRACK THUD CRINK CRUNK
...NH!
SHIT!
THAT'S STRESS, DUDE! YA REALLY OUGHT NOT EAT SO MUCH! NEVER KNOW WHEN YA GOTTA RUN, SEE?
HURGTH!
PEPTIC ULCER? CRIPES, MAN, A CHEAP ANTIBIOTIC WOULDA FIXED THAT RIGHT UP!
NEVER MIND, I GOT IT--
OOH, BAD MITRAL VALVE! GOOD THING YOU DON'T HAVE TO WAIT IN THAT BULLSHIT LINE, YOU'D'A BEEN A DEAD 'UN FOR SURE!
HEY, SLOW DOWN, SHITHEAD! DON'T'CHA WANT THIS PUT BACK ON??
EEEE
FUCK'S SAKE, PAL!
I CAN FIX YA IF YOU'LL JUST SHUT UP A MINUTE!

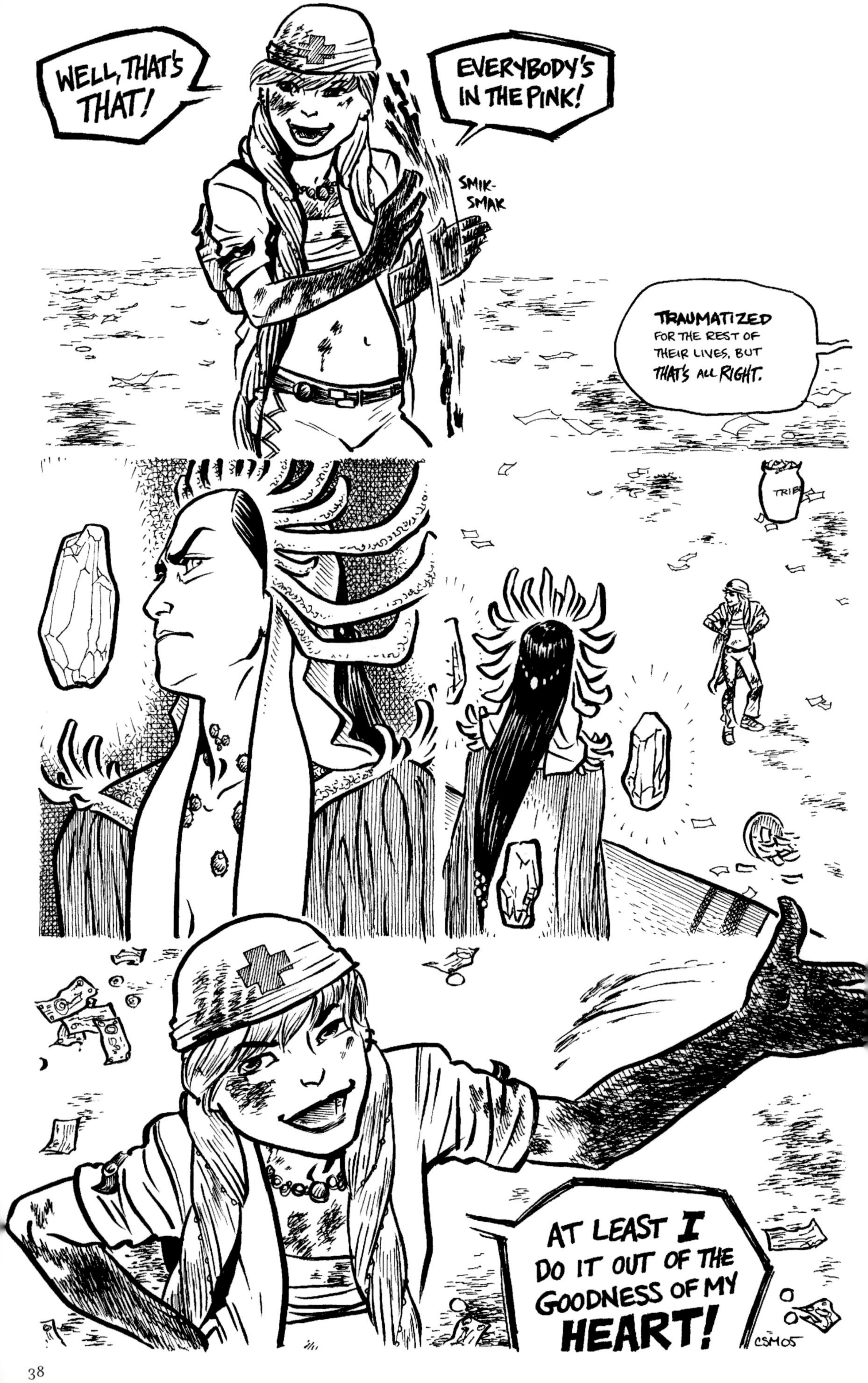
WELL, THAT'S THAT!
EVERYBODY'S IN THE PINK!
SMIK-SMAK
TRAUMATIZED FOR THE REST OF THEIR LIVES, BUT THAT'S ALL RIGHT.
TRIB
AT LEAST I DO IT OUT OF THE GOODNESS OF MY HEART!
CSM 05

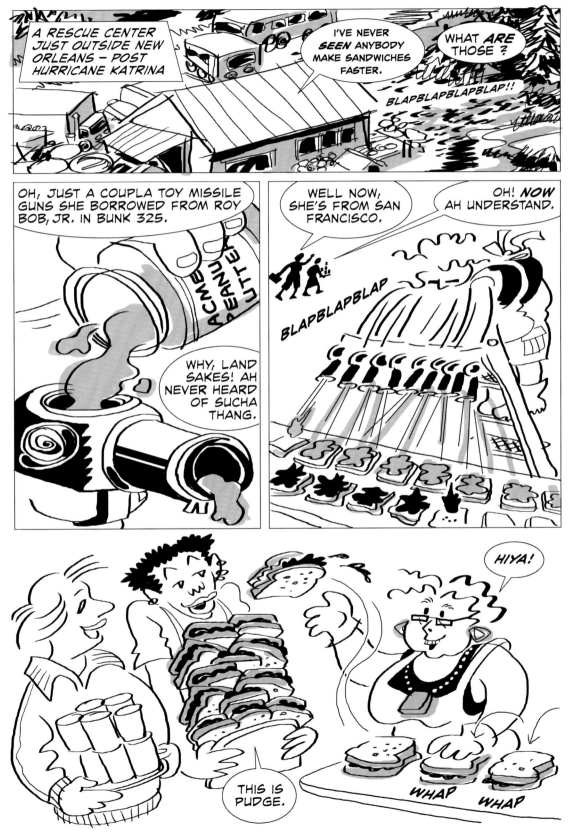

HURRICANE EYE FOR THE STRAIGHT GRRL

ANOTHER PUDGE, GIRL BLIMP™ TALE ©2005 LEE MARRS-

A RESCUE CENTER JUST OUTSIDE NEW ORLEANS – POST HURRICANE KATRINA

I'VE NEVER *SEEN* ANYBODY MAKE SANDWICHES FASTER.

WHAT *ARE* THOSE?

BLAPBLAPBLAPBLAP!!

OH, JUST A COUPLA TOY MISSILE GUNS SHE BORROWED FROM ROY BOB, JR. IN BUNK 325.

ACME PEANUT BUTTER

WHY, LAND SAKES! AH NEVER HEARD OF SUCHA THANG.

WELL NOW, SHE'S FROM SAN FRANCISCO.

OH! *NOW* AH UNDERSTAND.

BLAPBLAPBLAP

THIS IS PUDGE.

HIYA!

WHAP

WHAP

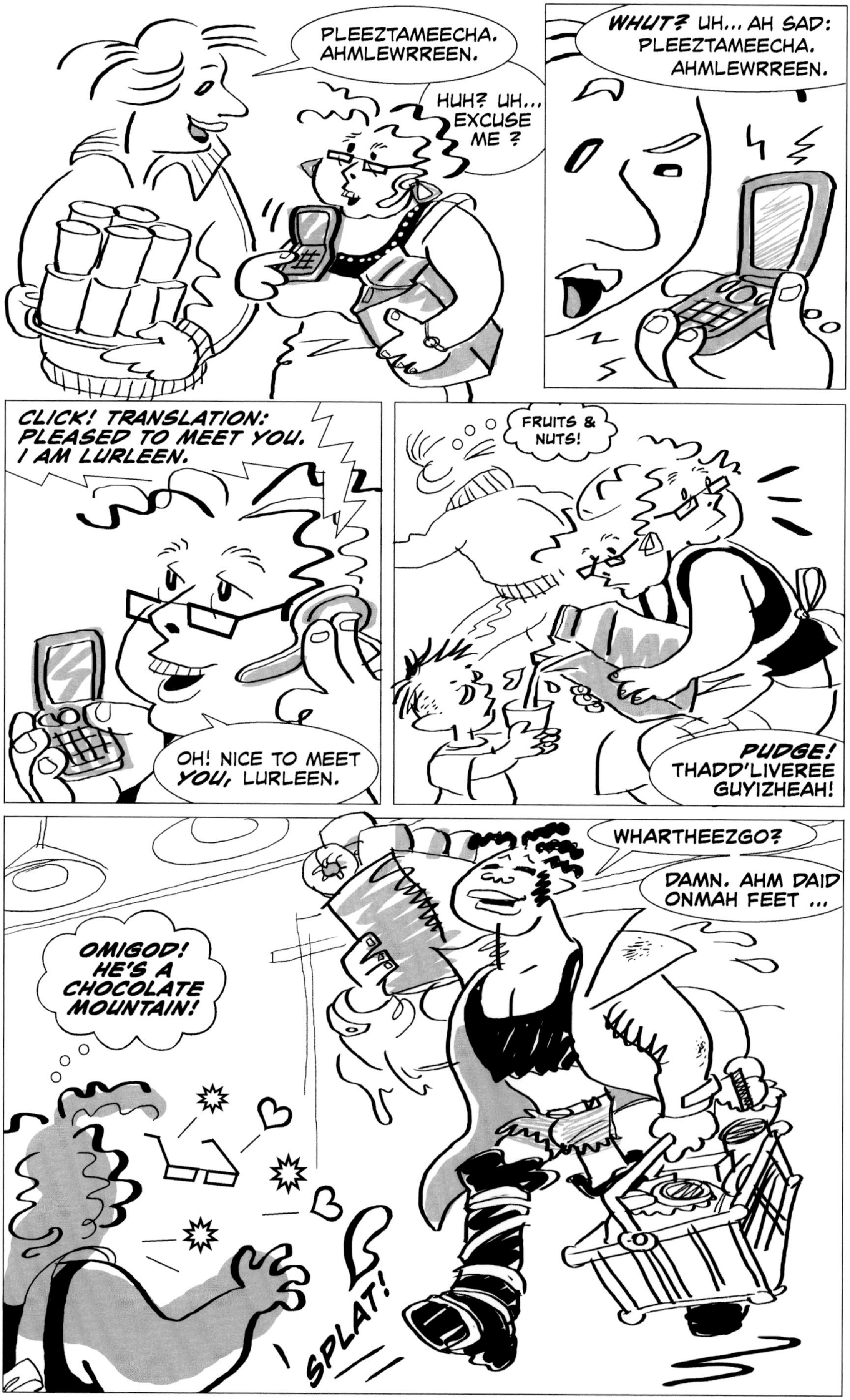
PLEEZTAMEECHA. AHMLEWRREEN.
HUH? UH... EXCUSE ME ?
WHUT? UH... AH SAD: PLEEZTAMEECHA. AHMLEWRREEN.
CLICK! TRANSLATION: PLEASED TO MEET YOU. I AM LURLEEN.
OH! NICE TO MEET YOU, LURLEEN.
FRUITS & NUTS!
PUDGE! THADD'LIVEREE GUYIZHEAH!
WHARTHEEZGO?
DAMN. AHM DAID ONMAH FEET ...
OMIGOD! HE'S A CHOCOLATE MOUNTAIN!
SPLAT!

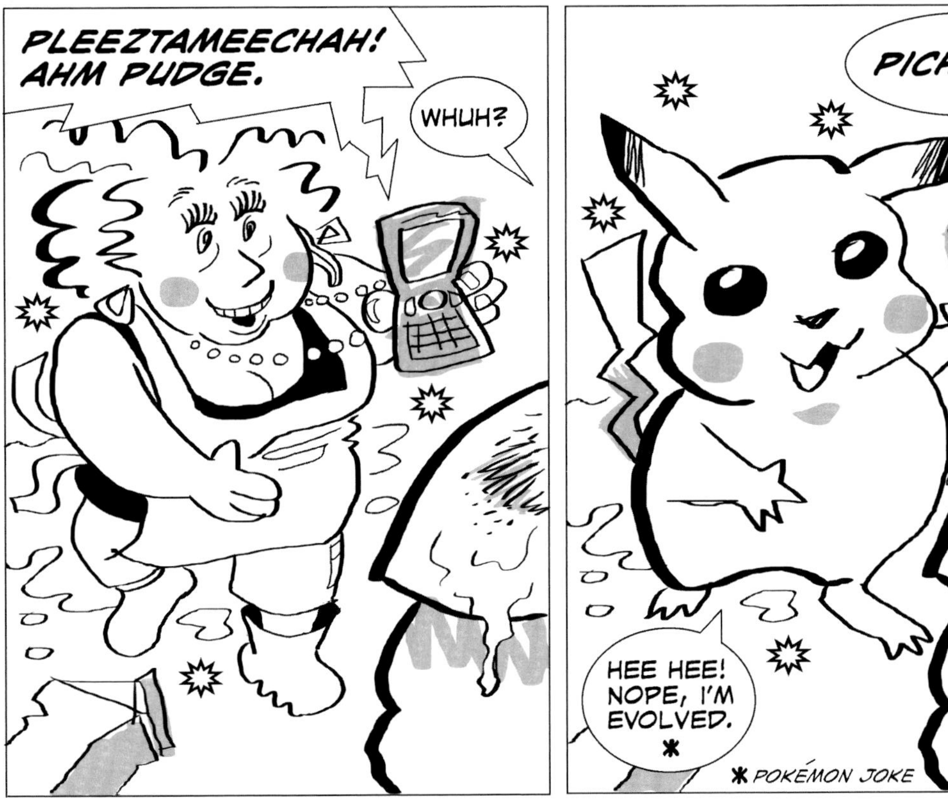
PLEEZTAMEECHAH! AHM PUDGE.
WHUH?
PICHAKU?
HEE HEE! NOPE, I'M EVOLVED. *
* POKÉMON JOKE

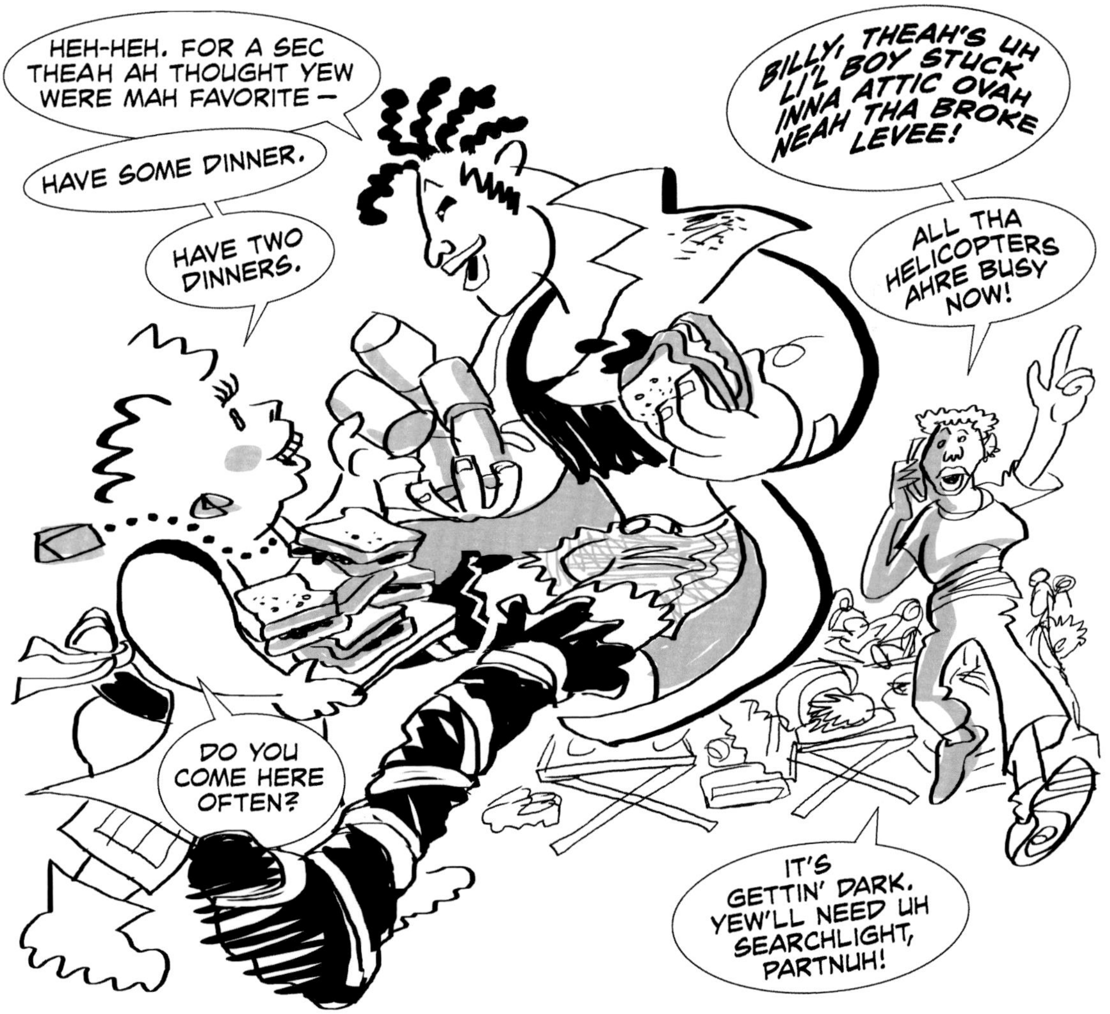
HEH-HEH. FOR A SEC THEAH AH THOUGHT YEW WERE MAH FAVORITE—
HAVE SOME DINNER.
HAVE TWO DINNERS.
BILLY, THEAH'S UH LI'L BOY STUCK INNA ATTIC OVAH NEAH THA BROKE LEVEE!
ALL THA HELICOPTERS AHRE BUSY NOW!
DO YOU COME HERE OFTEN?
IT'S GETTIN' DARK. YEW'LL NEED UH SEARCHLIGHT, PARTNUH!

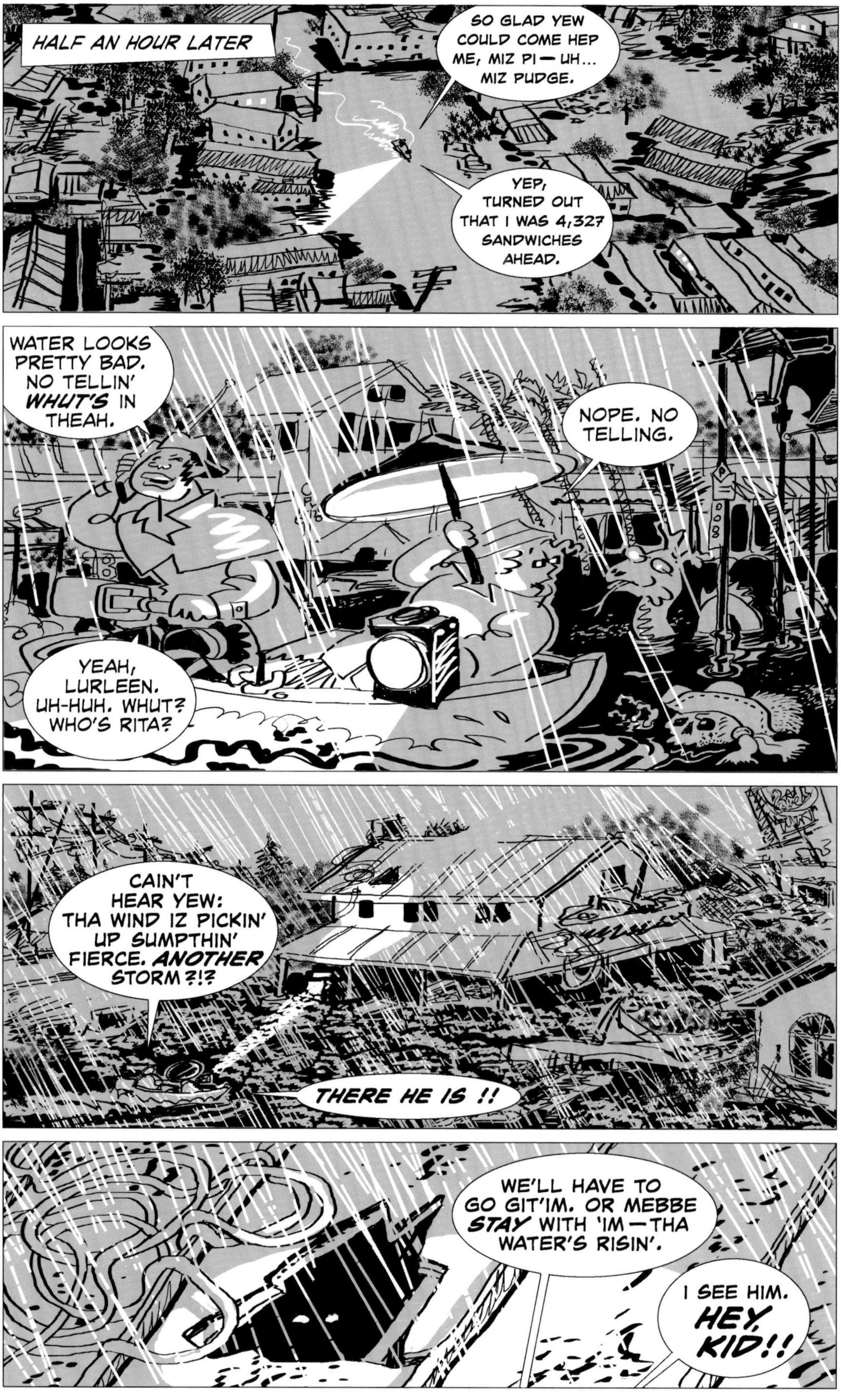
HALF AN HOUR LATER
SO GLAD YEW COULD COME HEP ME, MIZ PI—UH... MIZ PUDGE.
YEP, TURNED OUT THAT I WAS 4,327 SANDWICHES AHEAD.
WATER LOOKS PRETTY BAD. NO TELLIN' WHUT'S IN THEAH.
NOPE. NO TELLING.
YEAH, LURLEEN. UH-HUH. WHUT? WHO'S RITA?
CAIN'T HEAR YEW: THA WIND IZ PICKIN' UP SUMPTHIN' FIERCE. ANOTHER STORM?!?
THERE HE IS !!
WE'LL HAVE TO GO GIT'IM. OR MEBBE STAY WITH 'IM—THA WATER'S RISIN'.
I SEE HIM. HEY, KID!!

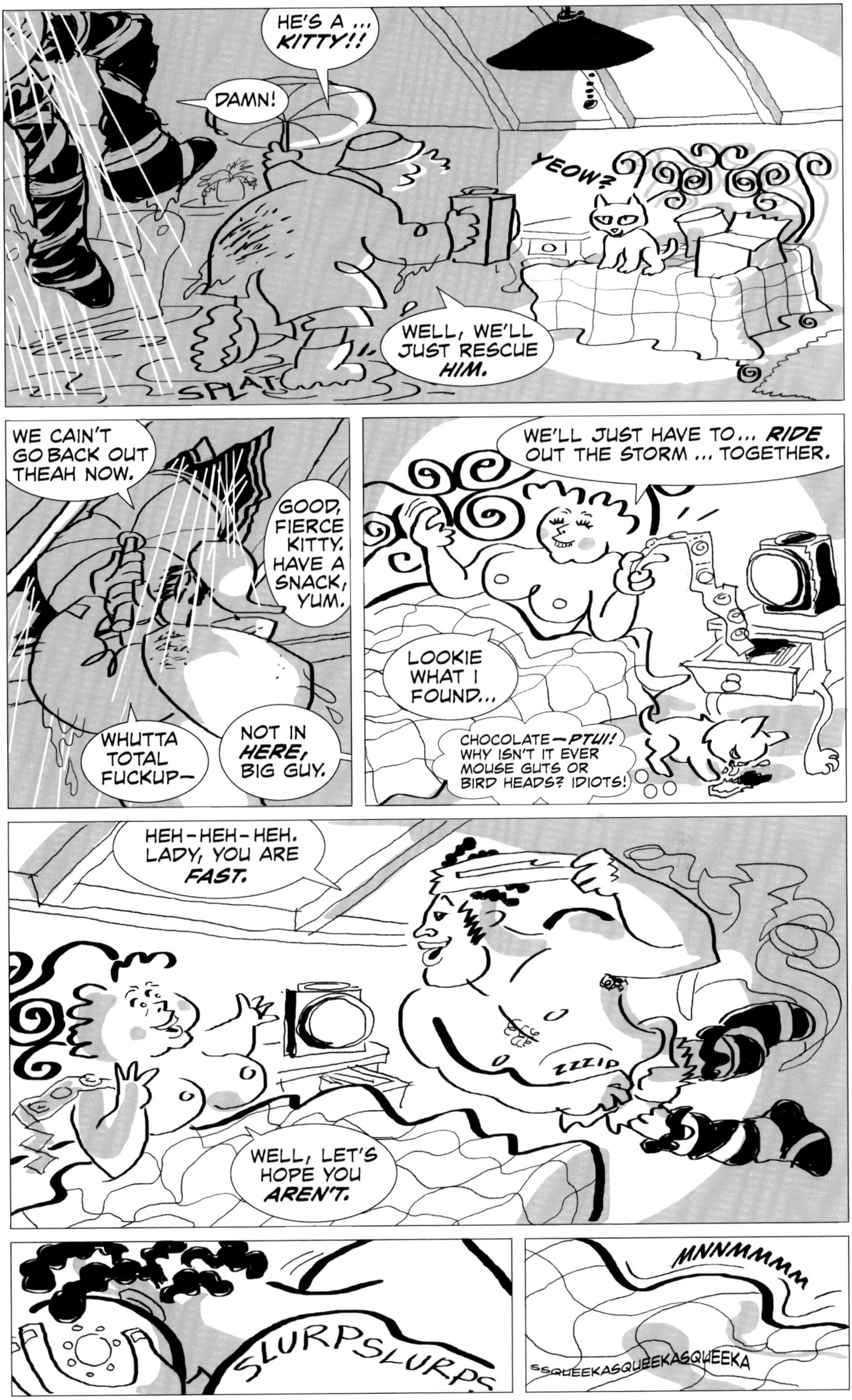
HE'S A ... KITTY!!
DAMN!
YEOW?
WELL, WE'LL JUST RESCUE HIM.
SPLAT
WE CAIN'T GO BACK OUT THEAH NOW.
GOOD, FIERCE KITTY. HAVE A SNACK, YUM.
WHUTTA TOTAL FUCKUP—
NOT IN HERE, BIG GUY.
WE'LL JUST HAVE TO... RIDE OUT THE STORM ... TOGETHER.
LOOKIE WHAT I FOUND...
CHOCOLATE—PTUI! WHY ISN'T IT EVER MOUSE GUTS OR BIRD HEADS? IDIOTS!
HEH-HEH-HEH. LADY, YOU ARE FAST.
ZZZIP
WELL, LET'S HOPE YOU AREN'T.
SLURPSLURPS
MNNMMMM
SSQUEEKASQUEEKASQUEEKA

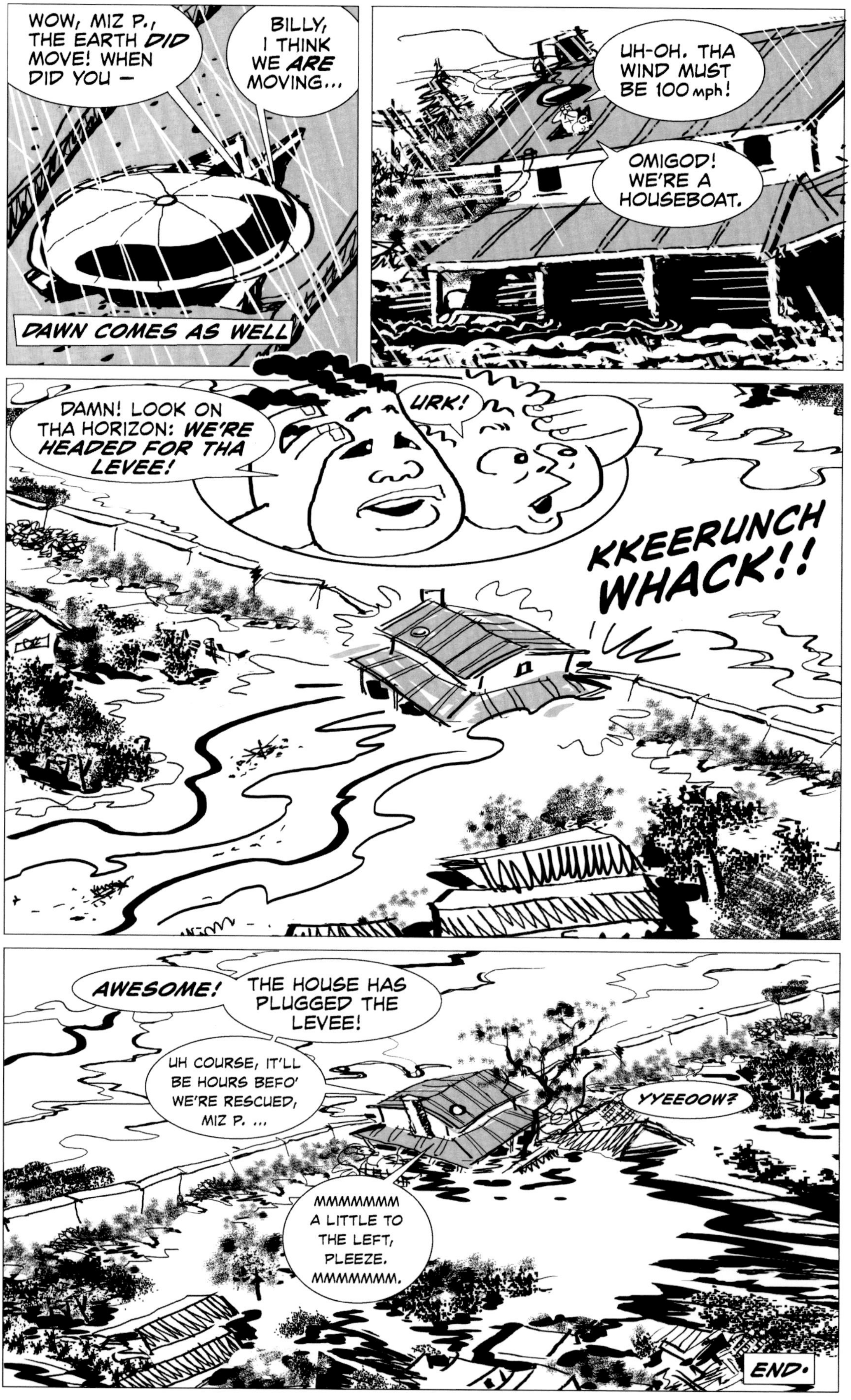
WOW, MIZ P., THE EARTH DID MOVE! WHEN DID YOU –
BILLY, I THINK WE ARE MOVING...
DAWN COMES AS WELL
UH-OH. THA WIND MUST BE 100 mph!
OMIGOD! WE'RE A HOUSEBOAT.
DAMN! LOOK ON THA HORIZON: WE'RE HEADED FOR THA LEVEE!
URK!
KKEERUNCH WHACK!!
AWESOME!
THE HOUSE HAS PLUGGED THE LEVEE!
UH COURSE, IT'LL BE HOURS BEFO' WE'RE RESCUED, MIZ P. ...
YYEEOOW?
MMMMMMM A LITTLE TO THE LEFT, PLEEZE. MMMMMMM.
END.

JEFF MACEY'S GIRLS

written by Diana Schutz, illustrated by Amanda Conner

The year is 1992, and Jaisa has had a bit too much to drink. It was that last shot of tequila that's done her in—straight up: a kiss of salted wrist to forewarn the taste buds and a pinch of lime to ease the afterburn. Jaisa knows her way around the bar pretty well for someone who's barely crested voting age, and she knows she's flipped over the edge now—from giggly to . . . well, just plain drunk.

"I shouldn'a had that las' shot," she announces—to anyone who will listen, really. But she's waggling an unsteady finger at Trisha, her partner in crime, though Trisha was long gone, plowed, looped, wasted—*totalled*—well before little Jaisa's baby blues started to glaze over with tequila frosting. Trisha, however, is more adept at carrying her liquor. And why shouldn't she be? She's got about ten years and at least ten pounds on Jaisa, maybe more. Jaisa's just a kid, after all, a tight-bodied teenager who can't afford to surrender many more of her still developing brain cells to that demon tequila.

She's already given up her lungs to Marlboro Light 100s, and the normally forested air is splintered with spires of smoke curling up into lazy rafters that hang, heavy and unmoving, in the hot, congested Saturday afternoon. In fact, there are an unusual number of smokers in this Lake Oswego backyard. The normally staid suburb at Portland, Oregon's lush, southern fringes is more often host to those denizens of old-moneyed families, the Corbetts and Meiers and Pendleton Wool's Bishops, among whom smoking, even when still considered fashionable in most circles, was *always* frowned upon—with that quiet but disapproving lowering of the eyelids that let you know immediately, quite silently but with courtroom finality, that you could never hope to rise even to the bottom rung of this social ladder, one that *they* wouldn't have deigned to *climb* to begin with. They're here today, in 1992, those silver-coifed dwellers of the Street of Dreams, betraying not one single grain of sweat sprouting between folds of pink, untanned flesh—not even an oil-slicked skin sheen glistening in the hazy afternoon sun. No, these are the people whose puckered hide tells the tale of a life dried up long ago, dried up and soon to blow away like the frail crown of the lawn's dead dandelions. In the meantime, they're here this Saturday afternoon, forestalling something inevitable in this Lake Oswego backyard, wrinkling their noses at the peculiar perfume of Marlboro Light 100s wafting sultry in the stilled breeze.

Author's Note: This is a work of nonfiction. It was originally written in 1992, during the very early days of what would become the Internet. Names have been changed to protect the innocent as well as the guilty. Thanks go to former Dark Horse staffer, Jeff Macey, for allowing the use of his name for the title character.

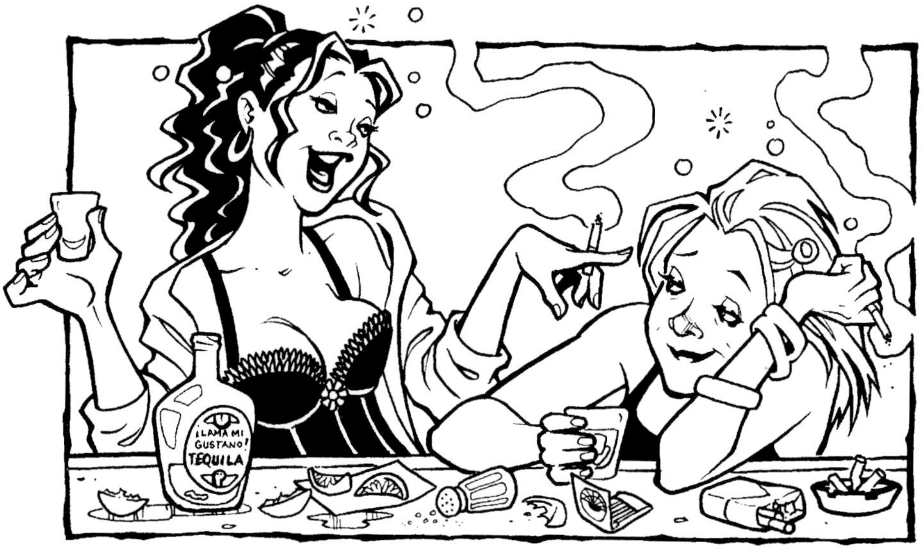
¡LAMA MI GUSTANO!
TEQUILA

Lake Oswego is home also to that younger breed of money-born, the thirtysomethings, whose healthy, browned bodies striding the lawn in Guess shorts admit of the sort of professional lifestyle that allows for daily Nautilus routines. These are the Lewis and Clark graduates, the relocated Californians, the new generation of lawyers and doctors and advertising execs whose lean wives dabble in real estate or interior design and wait 'til a *reasonable* age to have babies—two max, with the second usually coming in just under the wire, the wire that tenses and snaps at age forty when the female body is sure to turn into a pumpkin. These are the younger brothers and sisters of sixties youth, stretched between the socialism of the hippie movement and the nihilism of punk rock—who just said fuck it (but not in those words) and kicked around Europe, instead, on daddy's money, secure in securities, and returned to home and hearth and the warm though distant approval of their parents as if there weren't *any* generation gap to speak of. They're here today, too, endorphin junkies by birth, and you can bet *they're* not smoking, these freshly scrubbed children of the Surgeon General.

Jaisa's about to light up another, though, and lurches on high-heeled feet toward the patio table where Michelle, Trisha, and Angel suck in nicotine through carefully lipsticked mouths. A man's arm snakes out from behind, cupping Jaisa's elbow in a firm, almost reproving grasp.

"A lady doesn't walk like that," he admonishes in low but authoritative tones.

This is too much for Jaisa, who, guilty in her underage pleasure, collapses against her host, throwing her head back to brace on his shoulder as the rest of her body dissolves into innumerable sparks of laughter. Swiftly, with great skill, as if practiced a thousand times before, Jeff Macey maneuvers Jaisa into an open white garden chair, where her body collects itself once more, nervous titters scrambling to escape from behind her wide, drunken grin.

Jeff shoots a hard look over at Michelle, says nothing, speaks only through the arch of his eyebrows. "She's had a bit too much to drink," explains Michelle, belaboring the obvious. "Time to cut her off, Jeff."

For her own part, Michelle is sticking to soda today, or she'd "be just like that," she later confides. Even Trisha has suppressed her running giggles at the moment, reverting to the thin-lipped demeanor more characteristic of her now-lapsed Mormon upbringing. And Angel, well, Angel has already learned, at the tender age of just barely legal, to keep her voice a mere whisper. These girls understand the requirements of sophistication, after all. Mind you, *they* weren't born to wealth. This Lake Oswego afternoon crowd moves to a rhythm unheard in Michelle's small-town home of Newberg, Oregon—and Jeff Macey's suburban backyard might as well be a million miles away, rather than fifteen, or maybe ten as the crow flies, from Angel's North Portland neighborhood, where Friday night's excitement ranges from drive-by shootings to cops beating on the local, predominantly black, population. But they are Jeff Macey's girls, and they've learned their lessons well.

Except, perhaps, Jaisa, who even now suggests to Michelle that it's time for "table dances," and begins to mimic stripping off layers of clothing with a familiarity that hints of experience. This is the same wide-eyed girl who, just a few tequilas ago, was fretting over whether or not to dispense with her lightweight jacket in the afternoon swelter, heedful of the fact that her lacy black bustier might be just a touch too *daring* for Jeff Macey's Lake Oswego neighbors. And here she is, pretending to peel it back, gyrating in her seat to a remake of the Jackson Five's "I'll Be There" on some scratchy radio, singing along with not a bad voice and what she thinks is a seductive cast to her eyes—*and it is!* Obviously she's got Michelle concerned, who hisses, "Not here!" But Jaisa, so named because "her parents wanted a boy" (as the ever-helpful Michelle has already explained), has spent all of her not-yet-twenty years proving to her parents—and the world at large—that she's anything but.

Jaisa isn't one of Jeff Macey's girls—at least, not anymore. A former employee of Jeff's—one hesitates to inquire as to the exact *nature* of said employment—she's clearly struggling with what he's successfully taught the others regarding the better part of valor. As it turns out, though, Jeff *is* paying her today: "Six bucks an hour, just to sit here," she giggles, then inhales. She and Michelle have been at it since 9:00 A.M., supervising the last-minute preparations for a party that was planned only two days earlier. Yesterday they scoured Clackamas Town Center for ashtrays—and found one, for fifty dollars. "Fuck *that*," Jaisa pronounced. "We'll go to fuckin' Taco Bell and steal their little tin ashtrays before we spend fifty bucks on *one* fuckin' ashtray." Michelle knew better, however, and before too long they'd found what they needed, enough to supply every smoker at the party—though Jaisa seems to be having some trouble actually getting the ashes *into* hers—all for $1.59 apiece.

Another perk for smokers is a scattering of complimentary matches, royal blue covers with Jeff Macey's corporate logo imprinted in gold. And for those delicate types whose olfactory sensitivities might be offended by the pungent whiff of sulfur loosed by a struck match, Jeff Macey has thoughtfully provided divers lighters, multicolored Mini Bic Clics, sold in packages of two and faithfully purchased by Michelle and Jaisa, his lady foot soldiers of the day.

A temp agency has provided the catering staff. Lisa, all in black, her trim, muscular body sporting a casual halter and skirt, flips steaks on the grill, a brand-new outdoor barbecue acquired especially for the occasion—it seems Jeff Macey couldn't be bothered to clean the old one ("Don't tell anyone," breathes Michelle), so he bought new. And it's clear his girls appreciate this ability of Jeff's, despite Michelle's whispered warning. Then there's the woman tending bar in—*how can she stand it in this heat?*—dark nylons and a black, fitted short skirt, her long-sleeved white blouse wrapped tightly around her and fastened at the neck by a black bow tie. She's very striking, as she negotiates the long, linen-draped table teeming with more bottles than the local bistro, her thick black hair rippling into shades of blue and purple. "She had that *done* just yesterday," says Jaisa, whose last shot of tequila has taken her memory for the bartender's name along with it. Two more women dressed in black magically pop up in answer to empty glasses, plates, or hands, proffering drinks, donuts, potato or macaroni salads, brownies, olives and cauliflower, and small, tart wedges of mandarin orange. They could *all* be Jeff Macey's girls—and today, in fact, they are!

Jeff Macey's number one girl—"girl*friend*," he qualifies—is trailing behind him as he escorts some newly arrived neighbors on a tour of his Chandler Road home. Jeff likes a woman in a "nice spaghetti-strap dress," he admits, and Laurie does her best to accommodate him. Her abstract floral-print shift sports something more on the order of lasagna straps, but Jeff doesn't seem to mind, his arm circling so tight around Laurie's thin shoulders that her bony frame is sure to snap at any moment. Laurie doesn't say too much, but then what she does say is congenial in the extreme. She's not quite the *hostess* of the day, but the host's main squeeze, anyway, and plays out her role with a tentative grace that belies her not inconsiderable skill. She welcomes guests with a modest, silent smile, blushes over top of her painted cheekbones as Jeff self-consciously kicks her white flat sandals under the loveseat from their brazen presence on his bedroom floor—an unwitting concession that the unmarried Laurie spent last night in this $695,000 Lake Oswego house with the unmade master bed. But if Jeff Macey had thought this would shock his current tour group, he needn't have worried. The sexual revolution of two decades past has finally infiltrated the air-conditioned bedrooms of Portland's purlieus, and even Lake Oswegans have been known to indulge their libido on occasion. Take Jeff Macey's neighbor, for instance, whose suburban freckles remain impassive as the accusatory shoes are scuttled out of sight. Five months pregnant under her Nordstrom maternity plaid, she's preoccupied with the interior decor—"very Ralph Lauren-ish" with its dark wooden hues—and apparently unfazed by the walk-in shower's double nozzles—*double your pleasure double your fun*—or the windowed jacuzzi at the foot of the bed.

This isn't the first tour Jeff Macey has given today—"I'll probably wind up doing it again in another hour," he sighs—and his two daughters are already so inured to the ceaseless introductions that they simply can't be bothered to greet this latest round

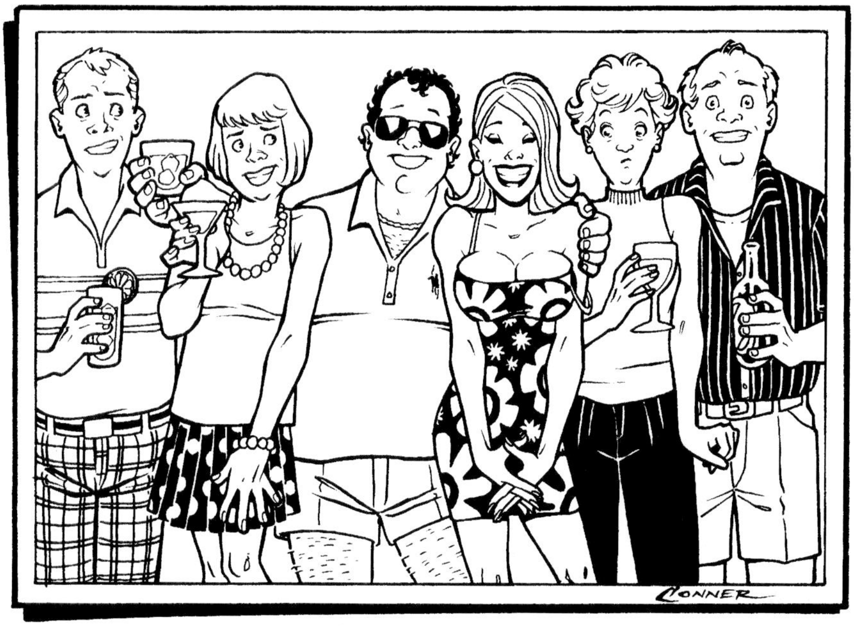
CONNER

of visitors intruding on their sometime home. The eleven-year-old Mariah is too absorbed in her PC, "just like her father," who in turn dismisses her current pursuit as "only a computer game," albeit one with surprisingly crisp screen resolution for 1992—Super Mario Brothers this ain't! Elder daughter Clarissa, tiny yet ample in all the right places, manages finally to acknowledge her father's guests with an ever-so-slight smile straining on a face with edges too hard for its 25 years.

Angel doesn't like Clarissa, and she makes no bones about it. "You can tell *exactly* what she's like just by *looking* at her," she counsels with that guileless, almost ruthless, opinionated honesty, second nature to female adolescents but bred out of them before they turn twenty. Michelle would no doubt shush her right about now, except that *she's* off on another of her frequent trips to the downstairs bathroom. "Look at her strut," Angel continues with a sneer, as Clarissa does indeed *strut* by, all bouncy and barefoot, tanned breasts bobbing in her summer sunsuit, eyes trained straight ahead, looking through aviator glasses at precisely no one.

It's not clear why Angel—*Angélique*—so vehemently despises Clarissa. Perhaps it's Clarissa's petite and perfect body. At eighteen, Angel still has yet to lose her baby fat, and her avowed taste—"*when* I eat"—for the sugar-glazed donuts, creamy potato salad, chocolate-frosted cakes, caramel rolls, and mesquite-flavored chips that are all being served today is testament to her tendency toward the corpulence born of inadequate nutrition, evidenced by Angel's own mother, sitting but a few tables away, her bloated, 200-plus-pound form draped in yards of hot pink—another of Jeff Macey's girls, oddly enough.

Perhaps it's Clarissa's perfect pearl-handled teeth, compact and even—that Close-Up smile she will not suffer herself to wear on this hot afternoon. Angel, on the other hand, hasn't been lying about her candy-coated diet, and her rotting mouth would send chills up the collective spine of the American Dental Association.

Perhaps it's Clarissa's perfect new neighborhood, sequestered here in Lake Oswego's exclusive Iron Mountain district, that burns Angel's young proletarian butt. She's already pronounced the elder Macey daughter a "snob," in that unforgiving tone of the poor for the rich, and she doesn't *want* to get to know her any better. Angel already knows everything she *needs* to know about Clarissa. And what she knows, absolutely and with conviction, though without the adult sophistication—or education—to understand its import, is this: Clarissa is Jeff Macey's *daughter*. And that is something Angel can't possibly hope to touch. Never mind the pot of gold; there isn't even a rainbow lurking in her stormy little life.

Because, in the end, it all comes down to Jeff Macey—this short, rumpled, 46-year-old unremarkable man—Jeff Macey, whose inky black curls are pasted to his forehead on this sweaty afternoon, whose eyes take wary shelter behind dark, dark sunglasses—Jeff Macey, who moved into this Chandler Road estate not two months ago, all 4,000 square feet to himself—well, to himself *and* Christina, another Jeff Macey girl, his 22-year-old housekeeper, conveniently absent today, out of the way of quizzical looks from uncomprehending neighbors—Jeff Macey, all in white, performing this juggling act, an *incredible* juggling act, in thigh-high shorts and open-necked polo shirt, Laurie in her lasagna straps trailing behind, always trailing behind Jeff Macey—who today has invited his new Lake Oswego neighbors to a block party in his backyard, an "at home," as they'd no doubt call it, a kinda sorta get-to-know-you scene, a backyard social on this steamy Saturday—in which Jeff Macey juggles old money, young money, and no money at all—neighbors and friends and the girls—Jeff Macey's girls, his employees and daughters and Laurie trailing behind—for whom it all comes down to. Jeff. Macey.

= = =

The year is still 1992, and Jeff Macey is an astronomy buff. His company, Event Horizons, borrows its name, in fact, from that discipline's jargon: an event horizon is, basically, the outer rim of a black hole. At this spherical edge, the escape velocity is equal to the speed of light, which means, if Einsteinian wisdom should continue to curry favor among physicists, that no electromagnetic information can ever leave a black hole. Scientists don't quite know *what* to make of these singularities. They presume, but cannot yet prove, and maybe never will, that a black hole is what's left after a massive star finally shoots its nuclear wad. At that point, exhausted and drained, this onetime sun gives up its cosmic ghost, collapsing in on itself just as if some celestial housewife had pulled its invisible plug. The resulting swirl sucks up everything in its wake, leaving an empty area of totally distorted and uncharacterizable space. The black hole's event horizon, rather than an actual, physical surface, is more akin to a demarcation line, a hairsbreadth between quantifiable, measurable, down-home reality and the no-man's-land of the mystical, magical, unexplainable, and terrifying *unknown*. An event horizon, in other words, doesn't exist. It is a *concept*, a rumor that rustles through astrophysics, a cautionary signpost at the sidereal doorway to nightmare: Abandon hope, all ye who enter.

As President and Chief Executive Officer of Event Horizons, Jeff Macey knows a great deal about black holes and other astral phenomena. In fact, he's in the business of selling just exactly this sort of information. One of a mushrooming crop of online services at a time when the only "wide web" most of the world understands is of the arachnid variety, Event Horizons is an electronic bulletin board, a nationwide network of digitized communiqués available to anyone with a telephone, computer, modem, and verifiable cash—enough cash to have moved Jeff Macey from his North Shore apartment by the lake to the brand new ("virgin," says Jeff) Chandler Road residence.

Jeff Macey isn't exactly wild about his office space—he'd much rather show off his high-ceilinged home—and hopes to relocate the business in the not-too-distant future. In the meantime, Event Horizons takes up a couple of rooms on the second floor of one of those low-rise neo-California hacienda-style commercial buildings springing up like plantain weed throughout the Northwest. The company shares the inhabited areas of the building—OFFICE SPACE FOR LEASE—with a handful of Lake Oswego lawyers, an upscale art gallery, Jennings Insurance Agency, and the mysterious MTEK, among others. Event Horizons' outer office, a large, open area, is cluttered with phones, PCs and printers, hard copy strewn like oversize confetti on every desk, and the girls—Jeff Macey's girls—dressed comfortably on a mid-July workday.

The inner office, Jeff Macey's *sanctum sanctorum*, is dark and claustrophobic in size, its conditioned air choked off by the boss' cigarettes. He sits, his back to a curtained window, dwarfed by the massive computer arsenal crowding out one full third of his desk. To his left: a bank of phone lines, presumably the 64 owned by Event Horizons, the company's lifeblood—or, more appropriately, its arteries, regularly pumping out electronic erythrocytes and leukocytes to the vascular VDTs of America!

All for the moderate fee of $12 per hour.

In fact, Jeff started his billing at $8 per hour, but that was six years ago, when he first created Event Horizons. He's had to raise the price twice since then—reluctantly, he claims, although his Lake Oswego mortgage cuts a hefty figure, no doubt. "I want to be the Ted Turner of online services," Jeff avers, but industry giants have so far kept him firmly in their considerable shadow—1992 giants like Sears and IBM's Prodigy, General Electric's GEnie, and the already venerable CompuServe. "That dork-ass communications company!" he says of the latter, despite the fact that CompuServe helps butter Jeff Macey's daily bread by using Event Horizons as the source for its own downloadable files of full-color scanned NASA photography.

But the year *is* 1992, and these pixel-ated images of outer space represent only a minor portion of the "services" offered by Event Horizons—the company's CEO is nothing if not versatile. In the true spirit of American entrepreneurship, Jeff Macey has expanded *his* database—all of which is for sale, at the right price—to include not only digitized depictions of Neptune or deep space galaxies seen through the bug eyes of Voyager II. No, Jeff Macey is a purveyor of all *kinds* of information, verbal and visual—from stock market updates to the bits and bytes of his pet subject, astronomy, to the ever-popular Northwest Girls Series.

Excuse me?

Yes, these are Jeff Macey's girls, too—representing a whopping 85 percent of his business—and he shares them with thousands of Event Horizons subscribers—those of legal age, at least. "It's all *some* form of heavenly bodies," quips Jeff. And only "$8 *more* per hour" note the ads, in fine print. 1-800-GO-MODEM, indeed!

In a classic ex post facto move, the FBI is only now scurrying to look into this multi-million-dollar industry, the latest in do-it-yourself sex, a 1990s version of the trend pioneered by Hugh Hefner four decades ago. And they're not the *only* ones looking!

The Feds don't worry Jeff Macey. He believes in . . . well, *money*. America, he says, is an "incredible country," in which a powerful puritan ethic, on the one hand, is pitted against extraordinary freedom on the other, the freedom even to burn the flag, a freedom unmatched anywhere else on the globe. And the thrust that cuts through that division, the singular tension that generates the energy to keep either potential boiler from meltdown is . . . pure, old-fashioned capitalism. Sex sells, he's decided, and the U.S. dollar will out.

Besides, Jeff Macey wants to give the average person "a good shake," he says, not intending the pun. He rants at a video culture that consistently underestimates the intelligence of the public, that proffers the lowest common denominator—*in every-thing*—like so much milky pabulum. Whatever Jeff Macey does, however, he likes to do well.

He's bright, he says more than once, and creative. An Oregon native—a breed that gets rarer with the daily influx of California's global warming escapees—Jeff Macey stuffed his University of Kansas journalism degree in a back pocket and hit the oft-traveled mid-seventies road, odd-jobbing through the red-necked South— North Carolina and Texas—moving west to the more liberal counties of San Diego and Ventura before migrating north once more. An Army Research Institute employee for a time, he developed computerized training programs for the military, in the course of which he did some bellwether work in the then-burgeoning field of computer graphics, marrying photography and electronics, he explains, by encoding images into the binary digits of the language spoken by IBM and Apple, among others. Says Jeff Macey, "I like to be the first."

The first image successfully digitized by Jeff Macey for high-resolution computer reproduction streaks down his monitor as if some electronic draftsman wielding an invisible palette were painting an on-the-spot tableau. A monarch butterfly, *Danaus plexippus*, fills the screen with its four-inch wingspread, all dark yellows and oranges with black veins limning the tips. Jeff Macey always did appreciate a thing of beauty.

Next, he punches up "Laura" onscreen, #2 in the Northwest Girls Series. A large-bosomed brunette begins to grind her naked hips, back and forth, back and forth, in a forested, suburban backyard. There's something not quite natural here, an infinitesimal twitch to her swaying, back and forth, forth and back. She's on a loop, the visual equivalent to the late-eighties' M-M-Max Headroom-room. "I shot this at my house," Jeff Macey says, admitting that he does all the filming for Event Horizons' "adult" services.

Lucky Jeff.

Laura #2 constricts and pops off the screen as another unclothed girl scrolls on, breasts slightly smaller, skin so pale. She walks toward the viewer, then back again, this time with none of Laura's digital spasming. She's outdoors, strolling the length of a wooden backyard deck scattered with patio tables and open white chairs. Jeff Macey fingers the keyboard, and she speeds up, slows down, speeds up again, returns to a casual saunter. She's got that innocent appeal, says Jeff, large-eyed, a modicum

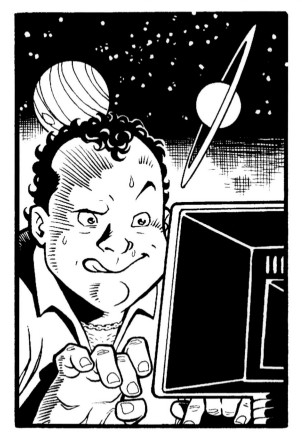

of Max Factor, pretty. "I like 'em pretty," he notes, eschewing the "barmaid" type for his computerized fantasies in favor of the girl-next-door, though it's doubtful that any of Jeff Macey's Lake Oswego neighbors would be inclined to model for his particular brand of home videos.

A Victoria's Secret blonde in a high-ceilinged boudoir, the last of today's Northwest Girls, pulls at an errant strap—a spaghetti strap, perhaps—and her black lace babydolls slink to the white carpet. She pauses for a moment. Then, as if suddenly aware of her dishabille—Eve, after her throaty swallow of the infamous golden delicious—her hand slithers to her pubis . . . stopping just short of another kind of event horizon. "That's nice," says Jeff Macey. And the screen goes blank.

= = =

"Sex is more private than death," Richard Rhodes once wrote, and online sex services—some of the safest sex in an AIDS-afflicted era—are more cloistered than a priest's confessional, though far less judgmental. And this is the sales pitch: gone is the middleman, the pimply 7-11 store clerk who, before the Southland Corporation capitulated to the demands of moral majority moms, stared at you over the brink of his stone-thick glasses as you fished dollar bills out of your wallet in exchange for the latest publications by Larry Flynt or the senior Guccione. Gone is the bopping teen, working weekends at West Coast Video, and her knowing leer as you creep out of the X-rated aisle, plunking your ill-gotten booty, face down, on the counter while you fumble for change, quickly. Gone is the face in the mirror, the accusing stare that you know is a reflection of Jeff Macey's puritan partisans but that you continue to confuse for . . . your own.

And all that's left is a secluded screen, a keyboard to caress, and Laura #2.

Social scientists theorize that with the advent of the telegraph, our wide world has hurled itself into an electronic age, distinct from both the chirographic and oral cultures that preceded it. In this new era of information influx, telephones, televisions, and other fantastical forms of telecommunications reach out their hard-wired hands to bind us in a McLuhanesque global village—while, paradoxically, pushing each and every one of us into our own solitary corner, complete with personal computer, sensory overload, and screaming alienation. Some communication scholars see this new electronic consciousness as a return to orality, a *secondary* orality—much as the cyberspace cowboys herd us even now into a secondary *reality*, a *virtual* reality. In an oral culture, sex was a pretty basic affair, by all accounts. The unlucky made do with a fertile imagination. In a print culture, sexual fantasies were mass-produced, from *Lady Chatterly's Lover* to the titillating, if crude, Tijuana bibles to the glossy, but admittedly cumbersome, *Playboy*. In 1992, while the electronic age is yet in its infancy, Hefner's still-life bunnies have already been supplanted by the Northwest Girls, and sex with magazines has gone the way of doctors' housecalls and the 12¢ comic, to be replaced by . . . sex with computers!

In 1844, when Samuel Morse tapped out the question, "What hath God wrought?" he couldn't possibly have dreamed that the answer would be: Jeff Macey.

= = =

Jaisa knows a thing or two about orality, though not of the type that's taught in university courses. In between trips to the bathroom with Trisha, she's been lighting up Marlboros, somewhat desultorily, through half-lidded eyes. Jeff Macey has taken Michelle's advice, and, with a hurried word to the blue-haired bartender, all booze is off-limits to Jaisa for the nonce, though Angel's fat, ponytailed brother Brett has snuck a Kahlua-and-cream her drunken way—heavy on the brown, light on the cow—which she proceeds, in most unladylike fashion, to spill down her black nylons, pearled rivulets collecting in the creases of her now-lopsided smile.

"She's drunk!" proclaims Mariah, too wise for her eleven years. "Jai-sa's dru-unk," she sing-songs.

Meanwhile, the Lake Oswego guests are having none of this. Demurely nibbling at Doritos while maintaining a safe distance from the antics of those . . . girls smoking at the patio table, Cathy watches her Gymboree-clad Ev-bo—"Evan-boy"—slurp down a soda. "Tha's my *fav'rite* joos," he squeals. "That's soda, not *juice*," his mother corrects, her voice rising in pitch, vainly attempting to protect her son's precious not-yet-two-year-old ears from the sound of . . .

"*Fuck!* Fuck is a *very* good word!" Trisha announces. The former Mormon finds it especially satisfying today. "Fuck! Fuck! Fuck!" she intones, like a mantra for the nineties . . .

As Clarissa goes bouncing by, on the balls of her bare feet, promenading down the white wooden deck like a Northwest Girl, past the Aerobics R Us encampment, where the clean-shaven crowd mobilizes forces with Lake Oswego's geriatric set, and on into the whitewalled kitchen where . . .

The fat, ponytailed Brett has just splurted New! Squeezable! 24-ounce Ranch dressing up Jaisa's nose—the most hysterical joke of her life, apparently—and she's

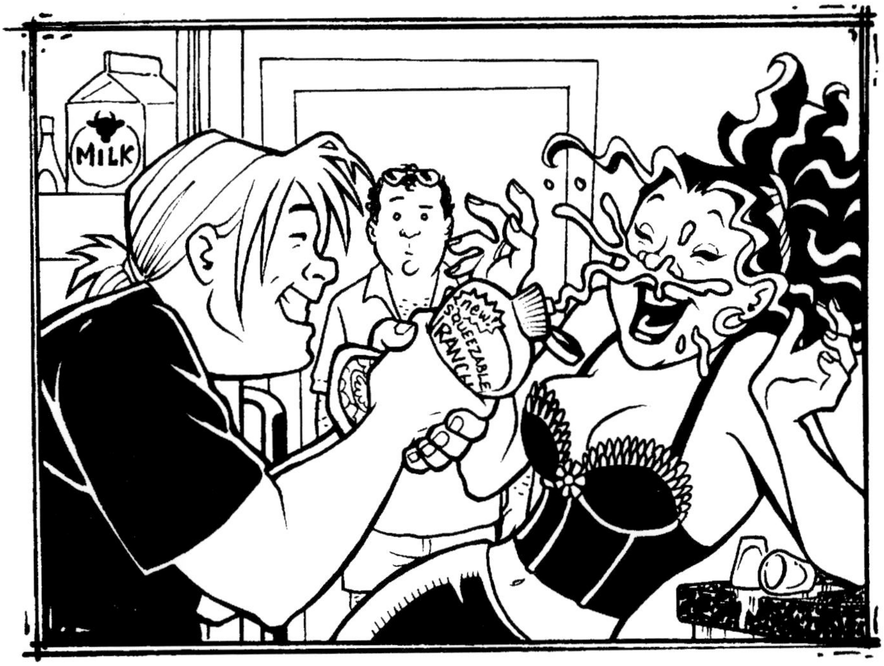
MILK
new!
SQUEEZABLE
RANCH

coughing and sneezing and dribbling and shrieking all at once, words tumbling out of her mouth like shiny-colored jacks, one on top of the other, as she tries to let Jeff Macey in on this a-*maz*-ing drollery. Jeff—a quick, wary chuckle as he darts a glance to the Chandler Road neighbors, now being courted by Laurie, all pinched but pleasant simper—"I hope that's *all* he put up your nose."

But Jeff Macey doesn't have to worry. Why should he, a former Girl Scout troop leader, give a shit for this Lake Oswego assemblage or its collection of wizened wallets? He knows the power of a buck, after all, has seen suited bankers loose their ties in the presence of his financial statements, their once-cocked eyebrows lowering innocuously into place. He doesn't need the bankers, their venture capital, this little El Dorado at the southernmost tip of Portland proper, or the condescending approbation of its residents—because he's already got what counts. He's got . . . his girls, Jeff Macey's girls, his daughters and housekeeper and girl*friend*—and the office girls, "a down-to-earth" bunch, he apologizes, but shouldn't, because they *are* down-to-earth, mired in a very real world, a world they can touch and smell and taste and desire with a passion forgotten by the Lake Oswego navigators whose noses are firmly anchored in the stratosphere—these girls of the office, Jeff Macey's customer-service-with-a-smile reps, Michelle and Trisha, and even little Angel, he's got her, too, though she won't move in with big daddy Jeff, not to his giant house on Iron Mountain with the white walls and high ceilings and unmade master bed, won't share her just-eighteen-year-old body with him at the expense of her North Portland boyfriend, the one who gropes her and hurts her and sucked the life out of her just last night, leaving two blotched, brown bruises on her bare, white neck for all of Lake Oswego to see—no, Angel won't give up her boyfriend any more than she could will away a disease, not for Jeff Macey or his virgin house or his absent housekeeper—but she's his girl just the same, and that's what really matters in the end—because in the end it *doesn't* come down to Jeff Macey, after all, but to his girls, to Jaisa and Michelle and Mariah and Clarissa, to all the girls, to Laura #2 and the rest of the Northwest Girls, who come from Newberg and North Portland and Anytown, U.S.A., whose lives would be vacant and stifled and go precisely nowhere, but who today at least, in this Saturday afternoon simmer, wrap their tinted lips around Salems and Camels and Marlboro Light 100s in a suburban backyard, Jeff Macey's backyard—and it is Jeff Macey who is their *savior* of a sort, for he has set their spirits free, and they know, in that curious, secret spot in their soul, that black hole that resides in us all at the outermost fringes of consciousness—*they know they are nothing*, after all. But in Jeff Macey's 46-year-old eyes, they are everything—they are . . . his girls, Jeff Macey's girls, and that is all they can hope for, all they will ever need.

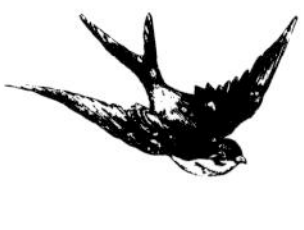

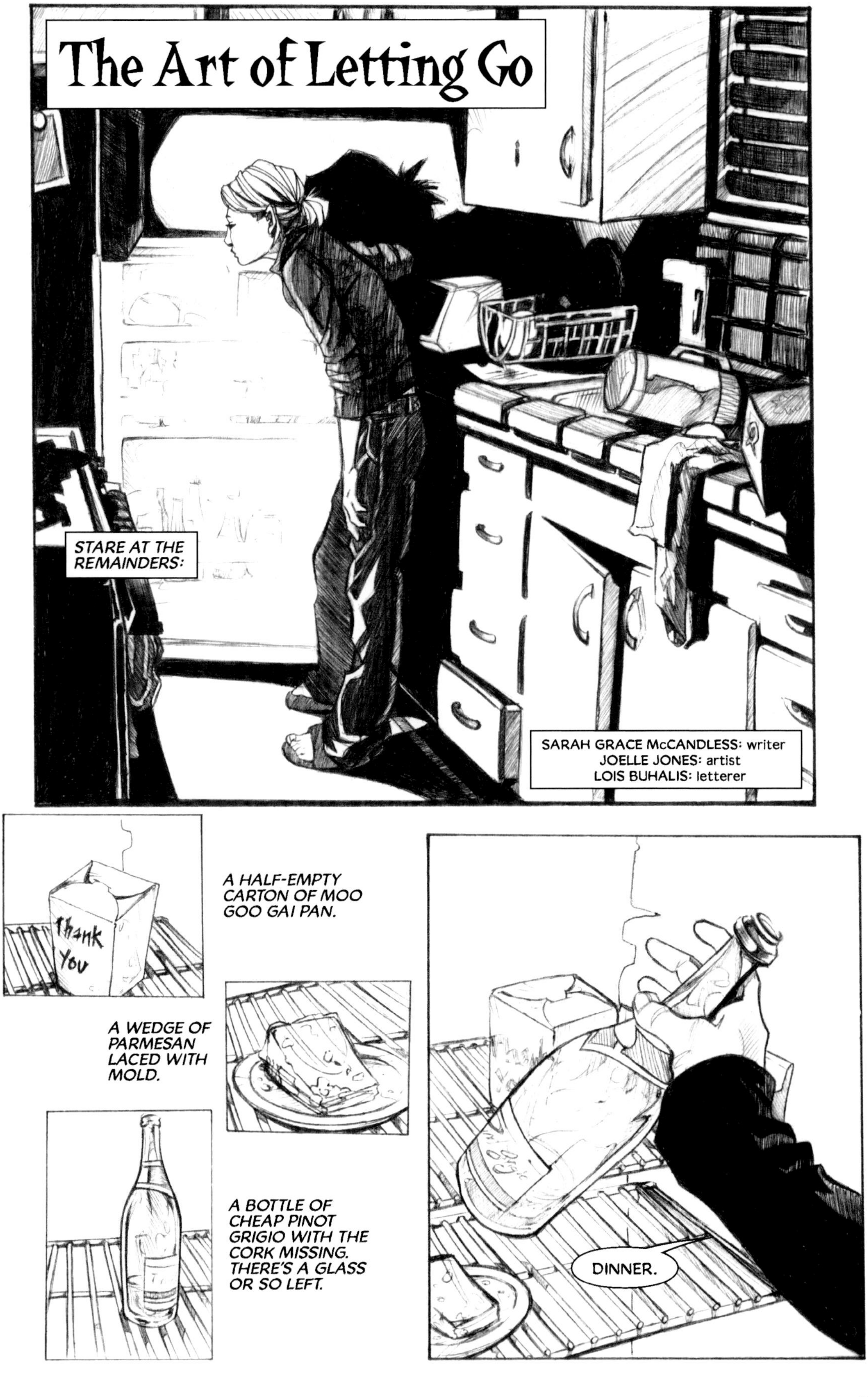

The Art of Letting Go
STARE AT THE REMAINDERS:
SARAH GRACE McCANDLESS: writer
JOELLE JONES: artist
LOIS BUHALIS: letterer
Thank You
A HALF-EMPTY CARTON OF MOO GOO GAI PAN.
A WEDGE OF PARMESAN LACED WITH MOLD.
A BOTTLE OF CHEAP PINOT GRIGIO WITH THE CORK MISSING. THERE'S A GLASS OR SO LEFT.
DINNER.

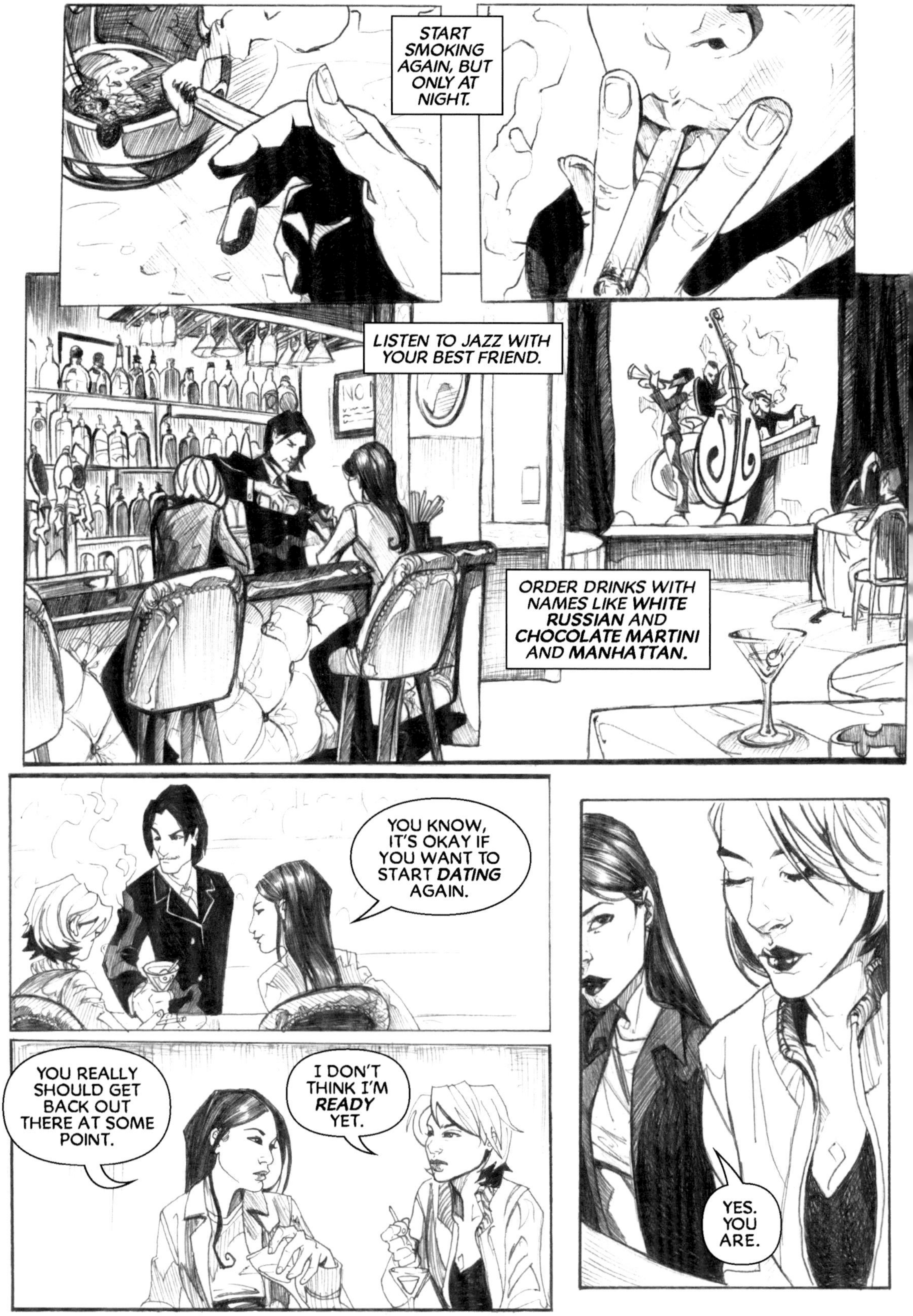
START SMOKING AGAIN, BUT ONLY AT NIGHT.
LISTEN TO JAZZ WITH YOUR BEST FRIEND.
NO
ORDER DRINKS WITH NAMES LIKE WHITE RUSSIAN AND CHOCOLATE MARTINI AND MANHATTAN.
YOU KNOW, IT'S OKAY IF YOU WANT TO START DATING AGAIN.
YOU REALLY SHOULD GET BACK OUT THERE AT SOME POINT.
I DON'T THINK I'M READY YET.
YES. YOU ARE.

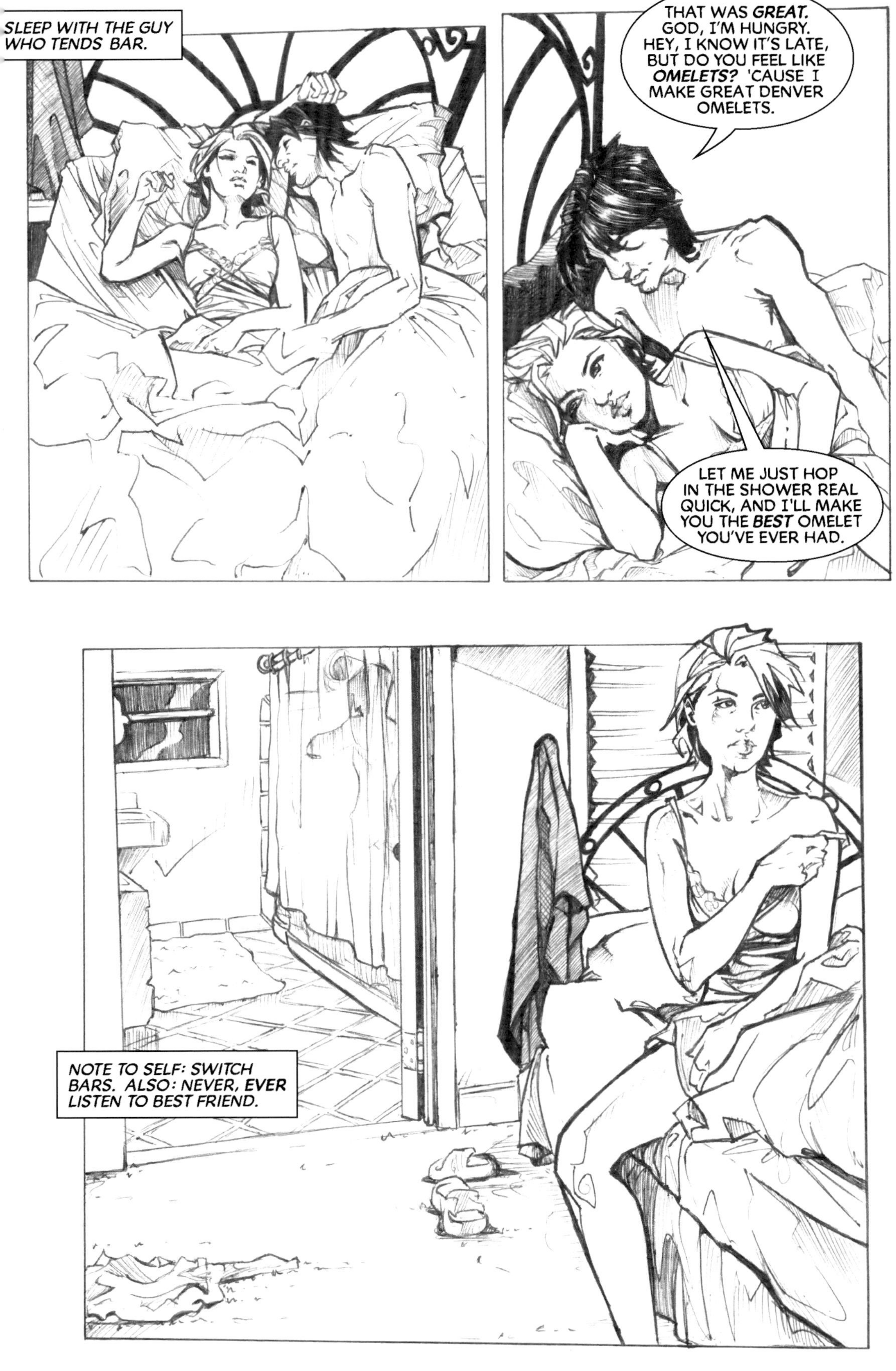
SLEEP WITH THE GUY WHO TENDS BAR.
THAT WAS GREAT. GOD, I'M HUNGRY. HEY, I KNOW IT'S LATE, BUT DO YOU FEEL LIKE OMELETS? 'CAUSE I MAKE GREAT DENVER OMELETS.
LET ME JUST HOP IN THE SHOWER REAL QUICK, AND I'LL MAKE YOU THE BEST OMELET YOU'VE EVER HAD.
NOTE TO SELF: SWITCH BARS. ALSO: NEVER, EVER LISTEN TO BEST FRIEND.

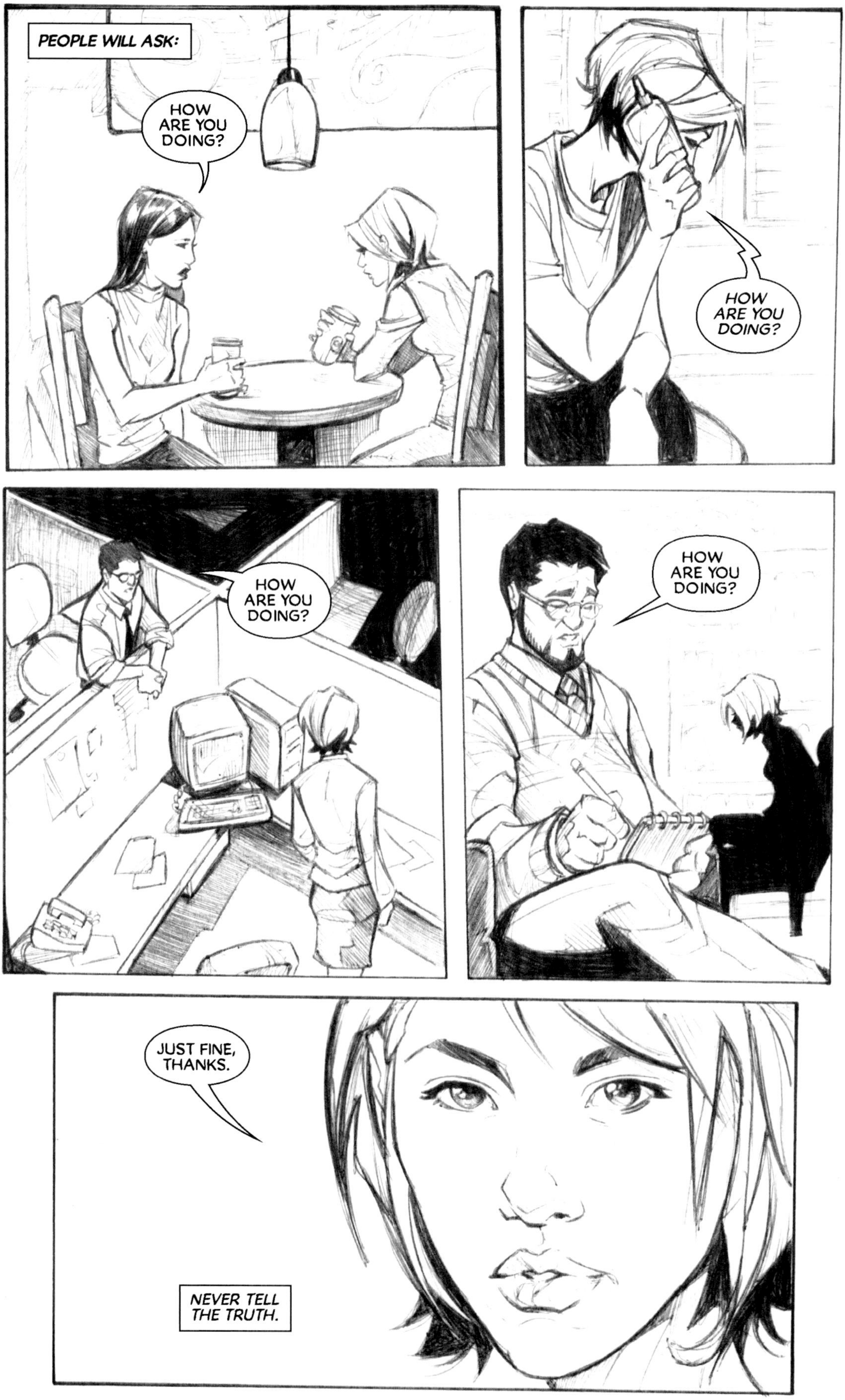
PEOPLE WILL ASK:
HOW ARE YOU DOING?
HOW ARE YOU DOING?
HOW ARE YOU DOING?
HOW ARE YOU DOING?
JUST FINE, THANKS.
NEVER TELL THE TRUTH.

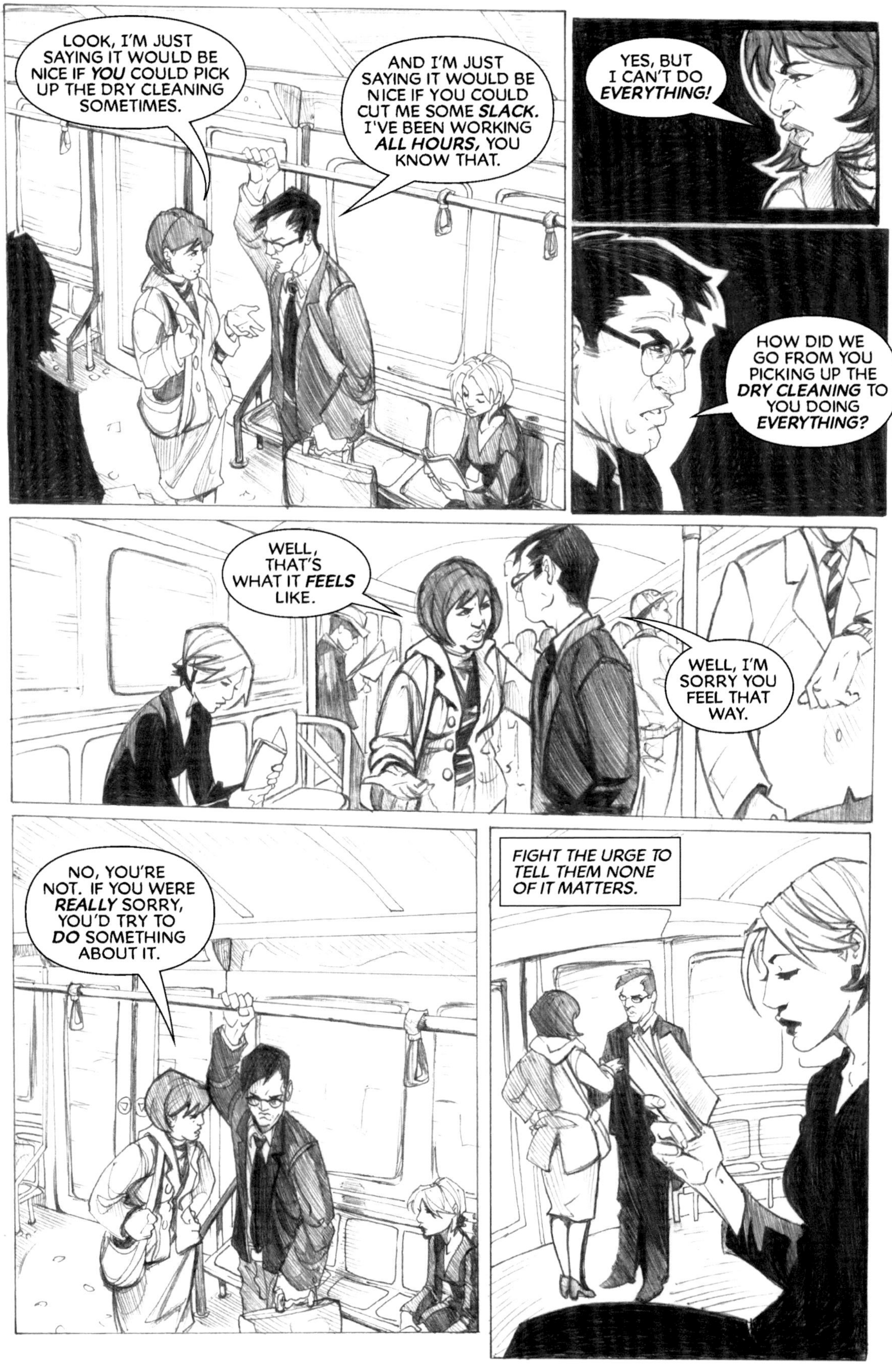
LOOK, I'M JUST SAYING IT WOULD BE NICE IF *YOU* COULD PICK UP THE DRY CLEANING SOMETIMES.
AND I'M JUST SAYING IT WOULD BE NICE IF YOU COULD CUT ME SOME *SLACK.* I'VE BEEN WORKING *ALL HOURS,* YOU KNOW THAT.
YES, BUT I CAN'T DO *EVERYTHING!*
HOW DID WE GO FROM YOU PICKING UP THE *DRY CLEANING* TO YOU DOING *EVERYTHING?*
WELL, THAT'S WHAT IT *FEELS* LIKE.
WELL, I'M SORRY YOU FEEL THAT WAY.
NO, YOU'RE NOT. IF YOU WERE *REALLY* SORRY, YOU'D TRY TO *DO* SOMETHING ABOUT IT.
FIGHT THE URGE TO TELL THEM NONE OF IT MATTERS.

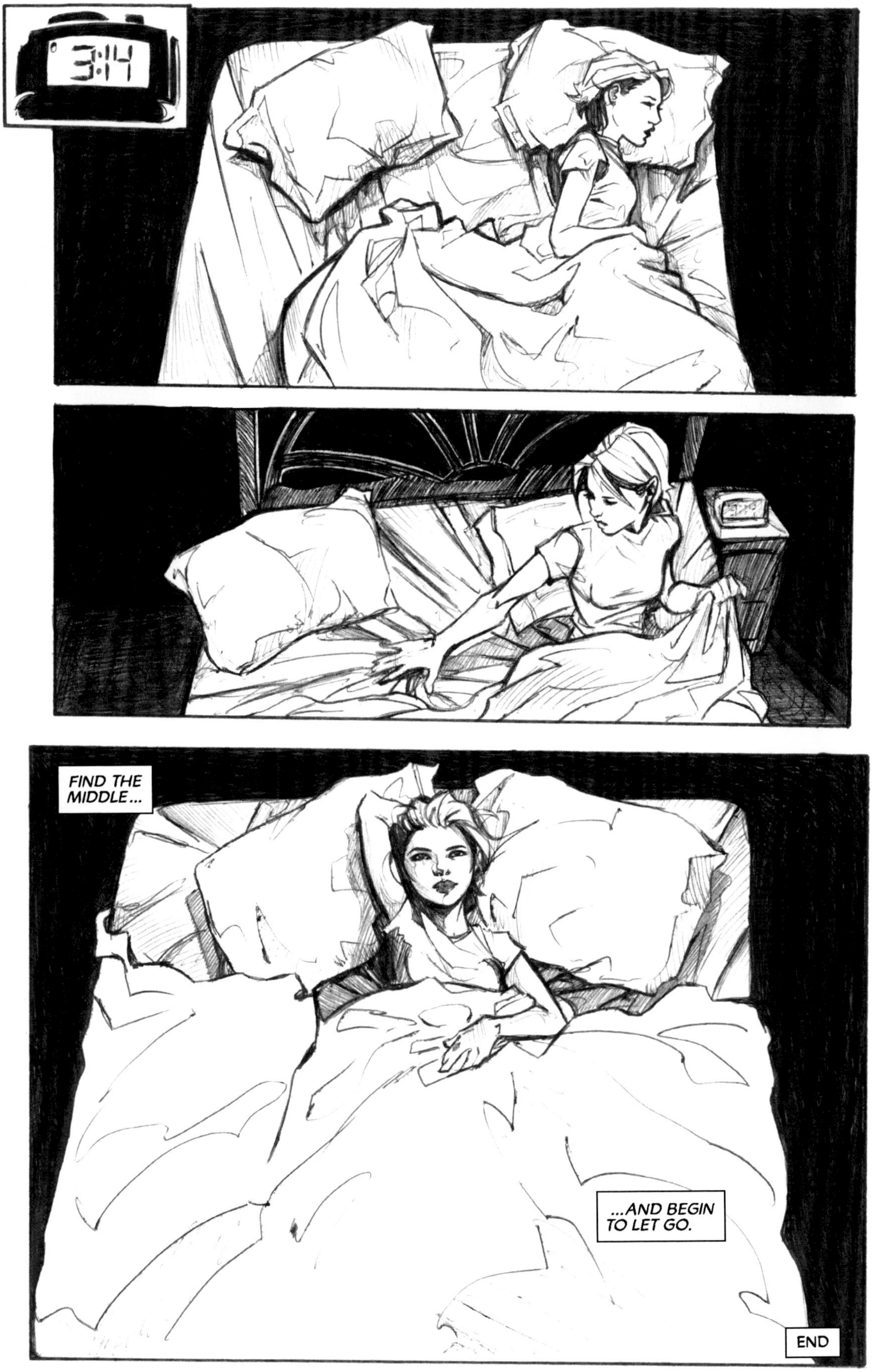
3:14
FIND THE MIDDLE...
...AND BEGIN TO LET GO.
END

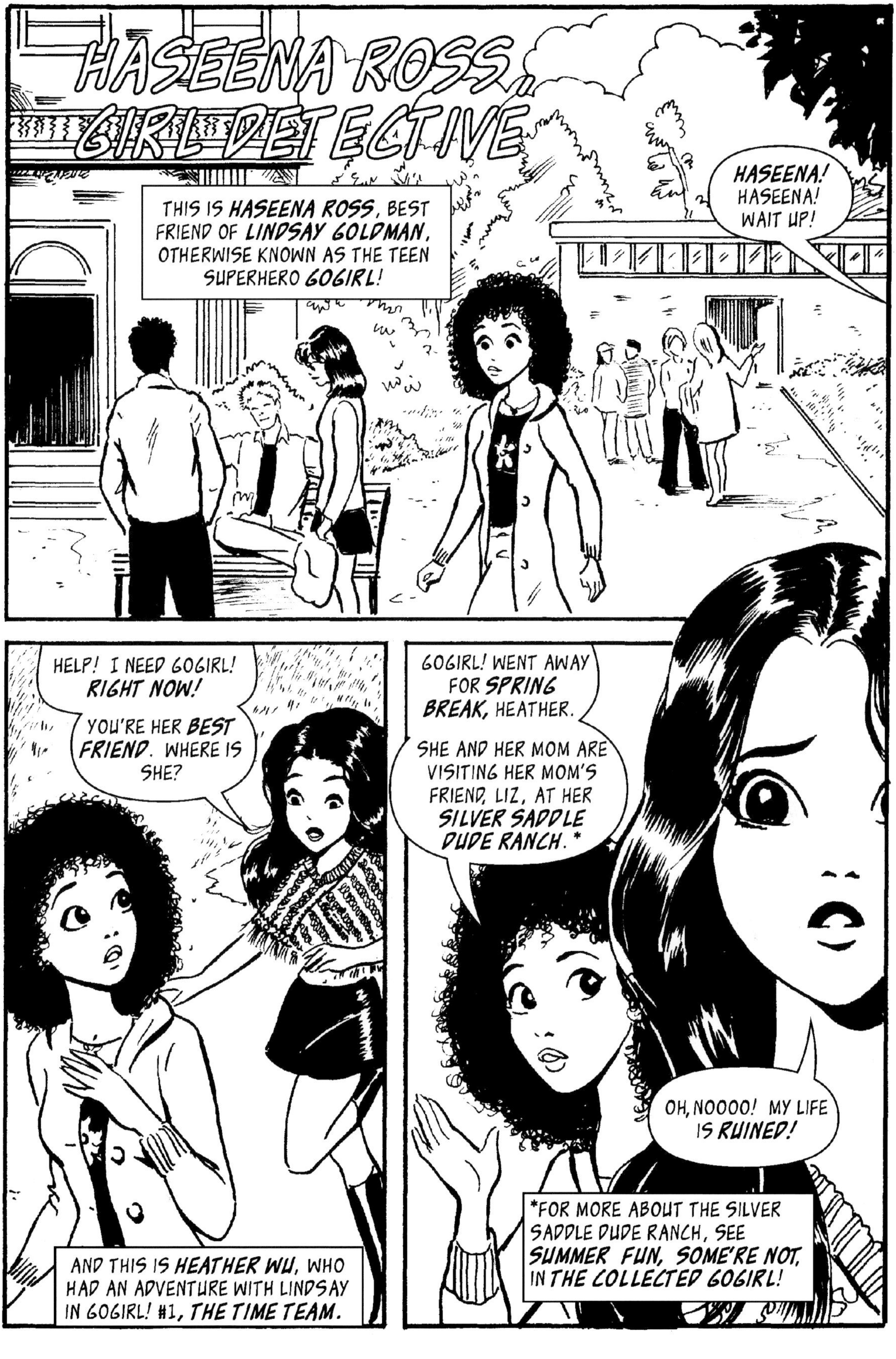
HASEENA ROSS, GIRL DETECTIVE
THIS IS HASEENA ROSS, BEST FRIEND OF LINDSAY GOLDMAN, OTHERWISE KNOWN AS THE TEEN SUPERHERO GOGIRL!
HASEENA! HASEENA! WAIT UP!
HELP! I NEED GOGIRL! RIGHT NOW!
YOU'RE HER BEST FRIEND. WHERE IS SHE?
AND THIS IS HEATHER WU, WHO HAD AN ADVENTURE WITH LINDSAY IN GOGIRL! #1, THE TIME TEAM.
GOGIRL! WENT AWAY FOR SPRING BREAK, HEATHER.
SHE AND HER MOM ARE VISITING HER MOM'S FRIEND, LIZ, AT HER SILVER SADDLE DUDE RANCH.*
OH, NOOOO! MY LIFE IS RUINED!
*FOR MORE ABOUT THE SILVER SADDLE DUDE RANCH, SEE SUMMER FUN, SOME'RE NOT, IN THE COLLECTED GOGIRL!

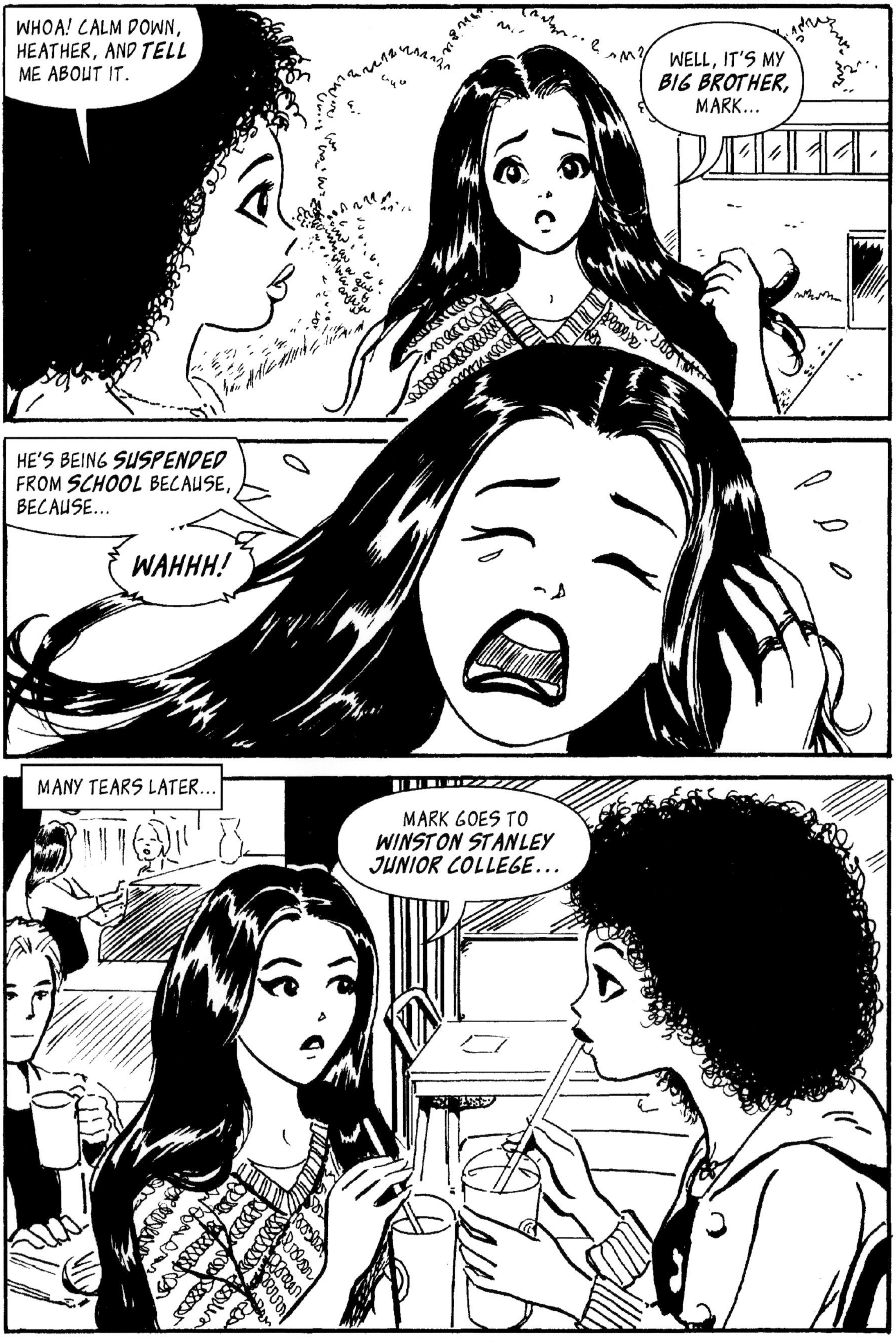
WHOA! CALM DOWN, HEATHER, AND TELL ME ABOUT IT.
WELL, IT'S MY BIG BROTHER, MARK...
HE'S BEING SUSPENDED FROM SCHOOL BECAUSE, BECAUSE...
WAHHH!
MANY TEARS LATER...
MARK GOES TO WINSTON STANLEY JUNIOR COLLEGE...

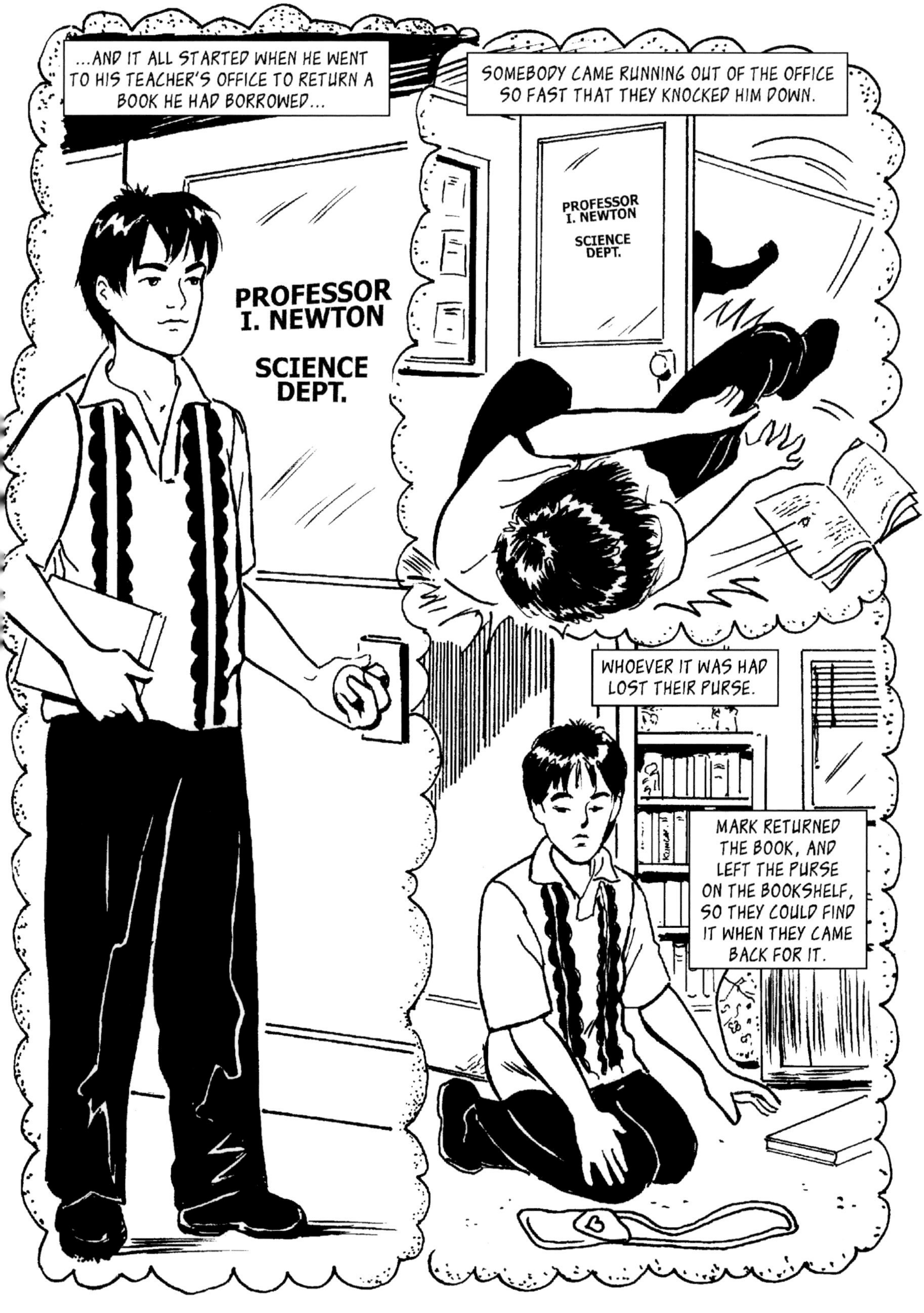
...AND IT ALL STARTED WHEN HE WENT TO HIS TEACHER'S OFFICE TO RETURN A BOOK HE HAD BORROWED...
PROFESSOR I. NEWTON
SCIENCE DEPT.
SOMEBODY CAME RUNNING OUT OF THE OFFICE SO FAST THAT THEY KNOCKED HIM DOWN.
PROFESSOR I. NEWTON
SCIENCE DEPT.
WHOEVER IT WAS HAD LOST THEIR PURSE.
MARK RETURNED THE BOOK, AND LEFT THE PURSE ON THE BOOKSHELF, SO THEY COULD FIND IT WHEN THEY CAME BACK FOR IT.

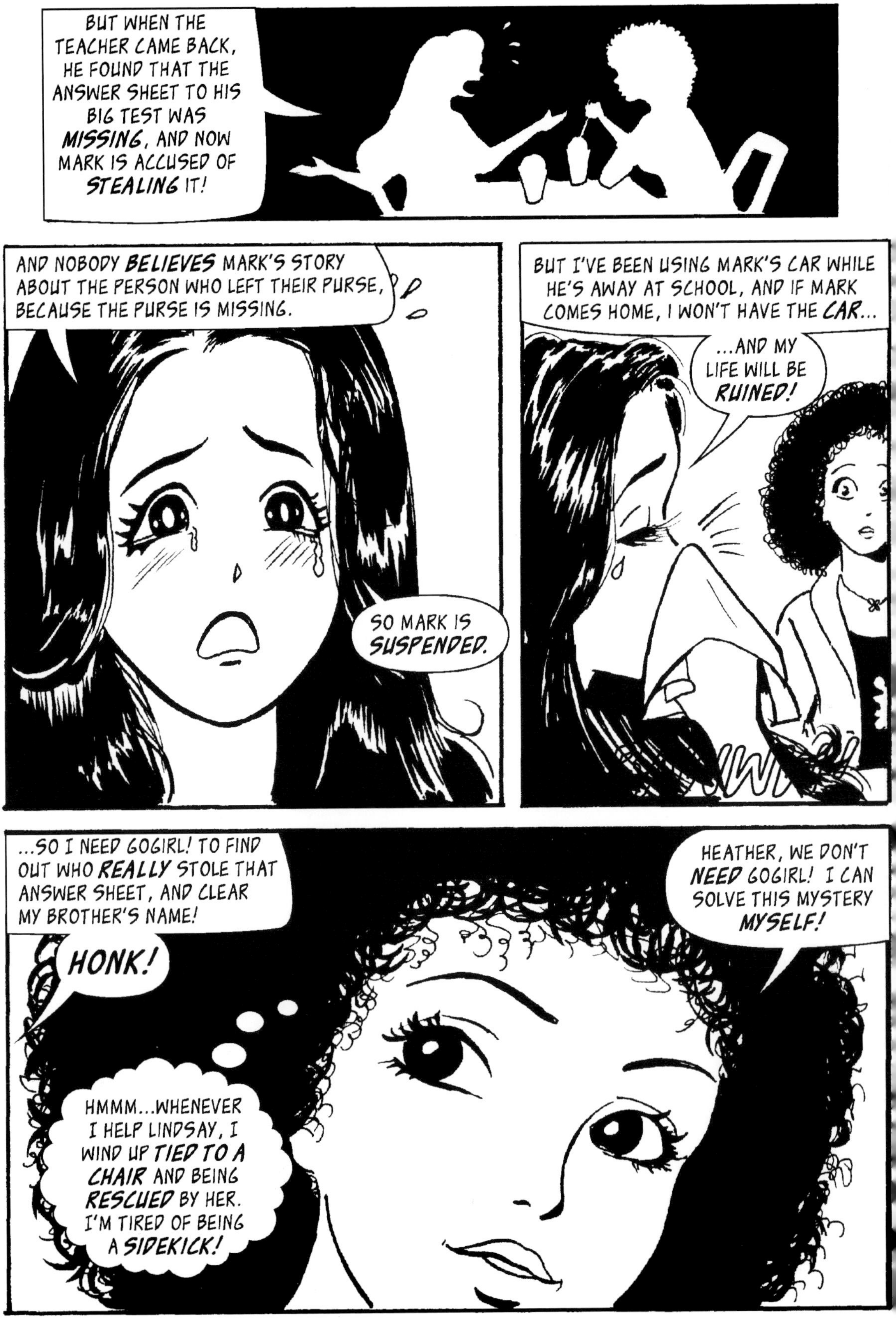
BUT WHEN THE TEACHER CAME BACK, HE FOUND THAT THE ANSWER SHEET TO HIS BIG TEST WAS MISSING, AND NOW MARK IS ACCUSED OF STEALING IT!
AND NOBODY BELIEVES MARK'S STORY ABOUT THE PERSON WHO LEFT THEIR PURSE, BECAUSE THE PURSE IS MISSING.
SO MARK IS SUSPENDED.
BUT I'VE BEEN USING MARK'S CAR WHILE HE'S AWAY AT SCHOOL, AND IF MARK COMES HOME, I WON'T HAVE THE CAR...
...AND MY LIFE WILL BE RUINED!
...SO I NEED GOGIRL! TO FIND OUT WHO REALLY STOLE THAT ANSWER SHEET, AND CLEAR MY BROTHER'S NAME!
HONK!
HEATHER, WE DON'T NEED GOGIRL! I CAN SOLVE THIS MYSTERY MYSELF!
HMMM...WHENEVER I HELP LINDSAY, I WIND UP TIED TO A CHAIR AND BEING RESCUED BY HER. I'M TIRED OF BEING A SIDEKICK!

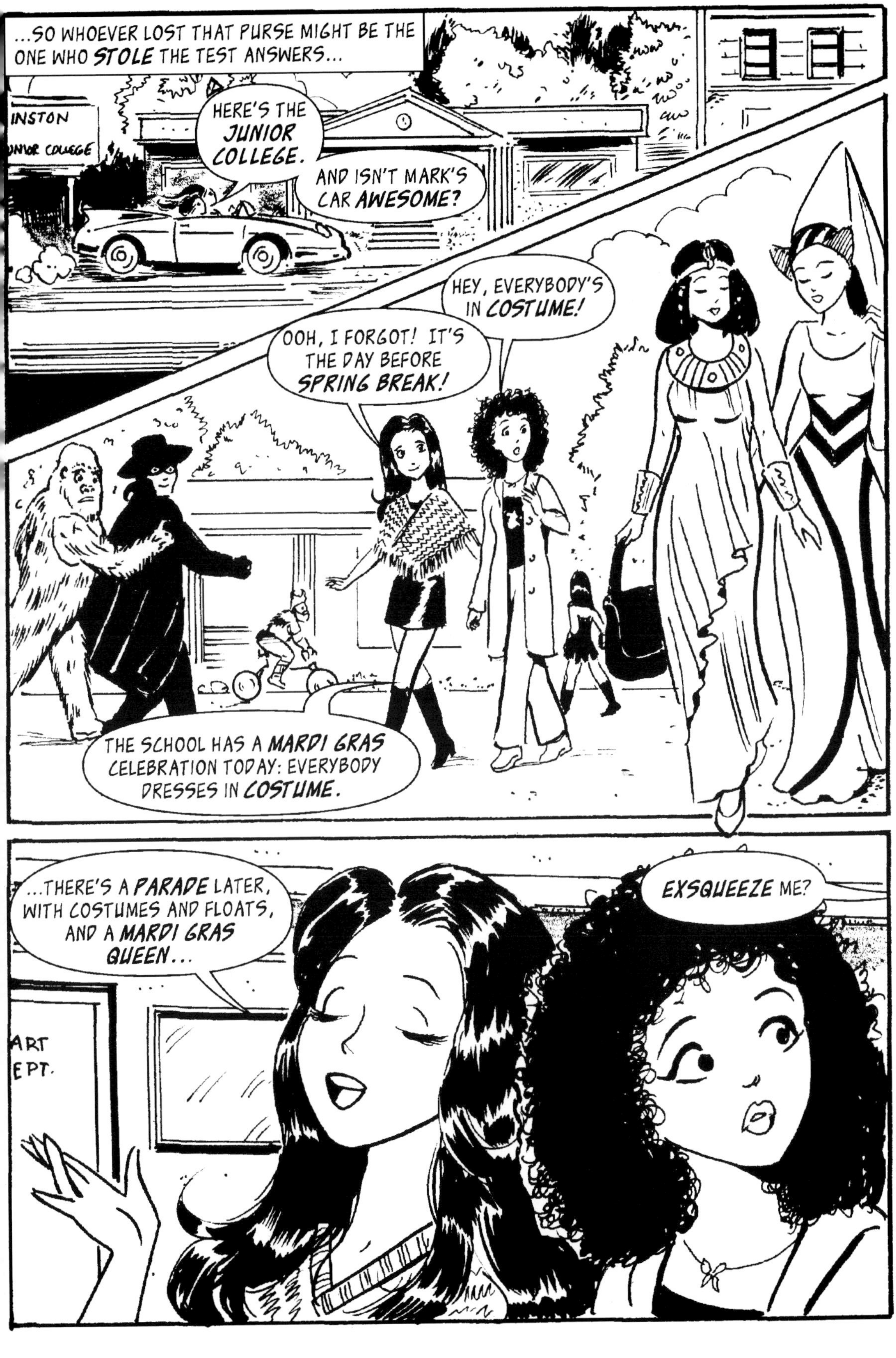
...SO WHOEVER LOST THAT PURSE MIGHT BE THE ONE WHO STOLE THE TEST ANSWERS...
INSTON
UNIOR COLLEGE
HERE'S THE JUNIOR COLLEGE.
AND ISN'T MARK'S CAR AWESOME?
HEY, EVERYBODY'S IN COSTUME!
OOH, I FORGOT! IT'S THE DAY BEFORE SPRING BREAK!
THE SCHOOL HAS A MARDI GRAS CELEBRATION TODAY: EVERYBODY DRESSES IN COSTUME.
...THERE'S A PARADE LATER, WITH COSTUMES AND FLOATS, AND A MARDI GRAS QUEEN...
EXSQUEEZE ME?
ART
EPT.

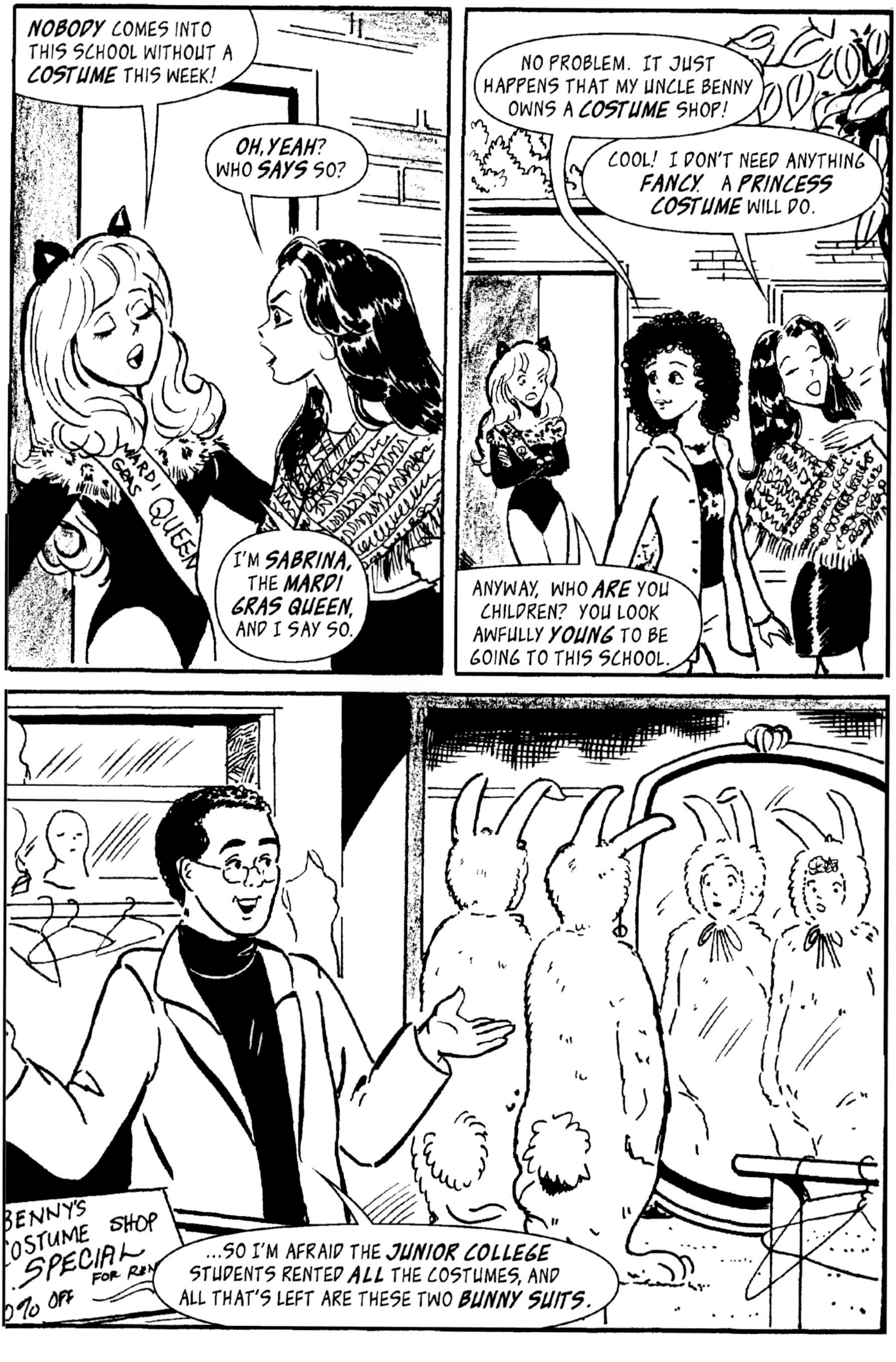
NOBODY COMES INTO THIS SCHOOL WITHOUT A COSTUME THIS WEEK!
OH, YEAH? WHO SAYS SO?
MARDI GRAS QUEEN
I'M SABRINA, THE MARDI GRAS QUEEN, AND I SAY SO.
NO PROBLEM. IT JUST HAPPENS THAT MY UNCLE BENNY OWNS A COSTUME SHOP!
COOL! I DON'T NEED ANYTHING FANCY. A PRINCESS COSTUME WILL DO.
ANYWAY, WHO ARE YOU CHILDREN? YOU LOOK AWFULLY YOUNG TO BE GOING TO THIS SCHOOL.
BENNY'S COSTUME SHOP SPECIAL FOR REN
0% OFF
...SO I'M AFRAID THE JUNIOR COLLEGE STUDENTS RENTED ALL THE COSTUMES, AND ALL THAT'S LEFT ARE THESE TWO BUNNY SUITS.

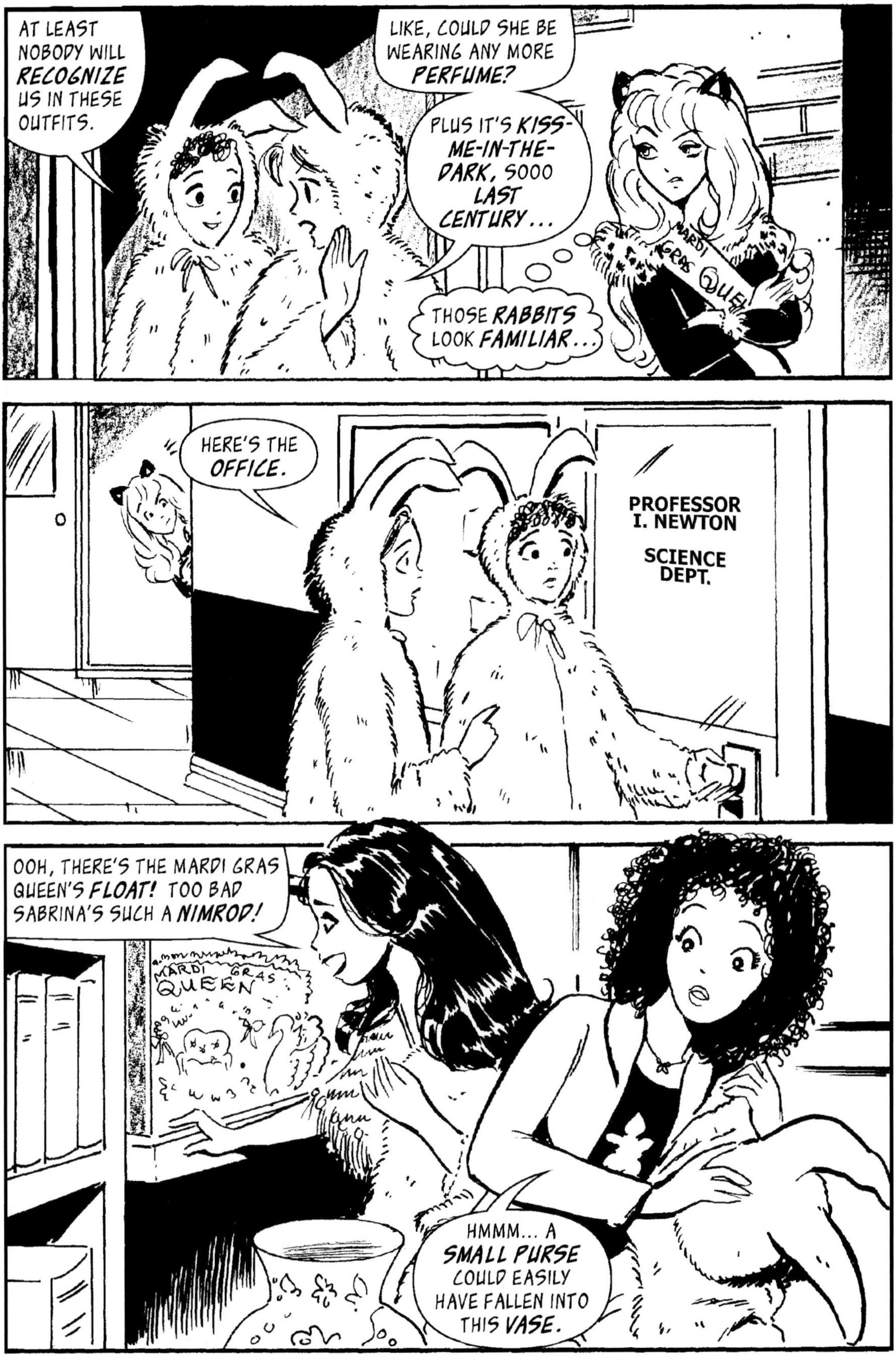
AT LEAST NOBODY WILL RECOGNIZE US IN THESE OUTFITS.
LIKE, COULD SHE BE WEARING ANY MORE PERFUME?
PLUS IT'S KISS-ME-IN-THE-DARK, SOOO LAST CENTURY...
THOSE RABBITS LOOK FAMILIAR...
MARDI GRAS QUEEN
HERE'S THE OFFICE.
PROFESSOR I. NEWTON
SCIENCE DEPT.
OOH, THERE'S THE MARDI GRAS QUEEN'S FLOAT! TOO BAD SABRINA'S SUCH A NIMROD!
MARDI GRAS QUEEN
HMMM... A SMALL PURSE COULD EASILY HAVE FALLEN INTO THIS VASE.

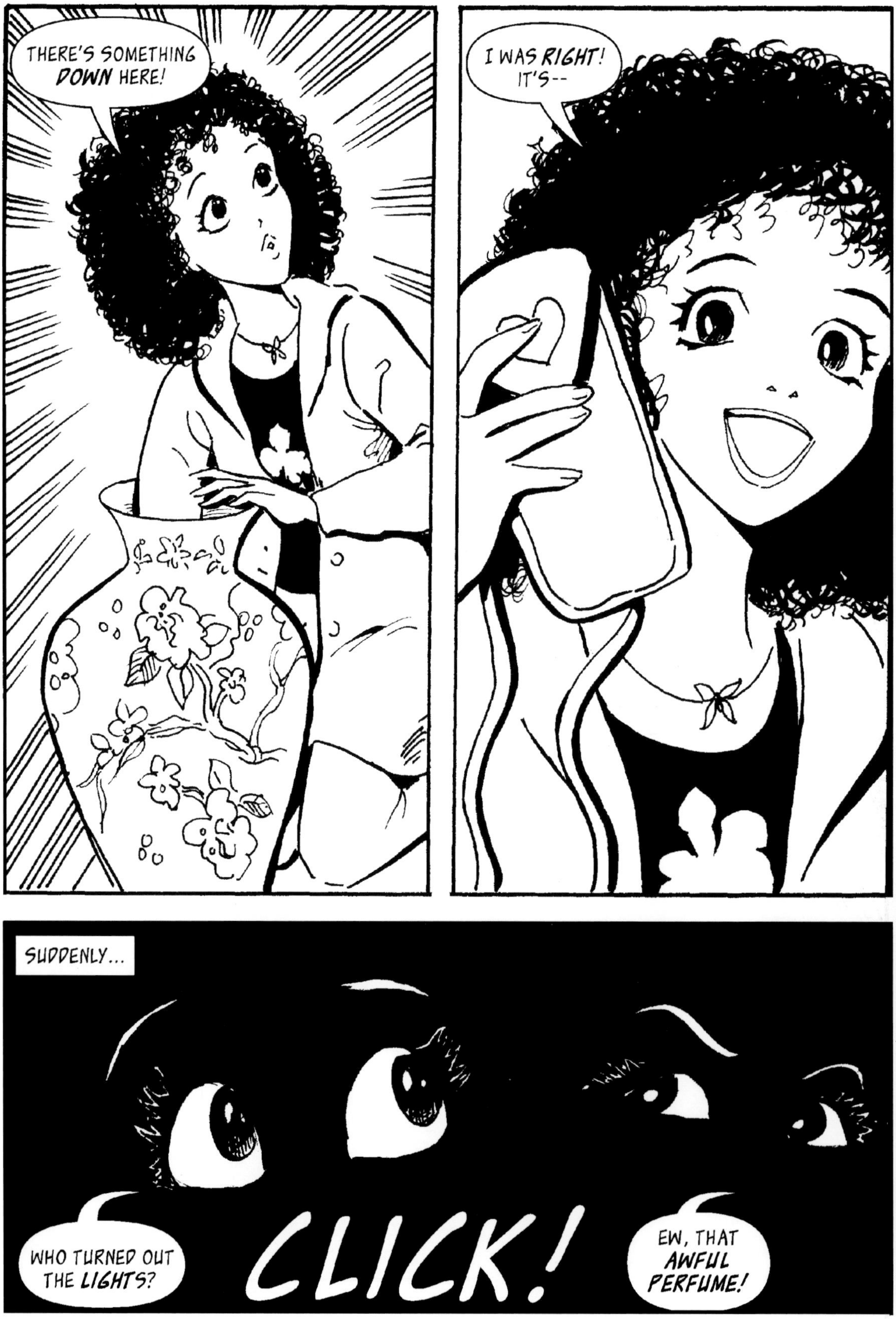
THERE'S SOMETHING DOWN HERE!
I WAS RIGHT! IT'S--
SUDDENLY...
WHO TURNED OUT THE LIGHTS?
CLICK!
EW, THAT AWFUL PERFUME!

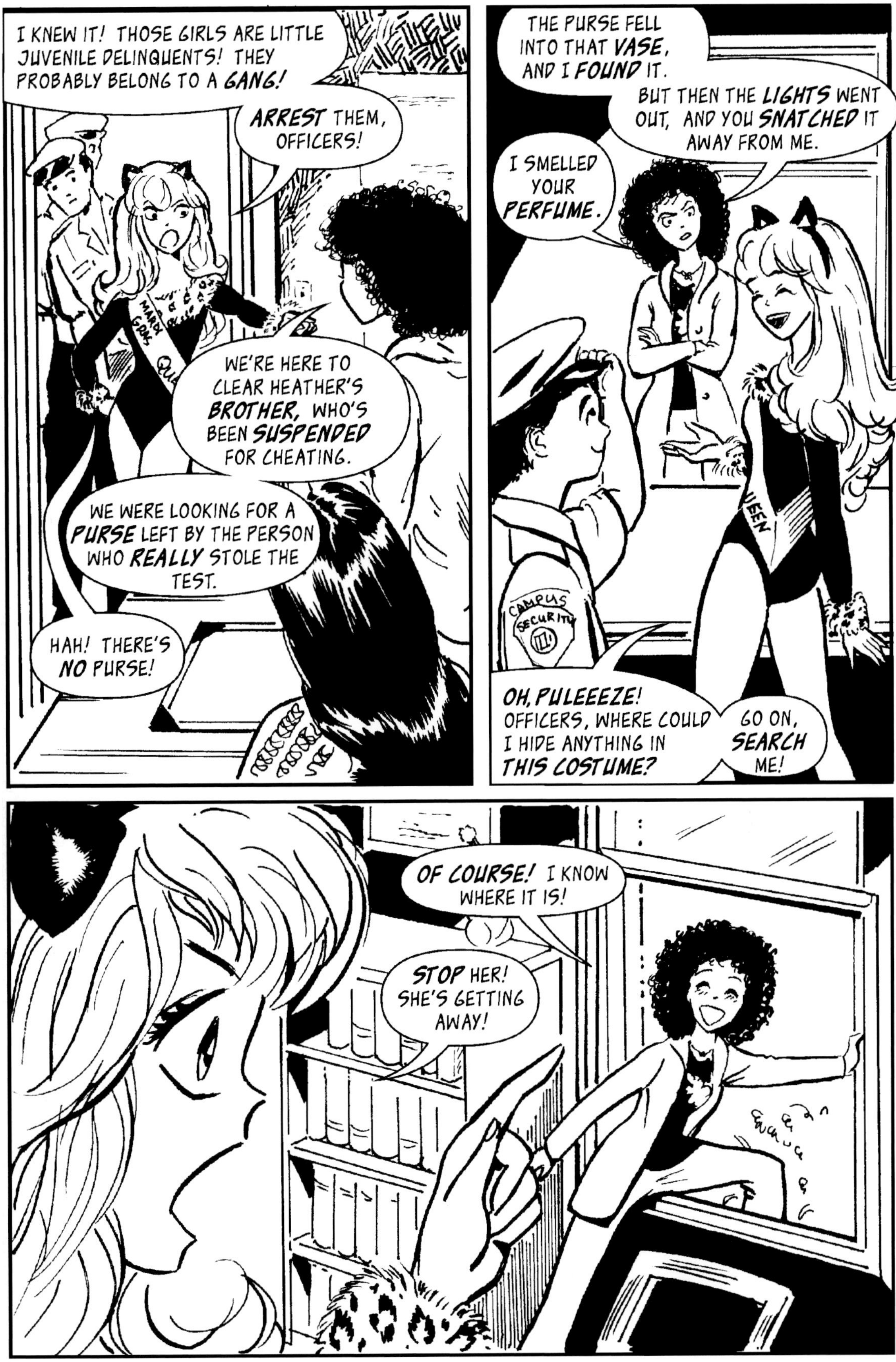
I KNEW IT! THOSE GIRLS ARE LITTLE JUVENILE DELINQUENTS! THEY PROBABLY BELONG TO A GANG!
ARREST THEM, OFFICERS!
WE'RE HERE TO CLEAR HEATHER'S BROTHER, WHO'S BEEN SUSPENDED FOR CHEATING.
WE WERE LOOKING FOR A PURSE LEFT BY THE PERSON WHO REALLY STOLE THE TEST.
HAH! THERE'S NO PURSE!
THE PURSE FELL INTO THAT VASE, AND I FOUND IT.
BUT THEN THE LIGHTS WENT OUT, AND YOU SNATCHED IT AWAY FROM ME.
I SMELLED YOUR PERFUME.
CAMPUS SECURITY
QUEEN
OH, PULEEEZE! OFFICERS, WHERE COULD I HIDE ANYTHING IN THIS COSTUME?
GO ON, SEARCH ME!
OF COURSE! I KNOW WHERE IT IS!
STOP HER! SHE'S GETTING AWAY!

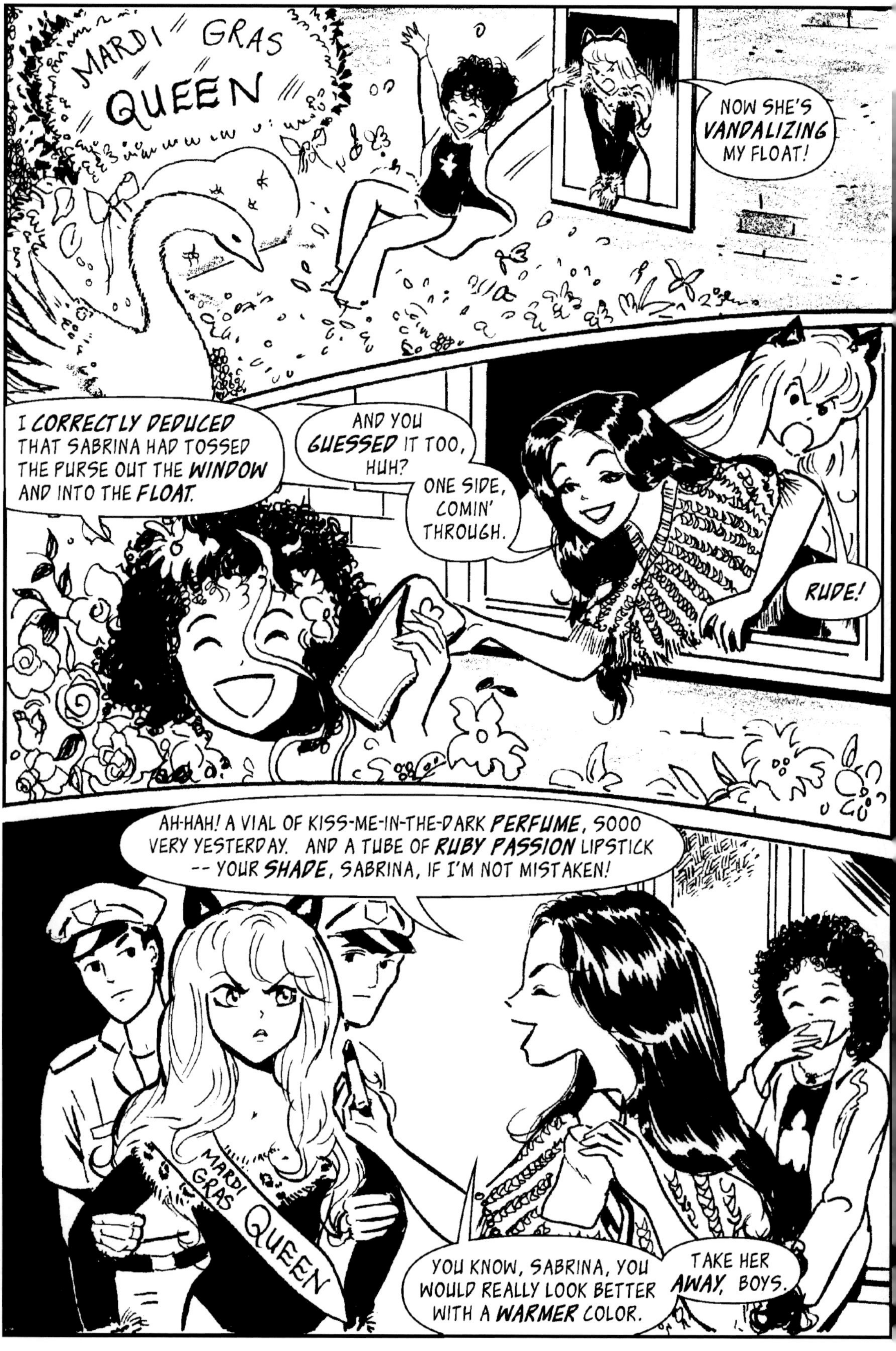
MARDI GRAS QUEEN
NOW SHE'S VANDALIZING MY FLOAT!
I CORRECTLY DEDUCED THAT SABRINA HAD TOSSED THE PURSE OUT THE WINDOW AND INTO THE FLOAT.
AND YOU GUESSED IT TOO, HUH?
ONE SIDE, COMIN' THROUGH.
RUDE!
AH-HAH! A VIAL OF KISS-ME-IN-THE-DARK PERFUME, SOOO VERY YESTERDAY. AND A TUBE OF RUBY PASSION LIPSTICK -- YOUR SHADE, SABRINA, IF I'M NOT MISTAKEN!
MARDI GRAS QUEEN
YOU KNOW, SABRINA, YOU WOULD REALLY LOOK BETTER WITH A WARMER COLOR.
TAKE HER AWAY, BOYS.

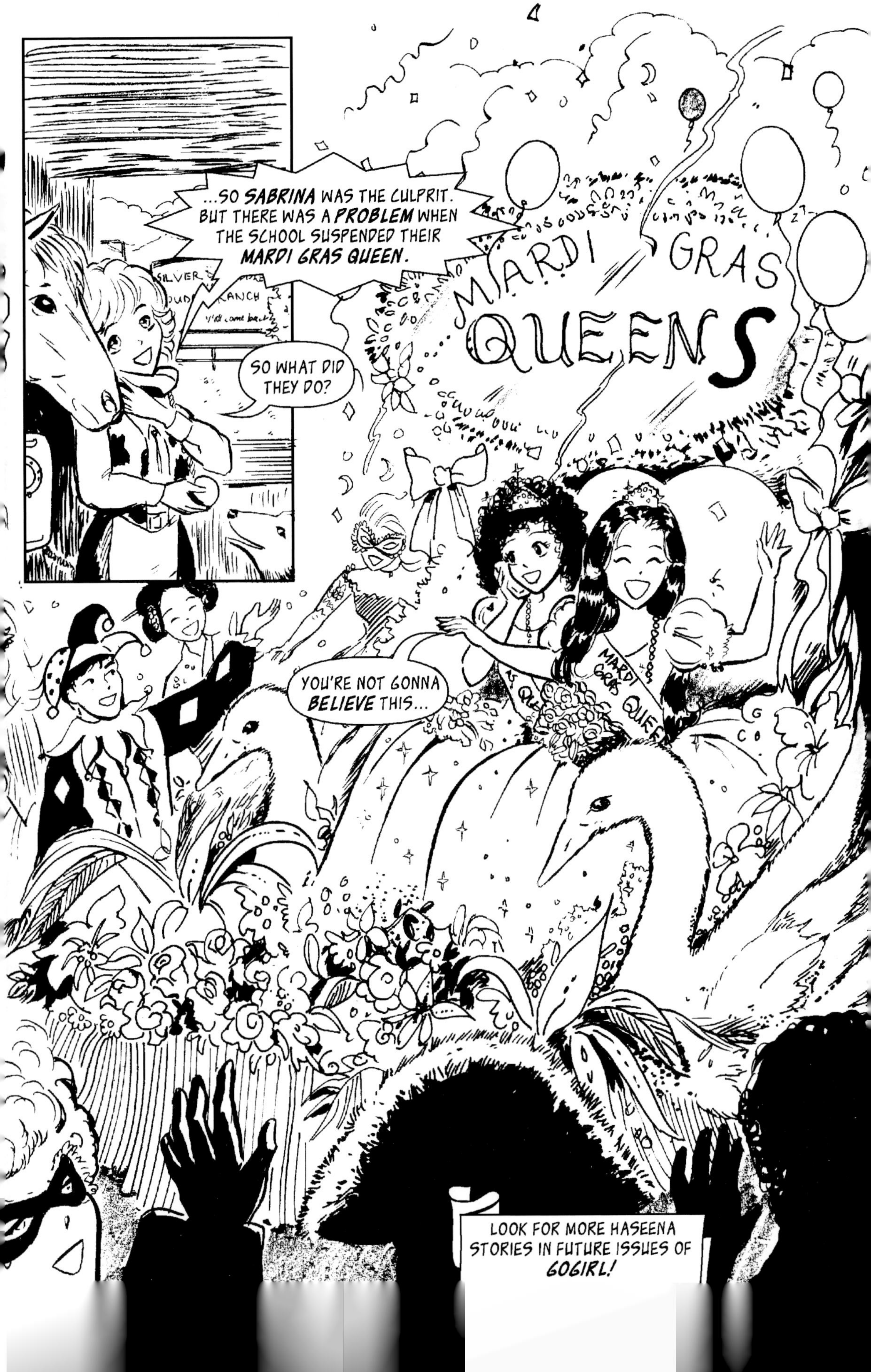

...SO SABRINA WAS THE CULPRIT. BUT THERE WAS A PROBLEM WHEN THE SCHOOL SUSPENDED THEIR MARDI GRAS QUEEN.
SO WHAT DID THEY DO?
MARDI GRAS QUEENS
YOU'RE NOT GONNA BELIEVE THIS...
LOOK FOR MORE HASEENA STORIES IN FUTURE ISSUES OF GOGIRL!

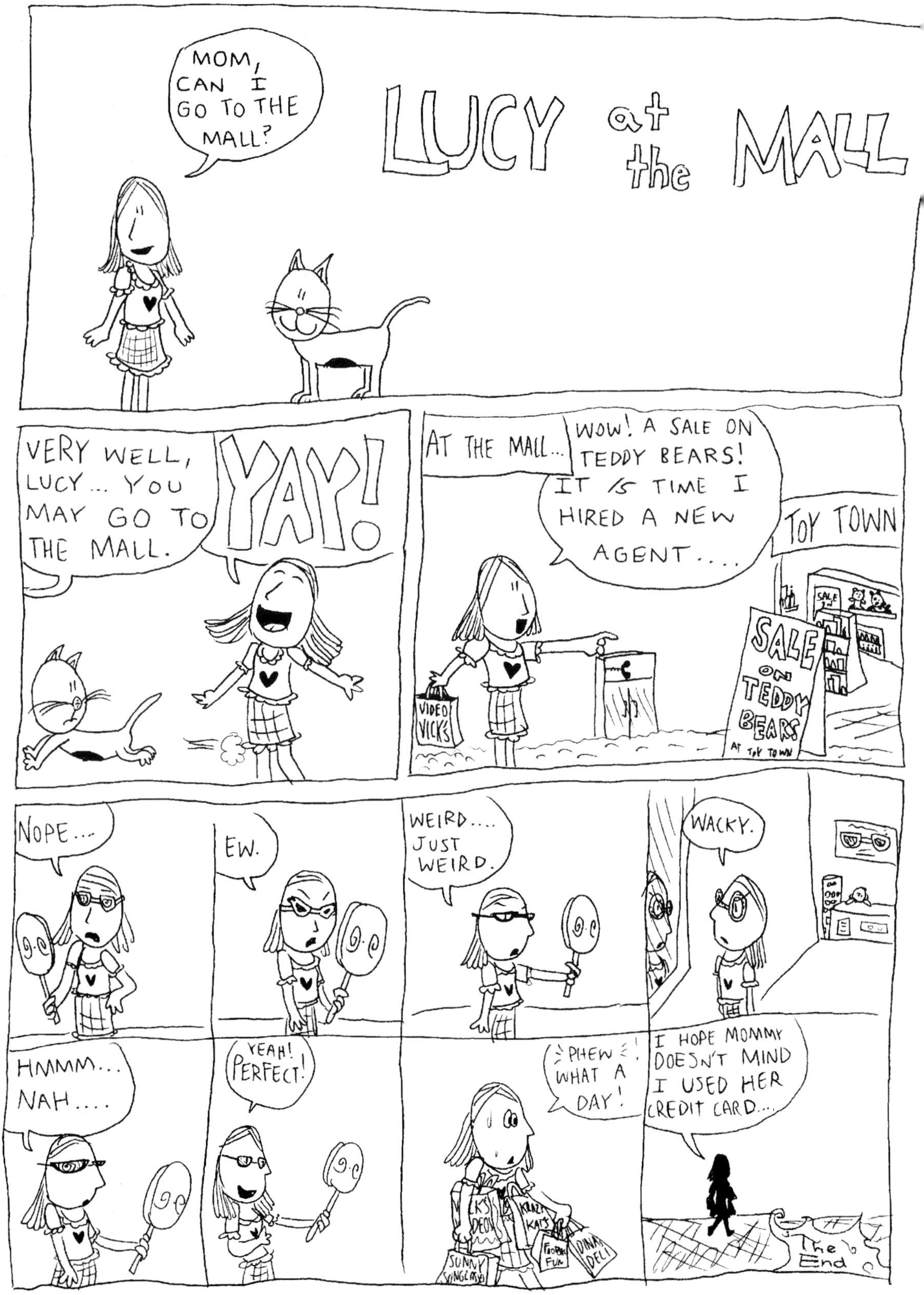
MOM, CAN I GO TO THE MALL?
LUCY at the MALL
VERY WELL, LUCY... YOU MAY GO TO THE MALL.
YAY!
AT THE MALL...
WOW! A SALE ON TEDDY BEARS! IT IS TIME I HIRED A NEW AGENT....
TOY TOWN
VIDEO VICK'S
SALE ON TEDDY BEARS AT TOY TOWN
NOPE....
EW.
WEIRD.... JUST WEIRD.
WACKY.
HMMM... NAH....
YEAH! PERFECT!
PHEW WHAT A DAY!
SUNNY SUNGLASSES
FOOD FUN
DINA'S DELI
I HOPE MOMMY DOESN'T MIND I USED HER CREDIT CARD...
The End

BOYS ARE SO ANNOYING

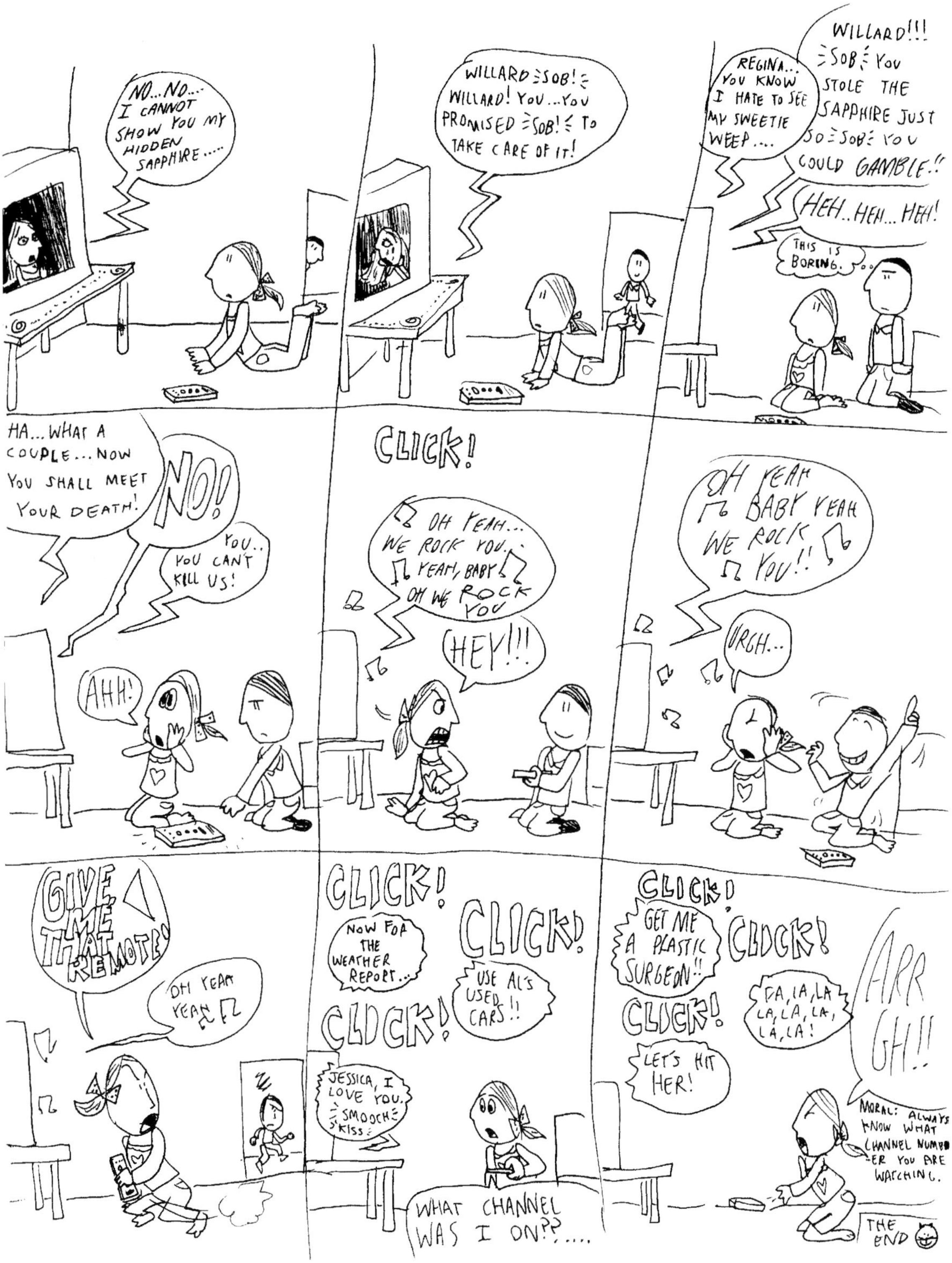
NO...NO... I CANNOT SHOW YOU MY HIDDEN SAPPHIRE.....
WILLARD SOB! WILLARD! YOU...YOU PROMISED SOB! TO TAKE CARE OF IT!
REGINA... YOU KNOW I HATE TO SEE MY SWEETIE WEEP....
WILLARD!!! SOB YOU STOLE THE SAPPHIRE JUST SO SOB YOU COULD GAMBLE!!
HEH..HEH...HEH!
THIS IS BORING.
HA...WHAT A COUPLE...NOW YOU SHALL MEET YOUR DEATH!
NO!
YOU.. YOU CAN'T KILL US!
AHH!
CLICK!
OH YEAH... WE ROCK YOU.. YEAH, BABY! OH WE ROCK YOU
HEY!!!
OH YEAH BABY YEAH WE ROCK YOU!!
URGH...
GIVE ME THAT REMOTE!
OH YEAH YEAH
CLICK!
NOW FOR THE WEATHER REPORT...
CLICK!
USE AL'S USED CARS!!
CLICK!
JESSICA, I LOVE YOU. SMOOCH KISS
WHAT CHANNEL WAS I ON??....
CLICK!
GET ME A PLASTIC SURGEON!!
CLICK!
CLICK!
LET'S HIT HER!
LA, LA, LA LA, LA, LA, LA, LA!
ARRGH!!
MORAL: ALWAYS KNOW WHAT CHANNEL NUMBER YOU ARE WATCHING.
THE END

NO RITES

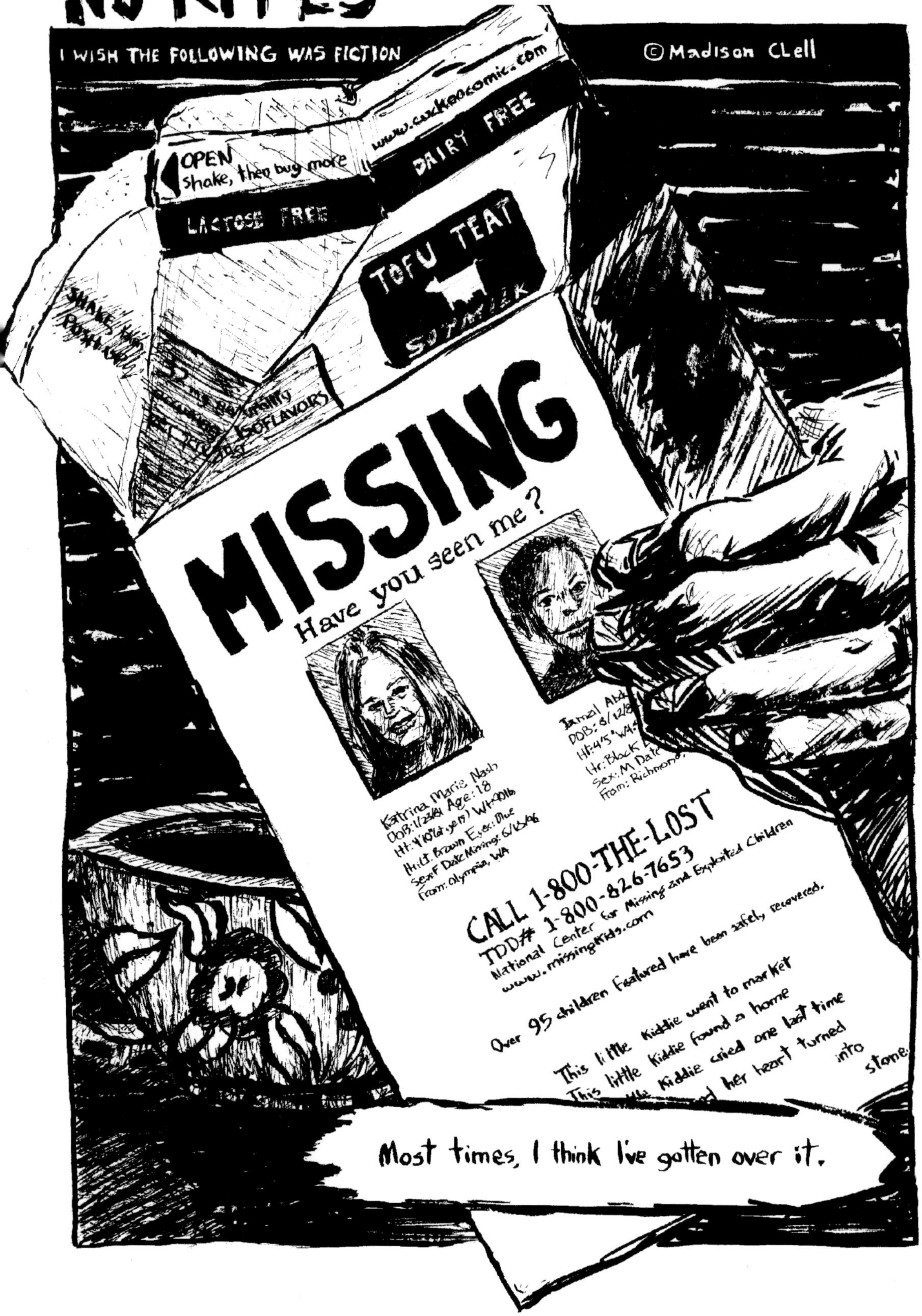

I WISH THE FOLLOWING WAS FICTION
©Madison CLell
www.cuckoocomic.com
OPEN
shake, then buy more
DAIRY FREE
LACTOSE FREE
TOFU TEAT
MISSING
Have you seen me?
Katrina Marie Nash
Age: 18
From: Olympia, WA
CALL 1-800-THE-LOST
TDD# 1-800-826-7653
National Center for Missing and Exploited Children
www.missingkids.com
Over 95 children featured have been safely recovered.
This little kiddie went to market
This little kiddie found a home
This little kiddie cried one last time
Most times, I think I've gotten over it.

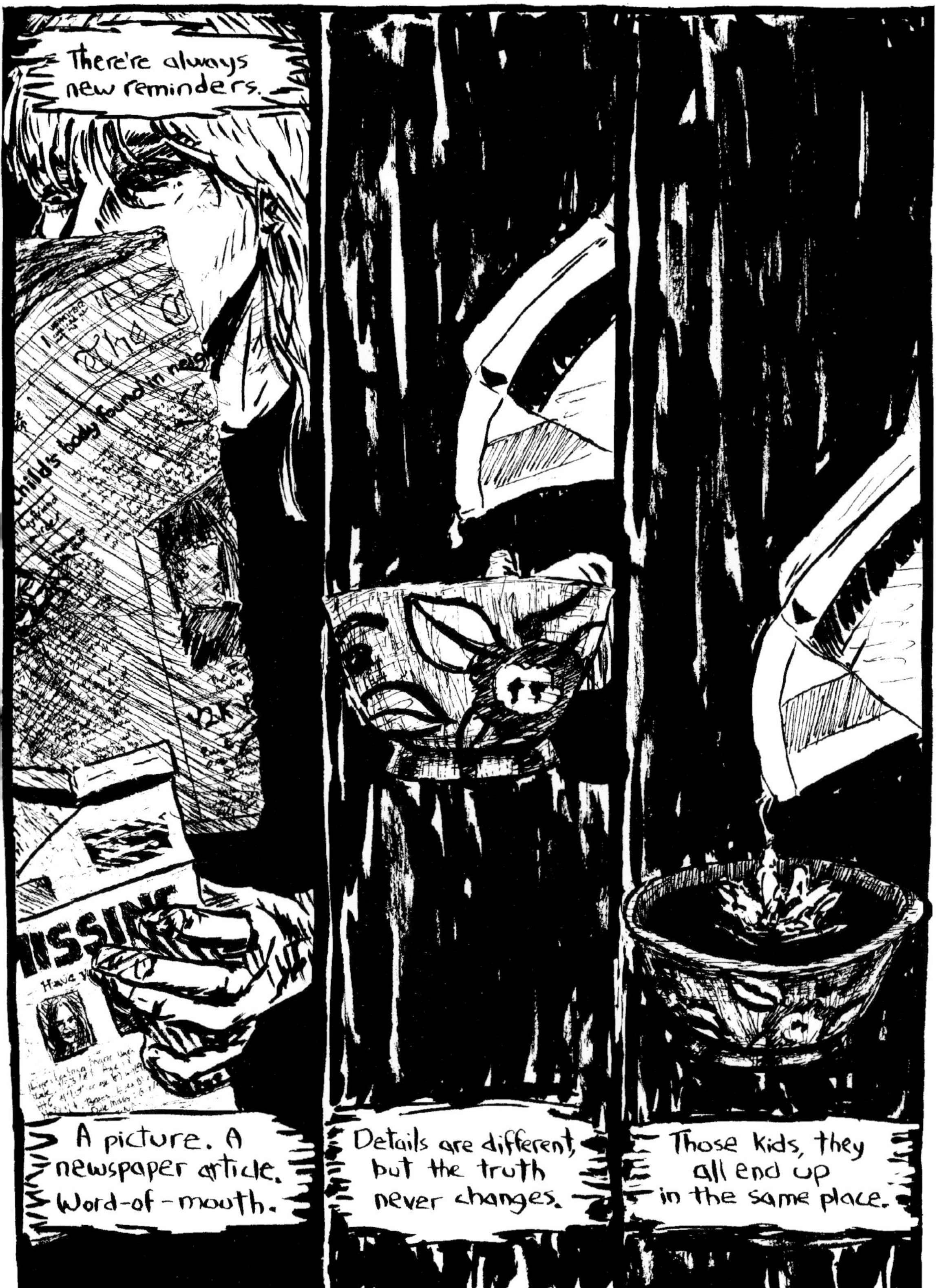
There're always new reminders.
A picture. A newspaper article. Word-of-mouth.
Details are different, but the truth never changes.
Those kids, they all end up in the same place.

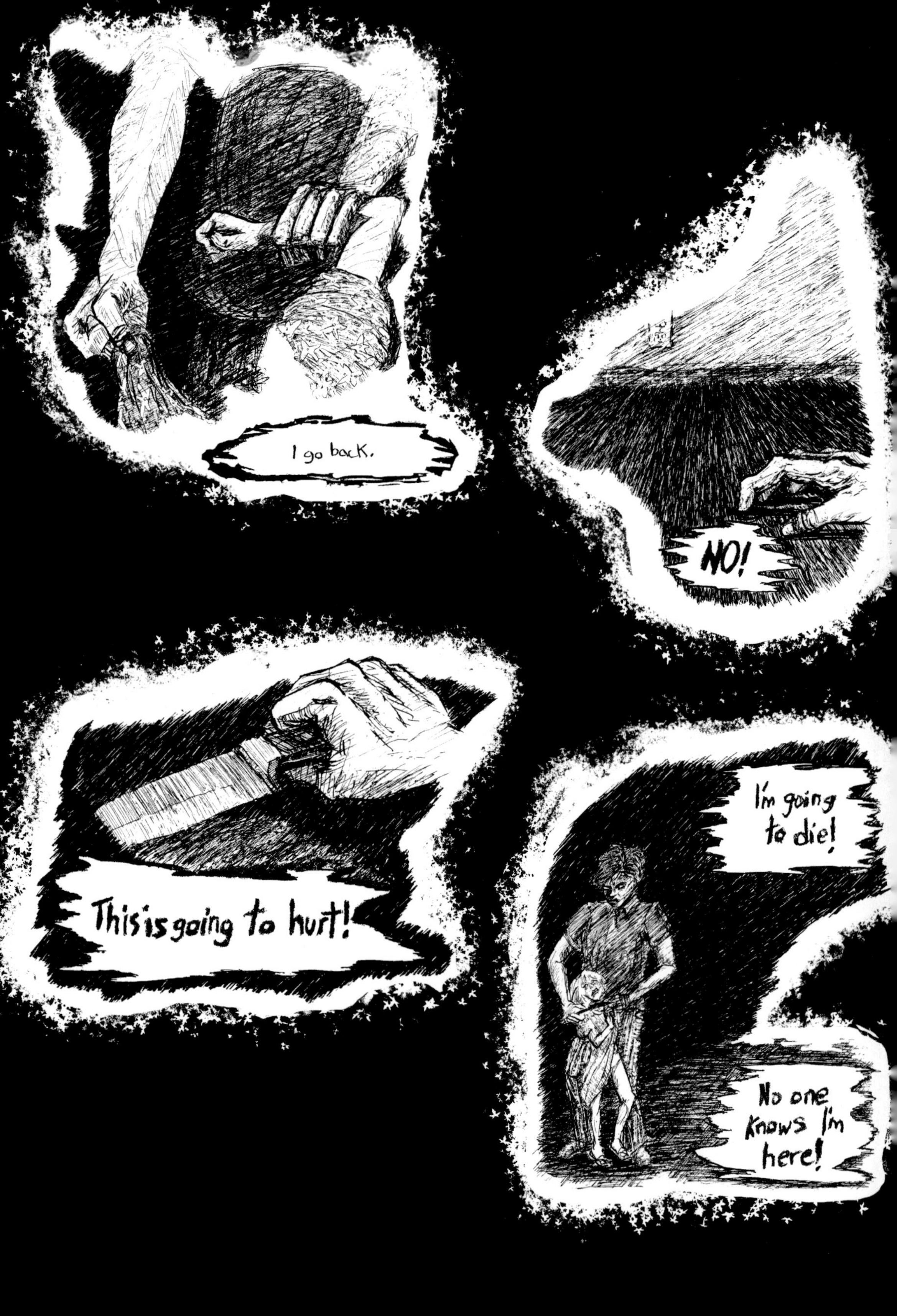
I go back.
NO!
This is going to hurt!
I'm going to die!
No one knows I'm here!

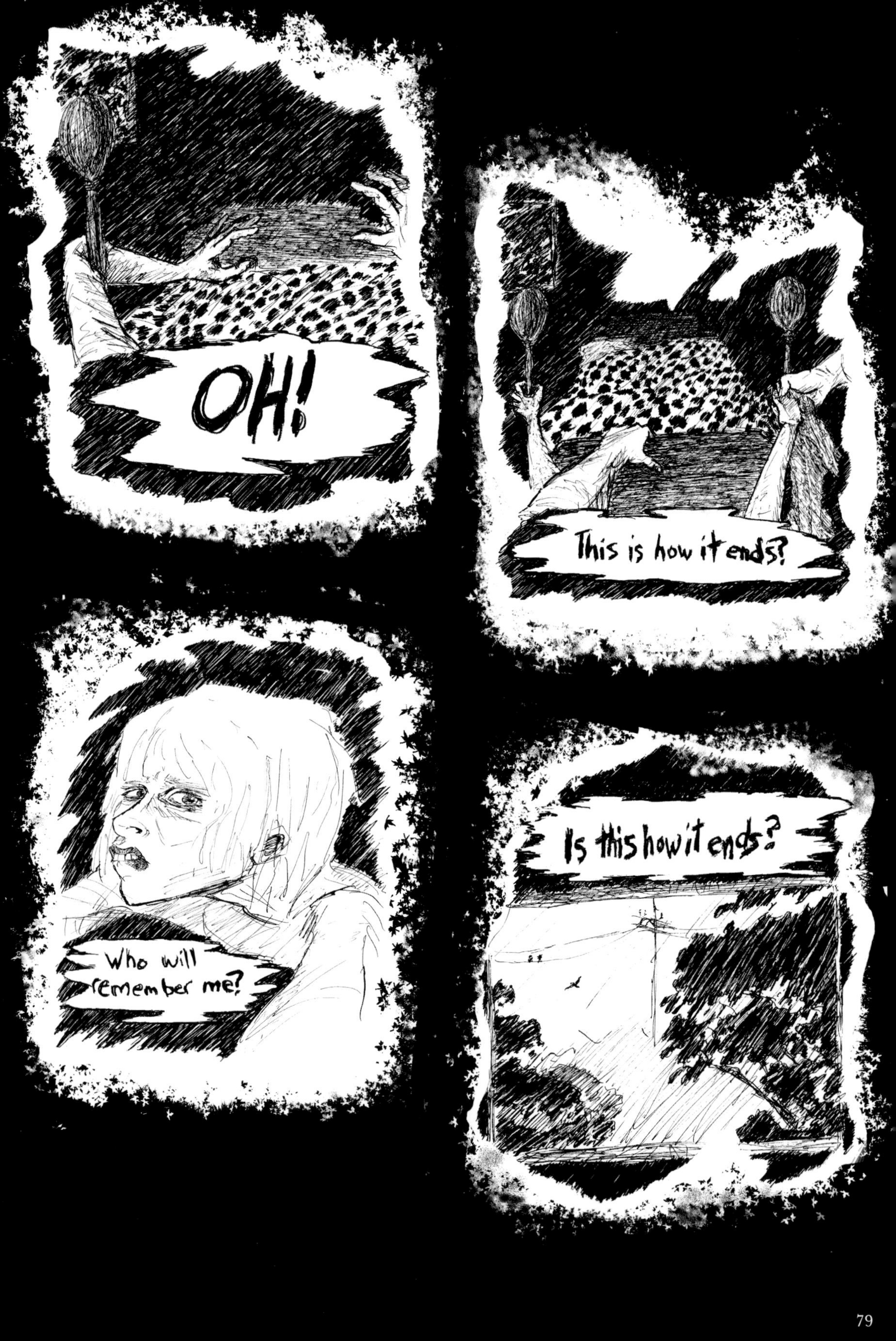
OH!
This is how it ends?
Who will remember me?
Is this how it ends?

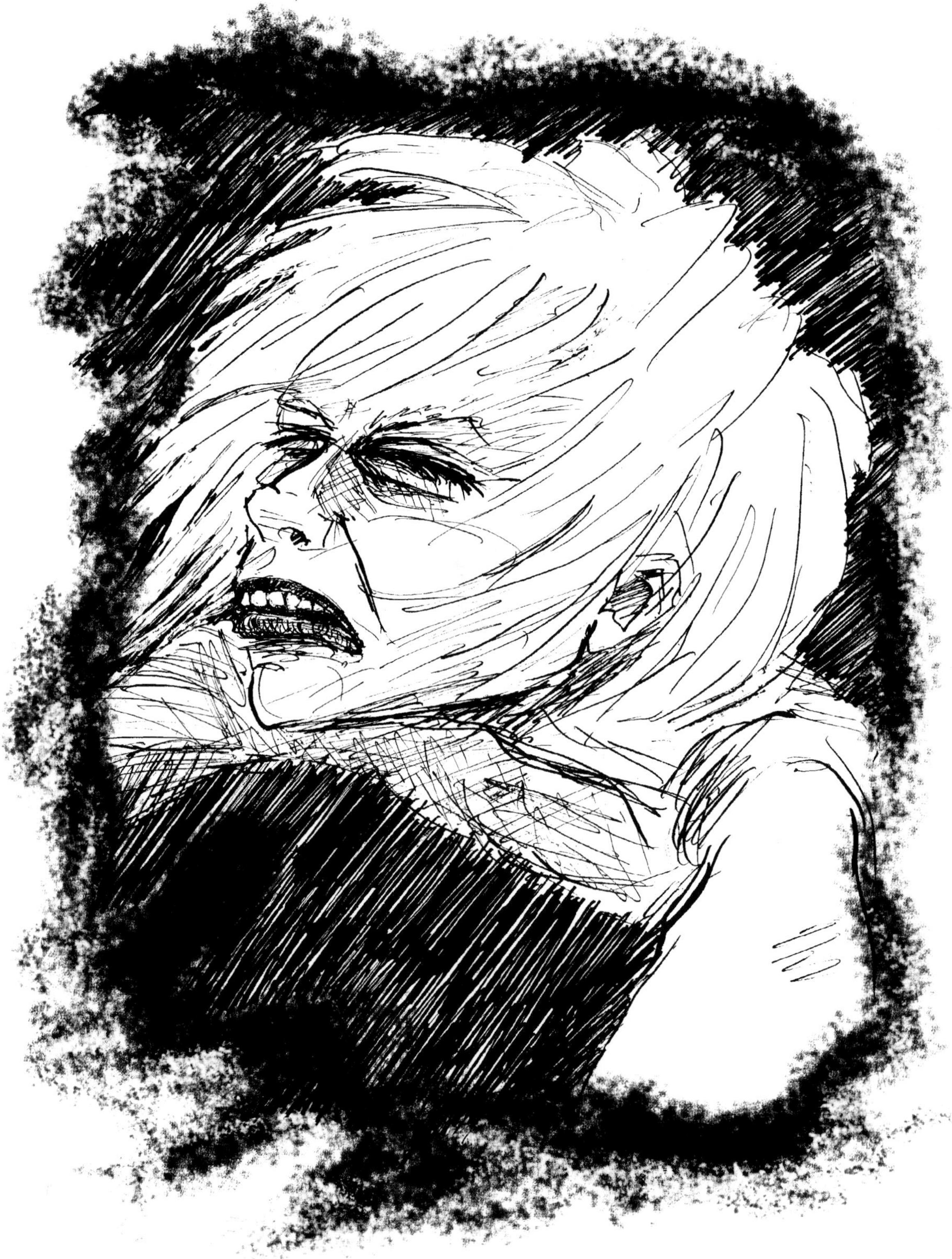

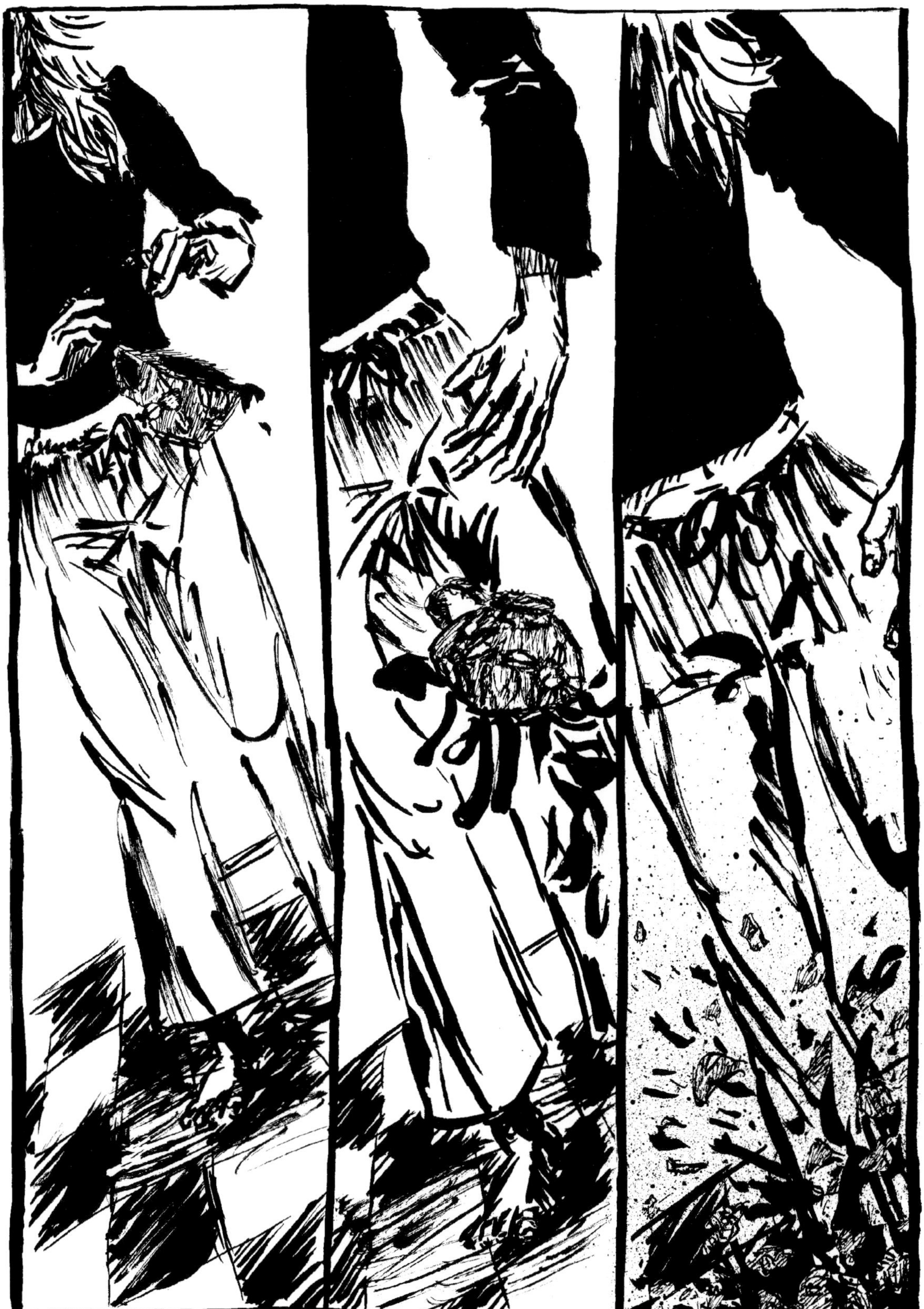

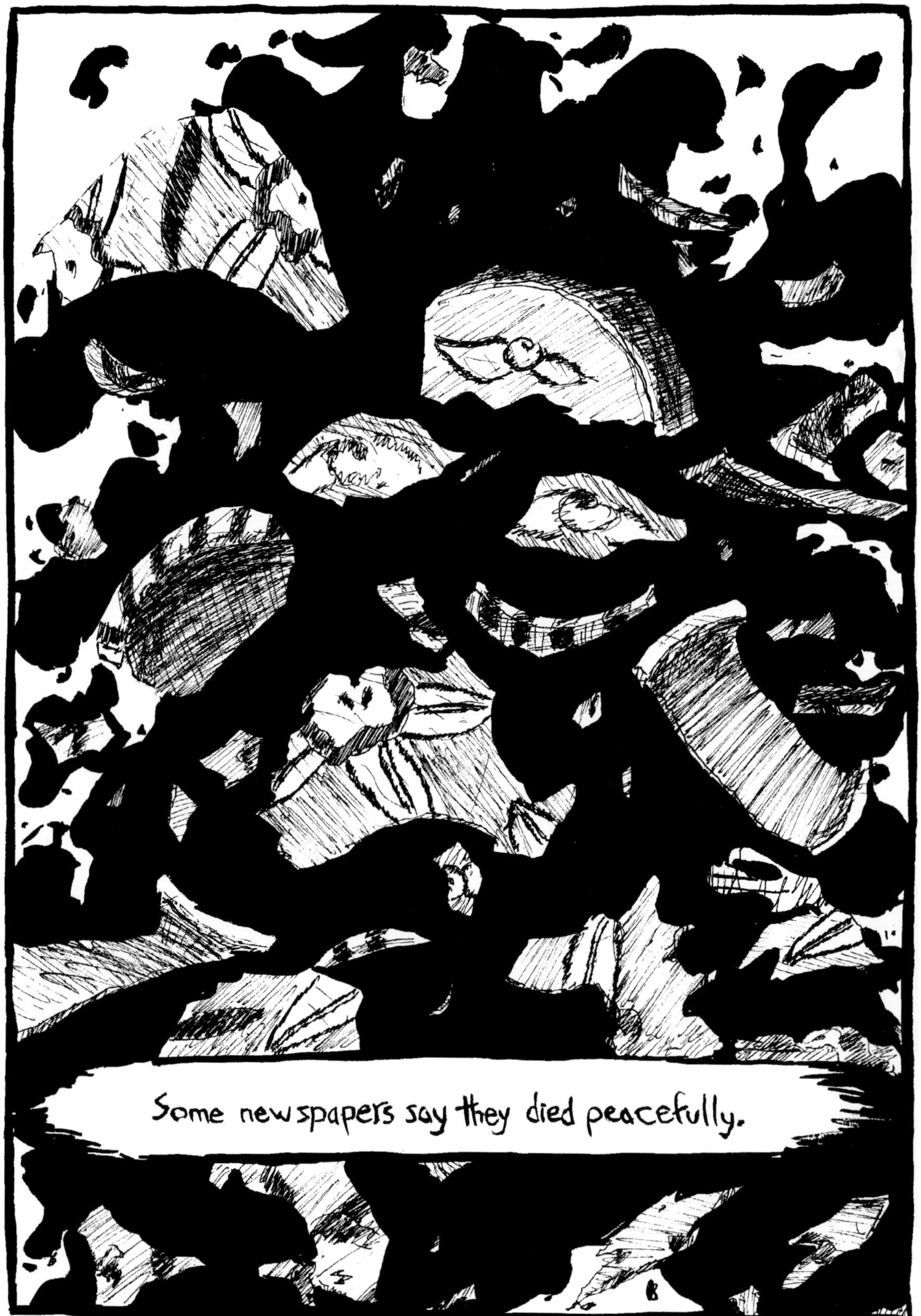
Some newspapers say they died peacefully.

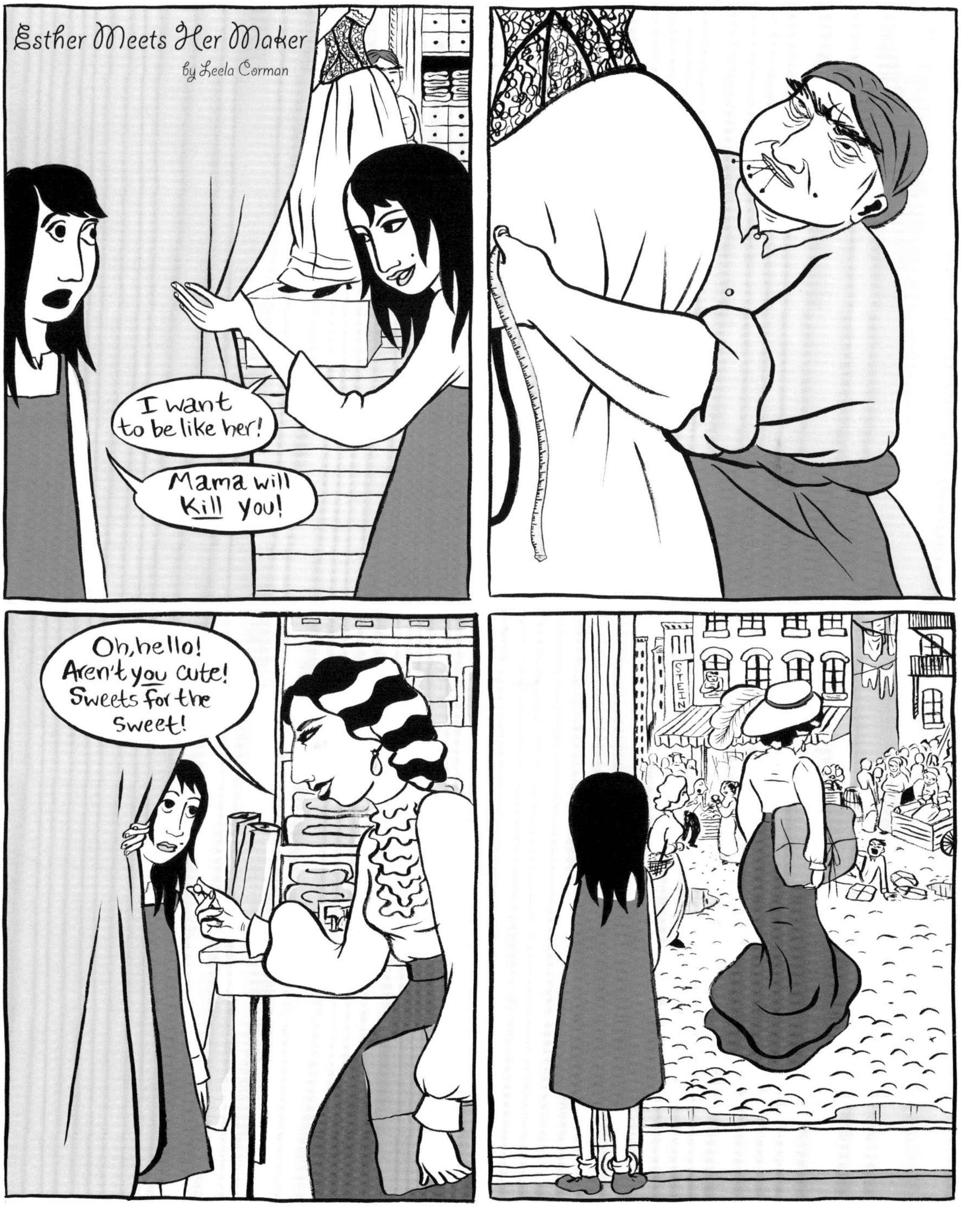
Esther Meets Her Maker
by Leela Corman
I want to be like her!
Mama will Kill you!
Oh, hello! Aren't you cute! Sweets for the sweet!
STEIN

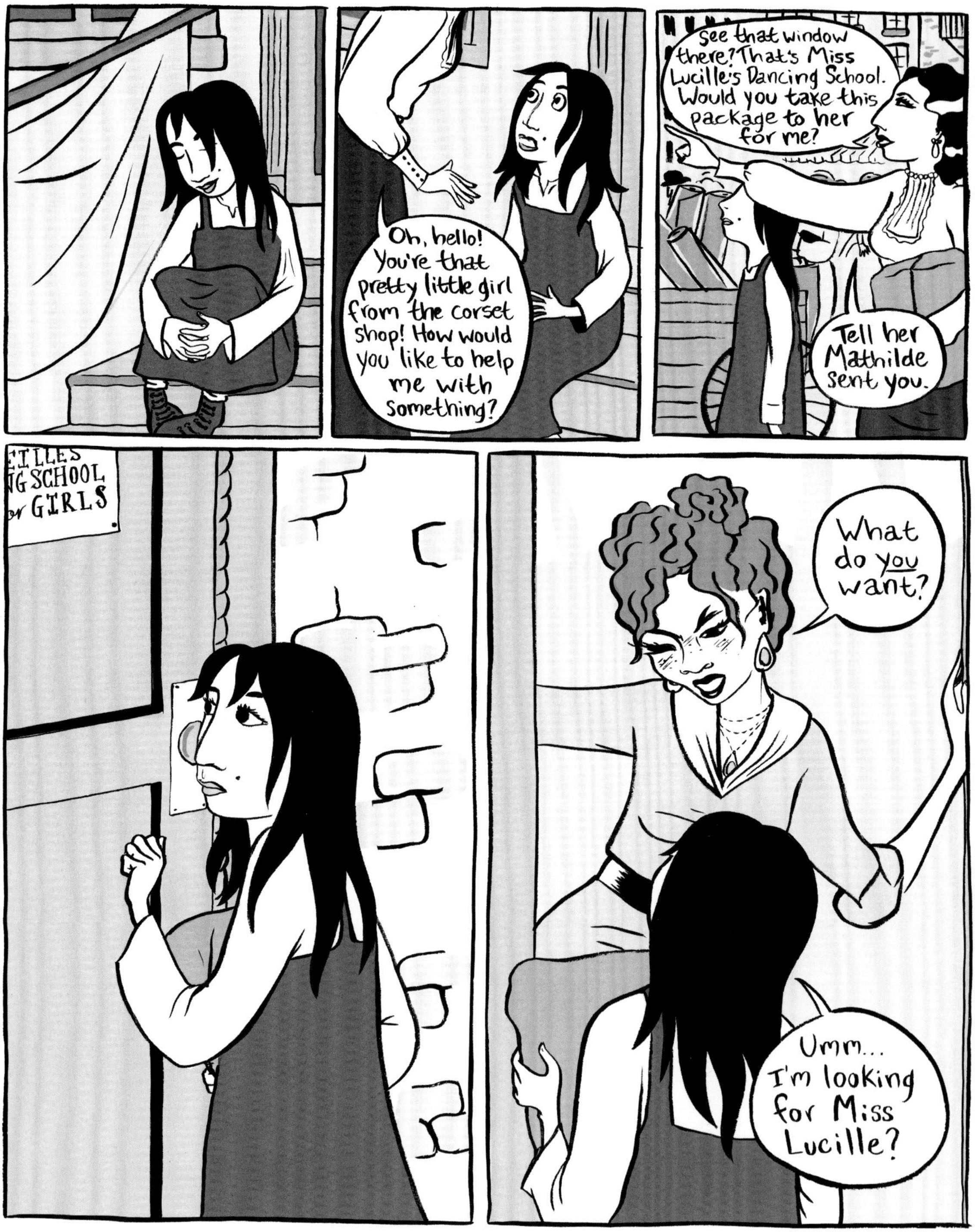
Oh, hello! You're that pretty little girl from the corset shop! How would you like to help me with something?
See that window there? That's Miss Lucille's Dancing School. Would you take this package to her for me?
Tell her Mathilde sent you.
What do you want?
Umm... I'm looking for Miss Lucille?

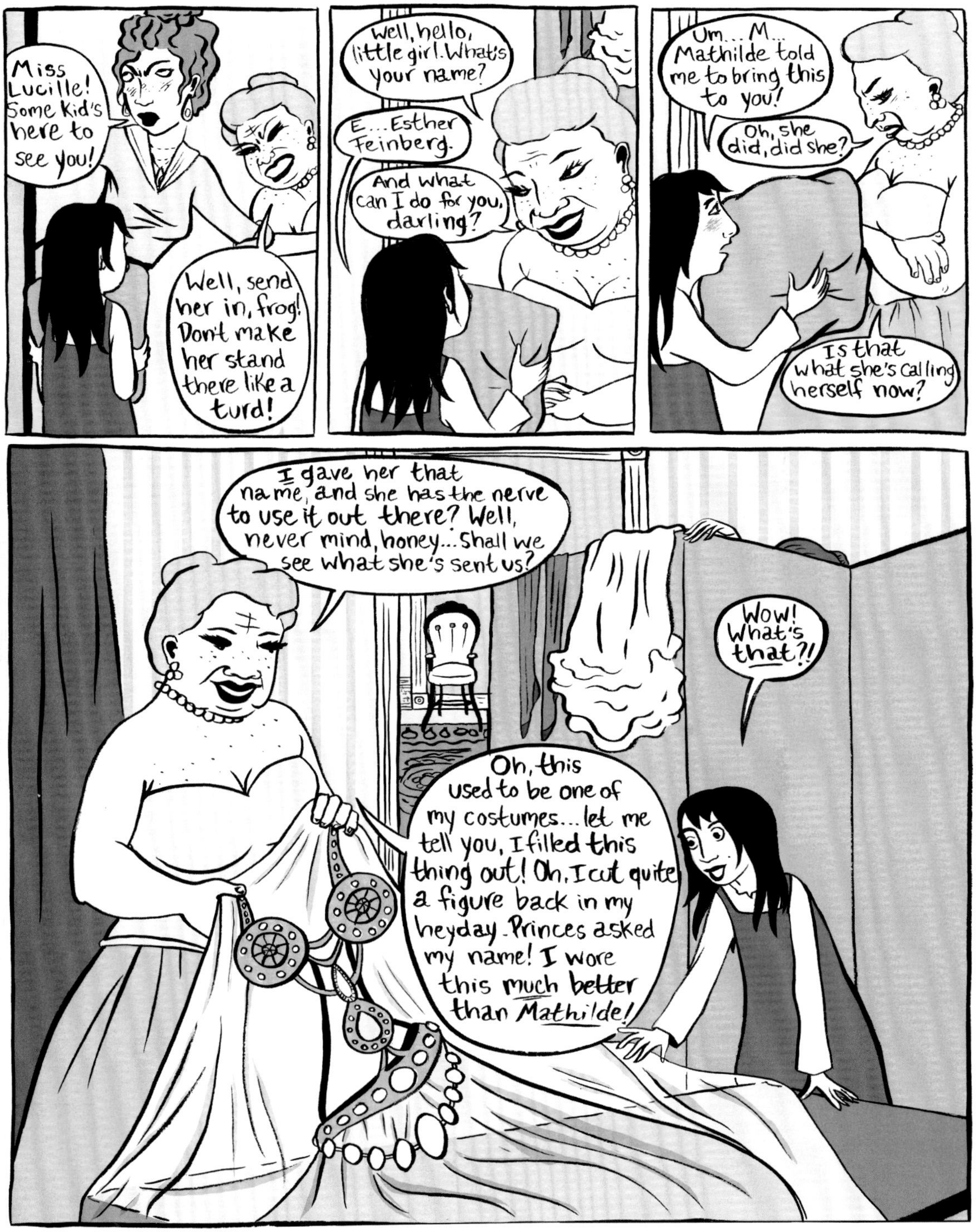
Miss Lucille! Some kid's here to see you!
Well, send her in, frog! Don't make her stand there like a turd!
Well, hello, little girl. What's your name?
E... Esther Feinberg.
And what can I do for you, darling?
Um... M... Mathilde told me to bring this to you!
Oh, she did, did she?
Is that what she's calling herself now?
I gave her that name, and she has the nerve to use it out there? Well, never mind, honey... Shall we see what she's sent us?
Wow! What's that?!
Oh, this used to be one of my costumes... let me tell you, I filled this thing out! Oh, I cut quite a figure back in my heyday. Princes asked my name! I wore this much better than Mathilde!

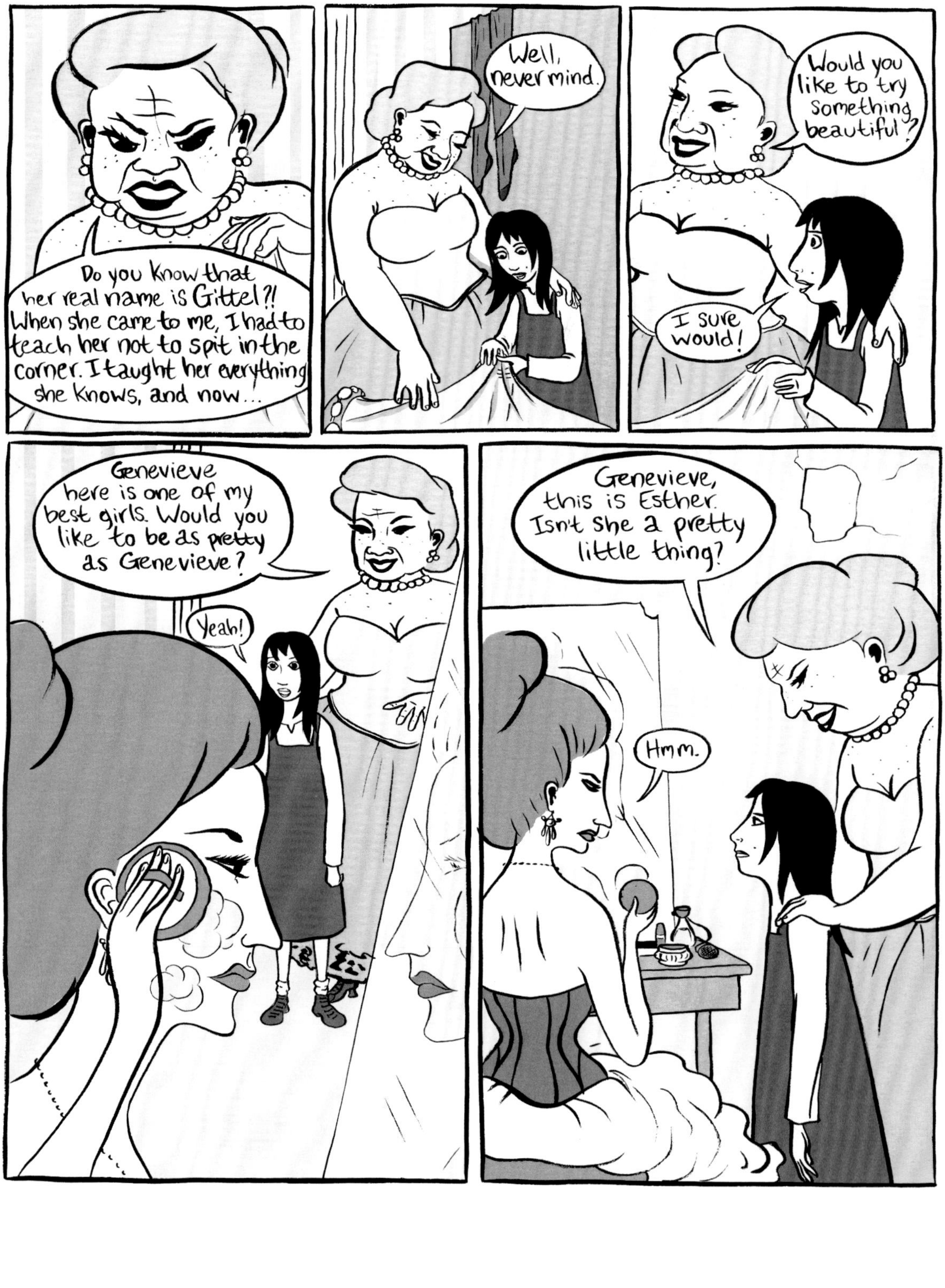
Do you know that her real name is Gittel?! When she came to me, I had to teach her not to spit in the corner. I taught her everything she knows, and now...
Well, never mind.
Would you like to try something beautiful?
I sure would!
Genevieve here is one of my best girls. Would you like to be as pretty as Genevieve?
Yeah!
Genevieve, this is Esther. Isn't she a pretty little thing?
Hmm.

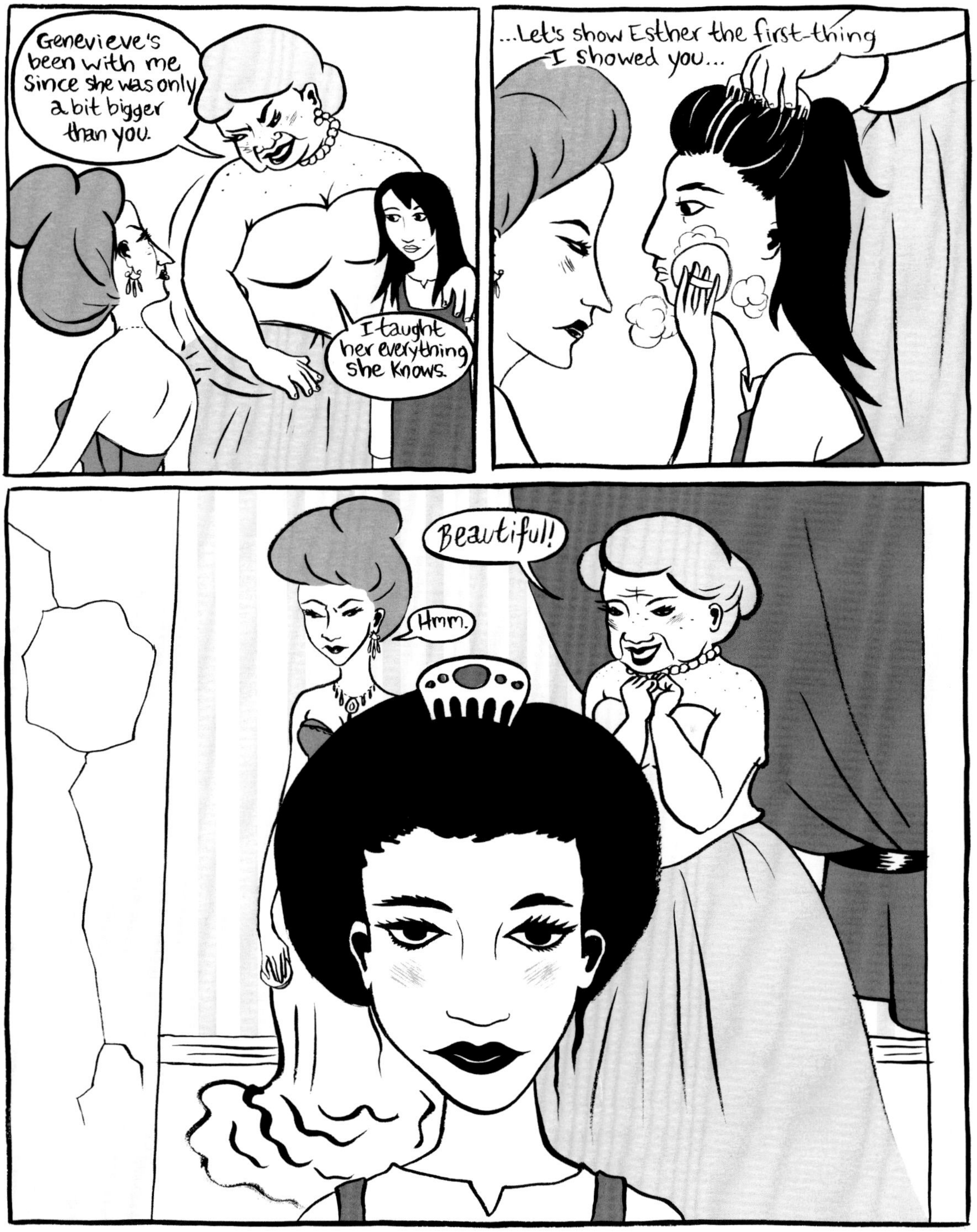
Genevieve's been with me since she was only a bit bigger than you.
I taught her everything she knows.
...Let's show Esther the first thing I showed you...
Beautiful!
Hmm.

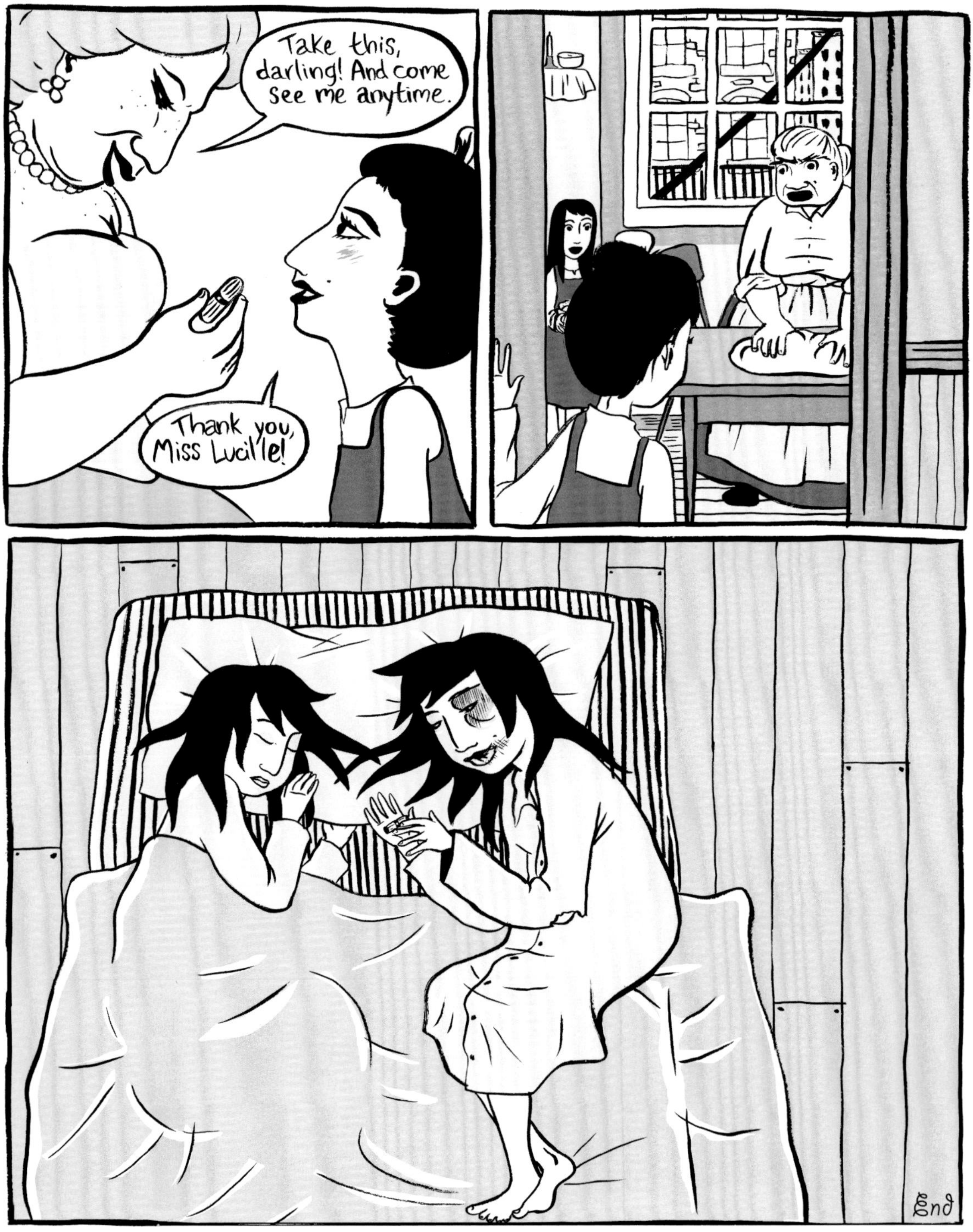
Take this, darling! And come see me anytime.
Thank you, Miss Lucille!
End

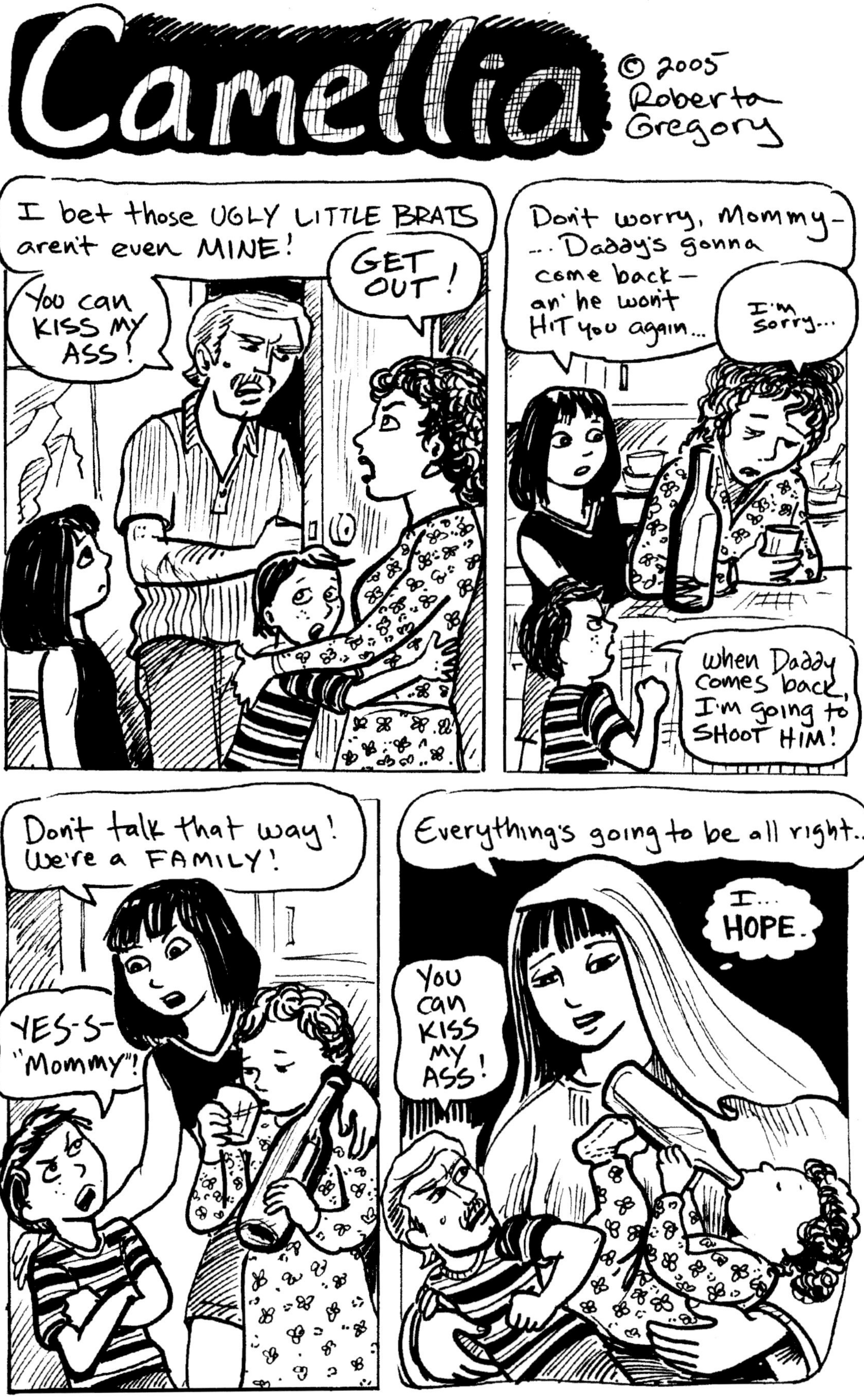
Camellia
© 2005 Roberta Gregory
I bet those UGLY LITTLE BRATS aren't even MINE!
You can KISS MY ASS!
GET OUT!
Don't worry, Mommy- ...Daddy's gonna come back- an' he won't HIT you again...
I'm sorry...
when Daddy comes back, I'm going to SHOOT HIM!
Don't talk that way! We're a FAMILY!
YES-S- "Mommy"!
Everything's going to be all right..
I... HOPE.
YOU can KISS MY ASS!

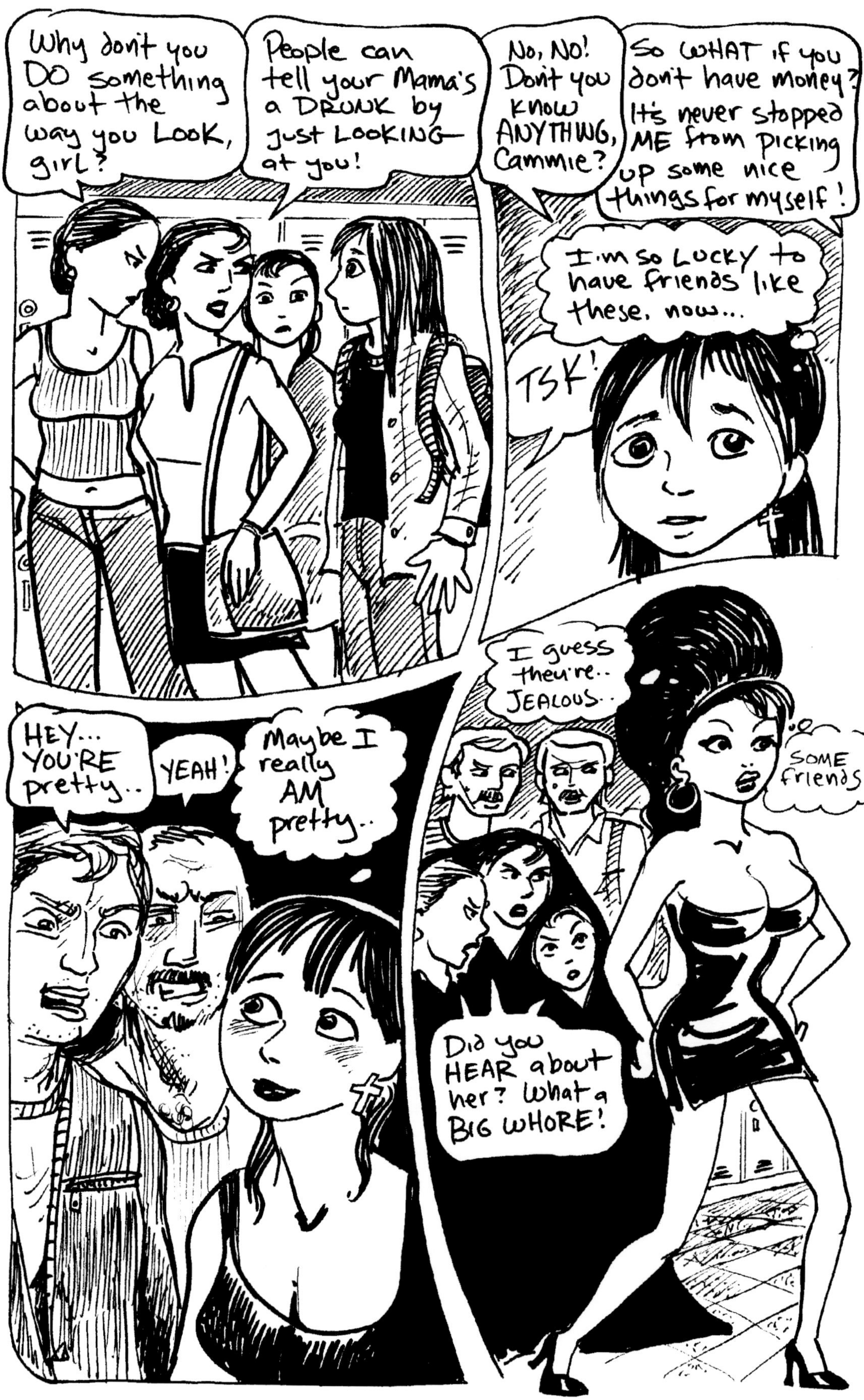
Why don't you DO something about the way you LOOK, girl?
People can tell your Mama's a DRUNK by just LOOKING at you!
No, NO! Don't you know ANYTHING, Cammie?
So WHAT if you don't have money? It's never stopped ME from picking up some nice things for myself!
I'm so LUCKY to have friends like these, now...
TSK!
HEY... YOU'RE pretty..
YEAH!
Maybe I really AM pretty..
I guess they're.. JEALOUS..
SOME friends..
Did you HEAR about her? What a BIG WHORE!

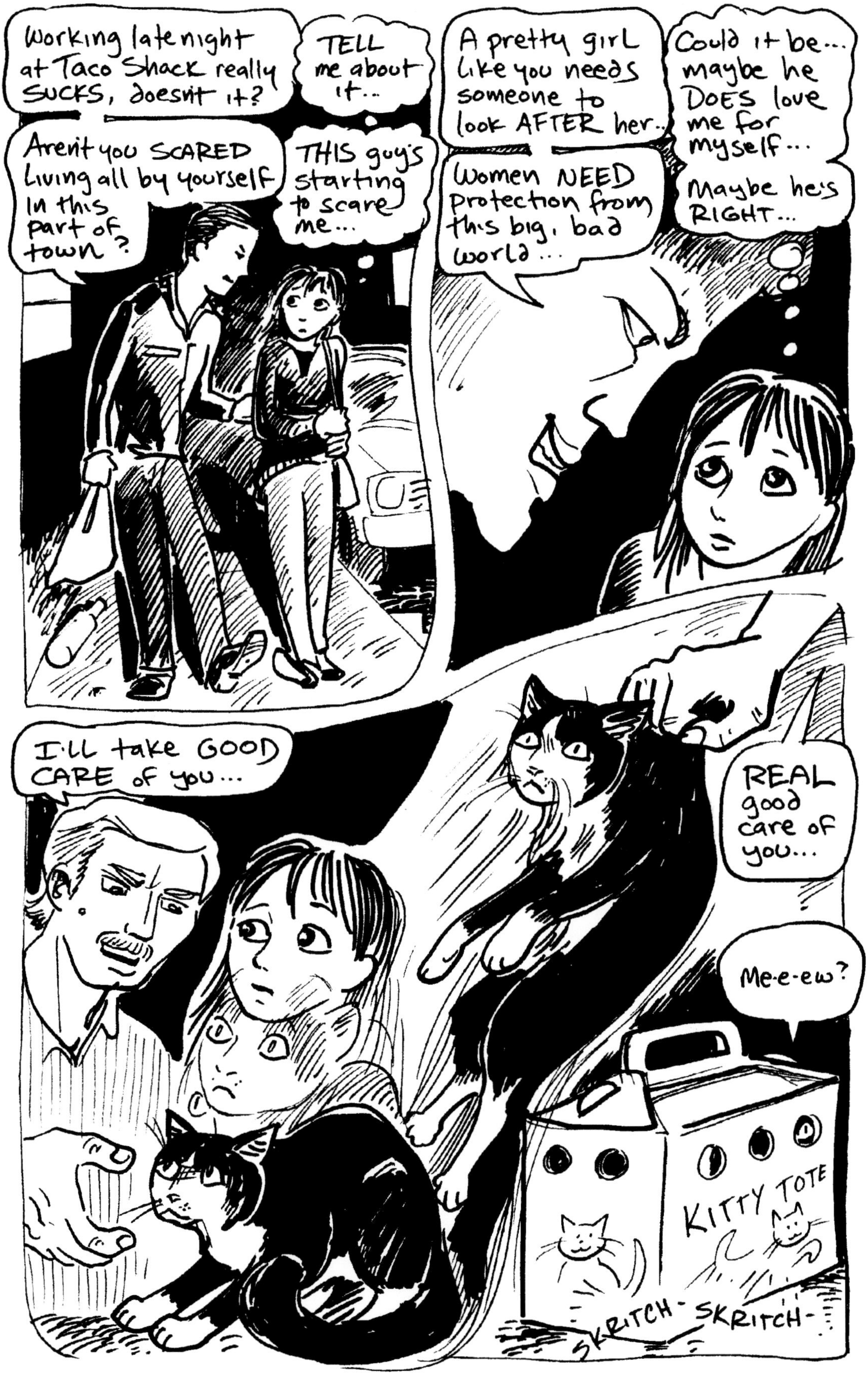
Working late night at Taco Shack really SUCKS, doesn't it?
TELL me about it...
Aren't you SCARED living all by yourself in this part of town?
THIS guy's starting to scare me...
A pretty girl like you needs someone to look AFTER her...
Women NEED protection from this big, bad world...
Could it be... maybe he DOES love me for myself...
Maybe he's RIGHT...
I'LL take GOOD CARE of you...
REAL good care of you...
Me-e-ew?
KITTY TOTE
SKRITCH-SKRITCH-

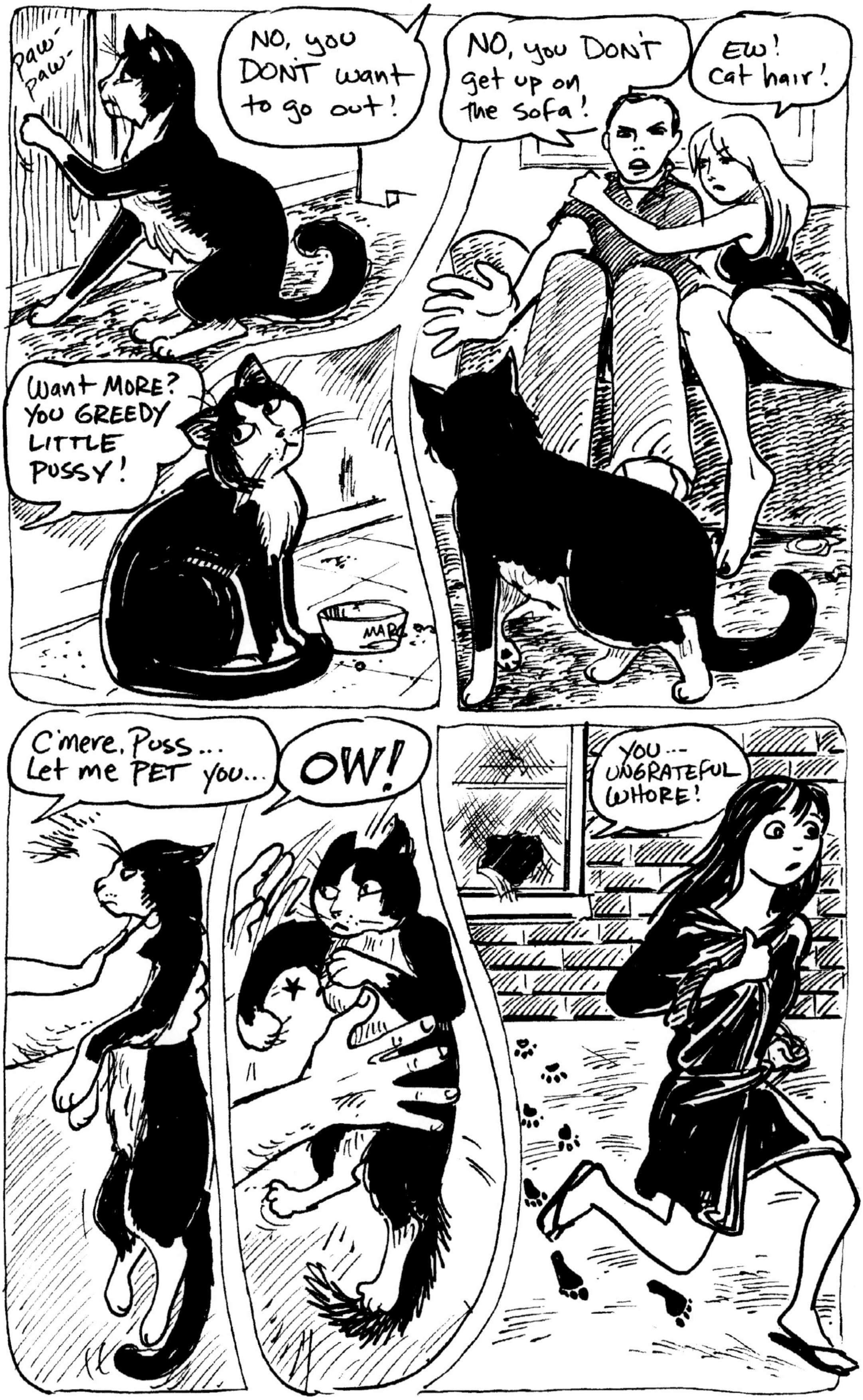
paw-paw-
NO, you DON'T want to go out!
NO, you DON'T get up on the sofa!
EW! Cat hair!
Want MORE? YOU GREEDY LITTLE PUSSY!
C'mere, Puss... Let me PET you...
OW!
YOU... UNGRATEFUL WHORE!

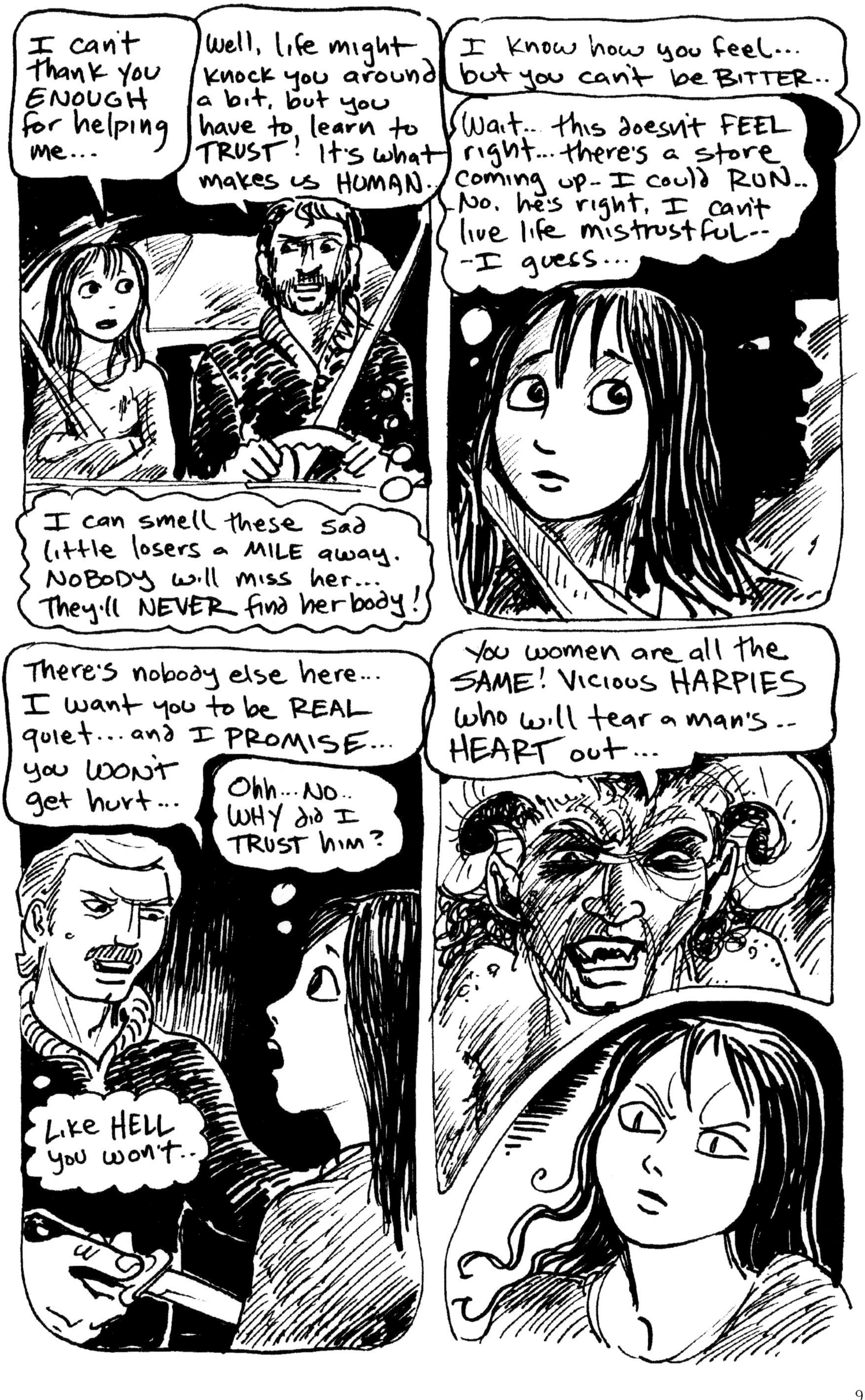
I can't thank you ENOUGH for helping me...
Well, life might knock you around a bit, but you have to learn to TRUST! It's what makes us HUMAN..
I can smell these sad little losers a MILE away. NOBODY will miss her... They'll NEVER find her body!
I know how you feel... but you can't be BITTER..
Wait.. this doesn't FEEL right... there's a store coming up.. I could RUN.. No, he's right, I can't live life mistrustful-- --I guess...
There's nobody else here... I want you to be REAL quiet... and I PROMISE... you WON'T get hurt...
Ohh... NO.. WHY did I TRUST him?
Like HELL you won't..
You women are all the SAME! Vicious HARPIES who will tear a man's.. HEART out...

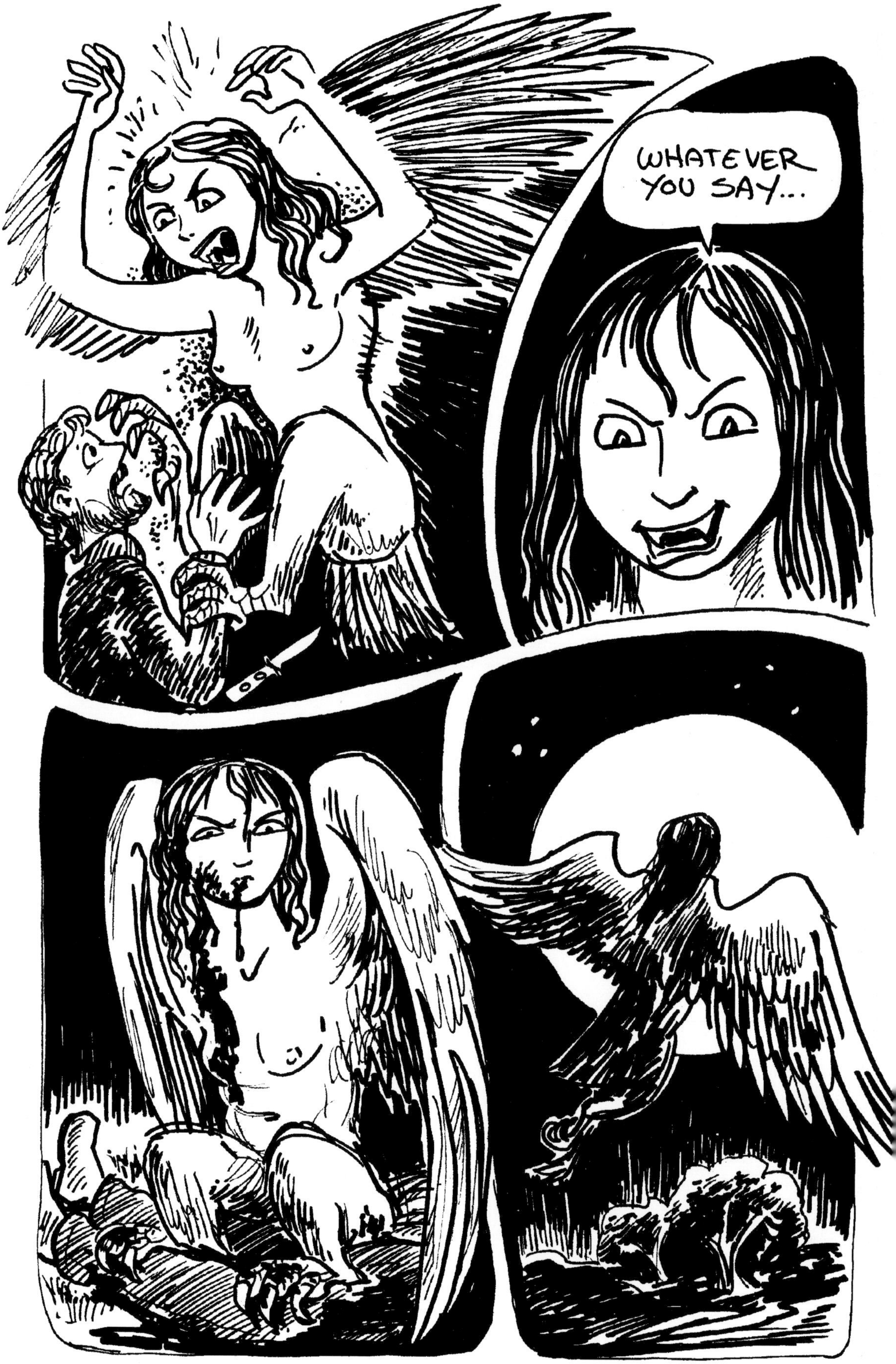
WHATEVER YOU SAY...

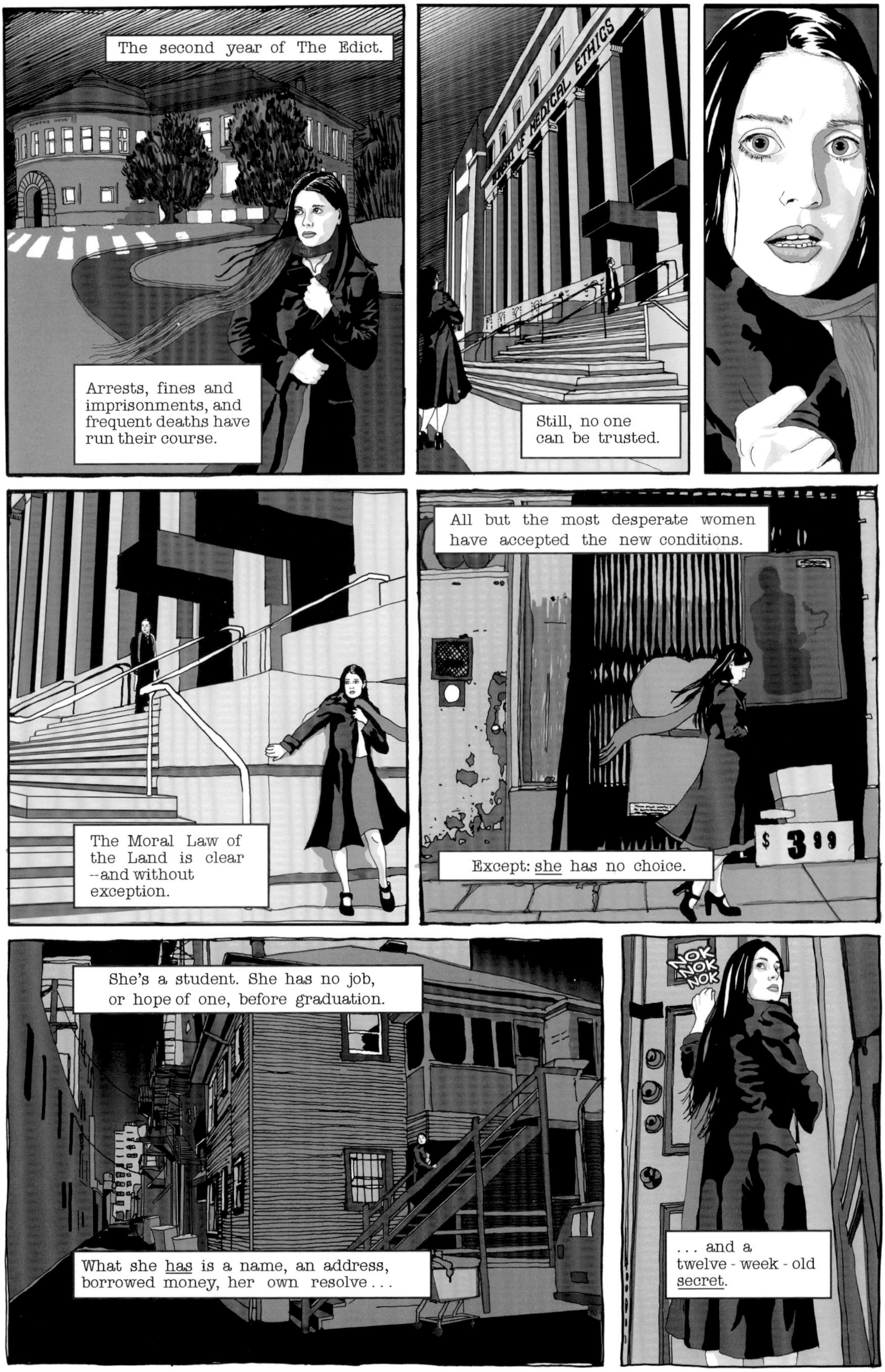
The second year of The Edict.
Arrests, fines and imprisonments, and frequent deaths have run their course.
OF MEDICAL ETHICS
Still, no one can be trusted.
The Moral Law of the Land is clear --and without exception.
All but the most desperate women have accepted the new conditions.
$ 3 99
Except: she has no choice.
She's a student. She has no job, or hope of one, before graduation.
What she has is a name, an address, borrowed money, her own resolve . . .
NOK NOK NOK
. . . and a twelve - week - old secret.

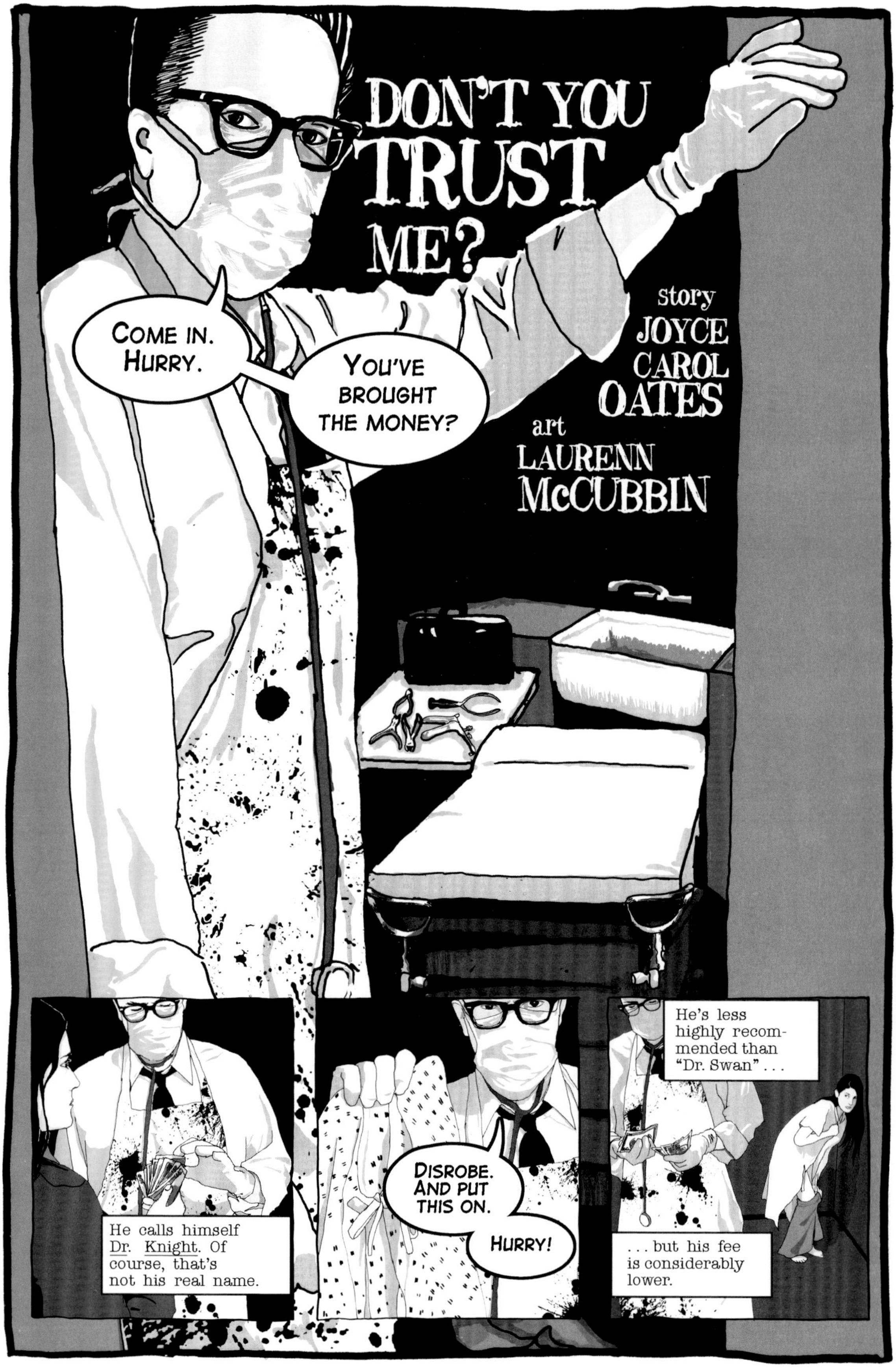
DON'T YOU TRUST ME?
story JOYCE CAROL OATES
art LAURENN McCUBBIN
COME IN. HURRY.
YOU'VE BROUGHT THE MONEY?
He calls himself Dr. Knight. Of course, that's not his real name.
DISROBE. AND PUT THIS ON.
HURRY!
He's less highly recommended than "Dr. Swan" . . .
. . . but his fee is considerably lower.

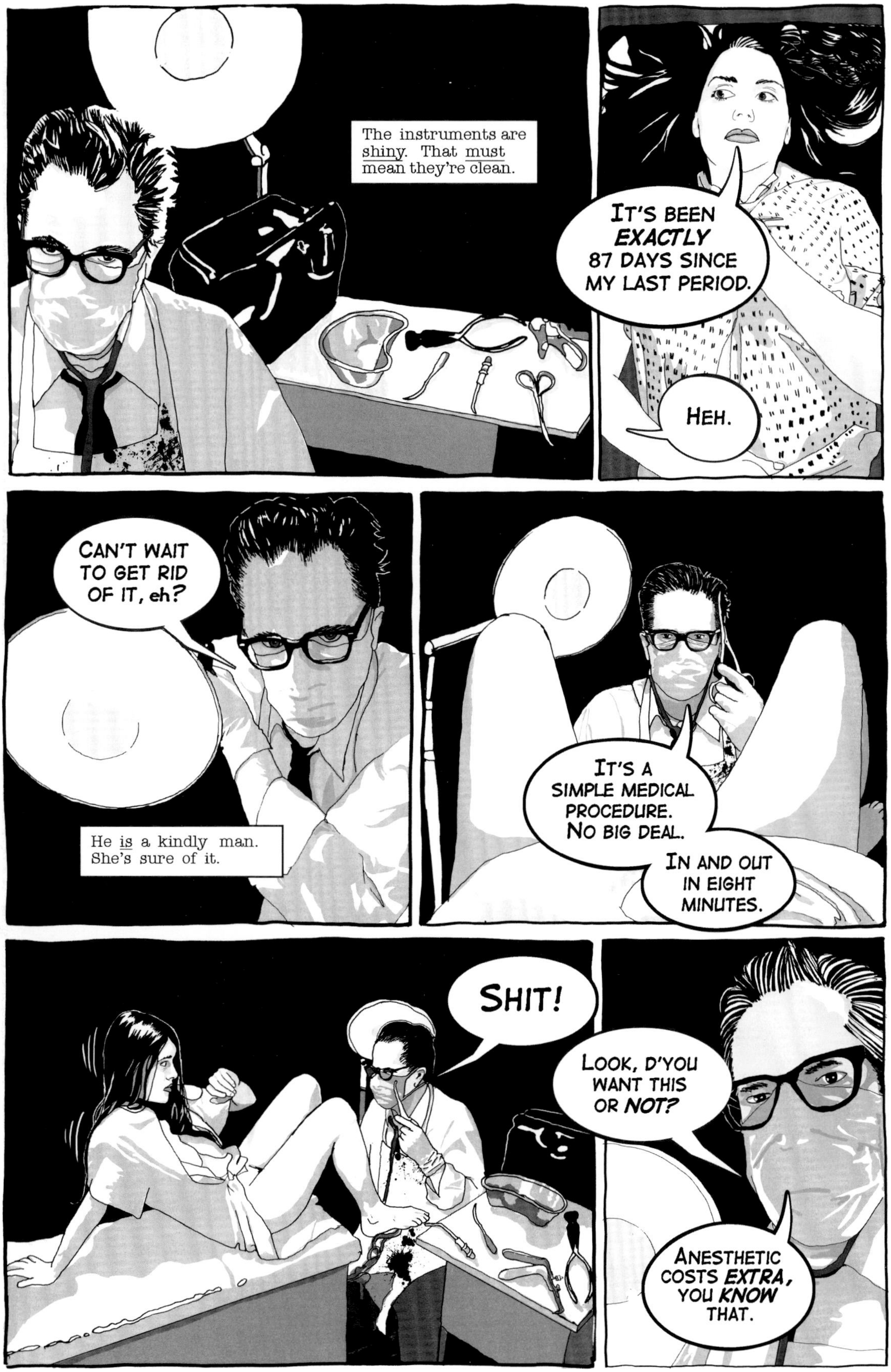
The instruments are shiny. That must mean they're clean.
IT'S BEEN EXACTLY 87 DAYS SINCE MY LAST PERIOD.
HEH.
CAN'T WAIT TO GET RID OF IT, eh?
He is a kindly man. She's sure of it.
IT'S A SIMPLE MEDICAL PROCEDURE. NO BIG DEAL.
IN AND OUT IN EIGHT MINUTES.
SHIT!
LOOK, D'YOU WANT THIS OR NOT?
ANESTHETIC COSTS EXTRA, YOU KNOW THAT.

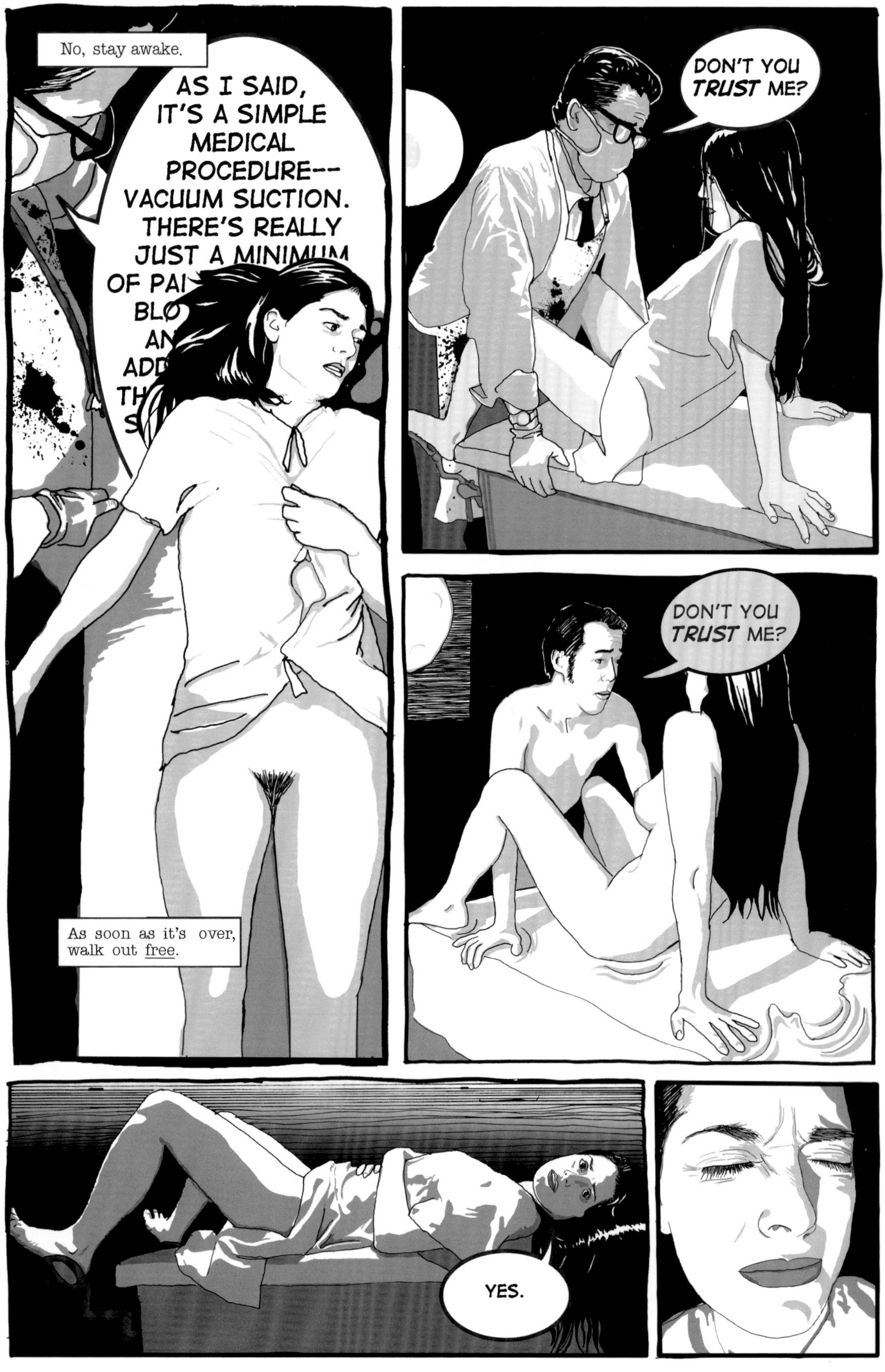
No, stay awake.
AS I SAID, IT'S A SIMPLE MEDICAL PROCEDURE-- VACUUM SUCTION. THERE'S REALLY JUST A MINIMUM
As soon as it's over, walk out free.
DON'T YOU TRUST ME?
DON'T YOU TRUST ME?
YES.

CREATOR BIOS

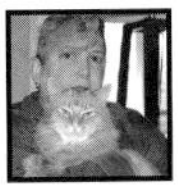

LOIS BUHALIS has been lettering comics for over twenty-two years. She lives in Portland, Oregon, with her husband and a variety of cats.

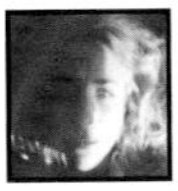

MADISON CLELL has turned down movie adaptations of her life. Fearing the truth too weird to print, she listed herself as a career steamboat historian for her high school reunion book. In reality, she's a former disco musician who paints, surfs, and is morphing her *Cuckoo* comics into performance art

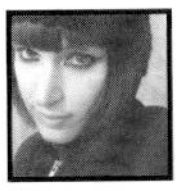

CHYNNA CLUGSTON FLORES is the Eisner and Harvey Award–nominated creator of *Blue Monday* and *Scooter Girl* from Oni Press. She also created the new graphic novel series *Queen Bee* from Scholastic, as well as the upcoming *Strangetown* from Oni. She currently lives in San Diego with her husband Jon, her bulldog, and an evil black cat. Her comic in this book originally appeared in *Punchthroat Anthology*.

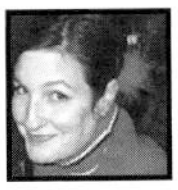

Former ad agency illustrator **AMANDA CONNER** began her comics career at Marvel and Archie Comics. Since then she has worked for Image, Vertigo, Harris, *Mad*, *Spin*, *Nightline* news, New Line Cinema, and the *New York Times*, and with such writers as Grant Morrison, Mark Millar, and Jimmy Palmiotti. She has also worked on *JSA Classified* for DC and icons for the L.A. Avengers football team.

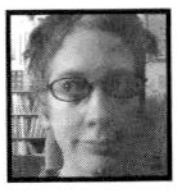

COLLEEN COOVER is a comic book artist and illustrator living in Portland, Oregon. She is the artist of *Banana Sunday*, a comedy for young readers written by Root Nibot, and is the creator of the erotic romance *Small Favors*. Her illustrations have appeared in the magazines *Curve*, *Girlfriends*, *On Our Backs*, and *Nickelodeon Magazine*.

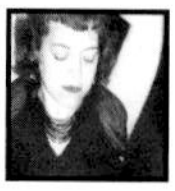

LEELA CORMAN is an illustrator. She lives in Brooklyn, New York. Her work can be seen at <www.glittercannon.com>. *Photo by Tom Hart.*

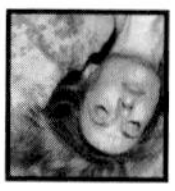

COLLEEN DORAN has been a professional artist since the age of fifteen. Her past clients include Marvel, DC, Image, Scholastic, and Lucasfilm. She illustrated *The Book of Lost Souls* for Marvel, and writes and illustrates *A Distant Soil* for Image. Her other credits include *Sandman*, *Wonder Woman*, *Amazing Spider-Man*, Clive Barker's *Hellraiser*, and Walt Disney's *Beauty and the Beast*.

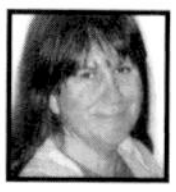

ROBERTA GREGORY is best known for her notorious Bitchy Bitch character, heroine of forty issues of *Naughty Bits*, many trade paperback collections in several languages, a weekly strip, a television cartoon, and three stage productions. But that's not all Roberta does; there are *Real Cat Toons*, *Mother Mountain*, *Winging It*, and loads of other projects. All the details are at <www.robertagregory.com>. *Photo by Carl Sloan.*

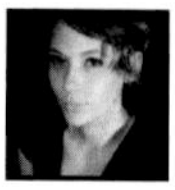

JOËLLE JONES spends her nights bartending and filling her sketchbook with images destined for future comics. She currently resides in Portland, Oregon, and her next project will be *12 Reasons Why I Love Her*, a collaboration with writer Jamie S. Rich, due from Oni Press in 2006.

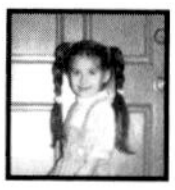

By age eight, **VIOLET KITCHEN** had already been featured in *Comic Book Artist* (twice) and *Comics Buyer's Guide*, and had been praised by *Publishers Weekly*. Alexa's first hardcover book—*Drawing Comics is Easy!*—was published in 2006.

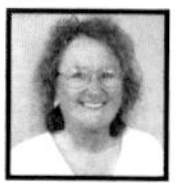

Inkpot Award–winner **LEE MARRS** is author/artist of hundreds of titles, reprinted in nine countries, for such characters as *Pudge, Girl Blimp*; *Batman*; *Wonder Woman*; and *Indiana Jones*. Also an Emmy Award–winning TV art director, Lee was a pioneer in computer graphics animation, with clients such as Disney/ABC, Apple Computer, IBM, Nickelodeon, Electronic Arts, and MTV. Her current comics can be found at DailyCandy. *Photo by Mike Friedrich.*

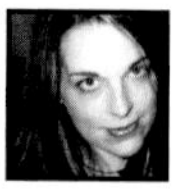

SARAH GRACE McCANDLESS's first novel, *Grosse Pointe Girl: Tales from a Suburban Adolescence* (Simon & Schuster) received accolades from *People* and *Entertainment Weekly*. Sarah Grace currently lives in Washington, D.C., and writes for various publications, including DailyCandy and *Venus Magazine*. Her second novel, *the girl i wanted to be*, was available from Simon & Schuster in June 2006.

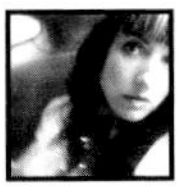

LAURENN McCUBBIN was the art director for Image Comics. She is also the illustrator of *Rent Girl* by Michelle Tea (Last Gasp), and the Xeric Award–winning *XXX LIVENUDEGIRLS* with Nikki Coffman. She will have work in *McSweeney's* #17 and in the anthology *Stumbling and Raging* (MacAdam/Cage). Her illustrations have been featured everywhere from Boing Boing to the *New York Times* to *On Our Backs*, and you can see more at <www.laurennmccubbin.com>.

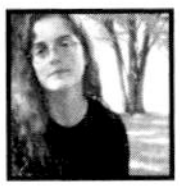

CARLA SPEED McNEIL is the writer, artist, and publisher of the critically acclaimed series *Finder*. Her company, Lightspeed Press, has released seven collections of the multiple Ignatz Award–winning comic so far. Carla was raised in southern Louisiana, and now resides peacefully in Maryland with a husband, two kids in various stages of development, and several large house pets. *Photo by Antony Johnston.*

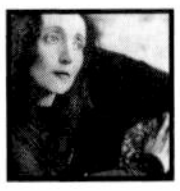

Guggenheim fellow, three-time Pulitzer Prize finalist, and *New York Times* best-selling author **JOYCE CAROL OATES** is a prolific novelist with over fifty books and hundreds of short stories to her credit. Among her many awards are the PEN/Malamud Award for Excellence in Short Fiction, the Kenyon Review Award for Literary Achievement, the Common Wealth Award for Distinguished Service in Literature, and the National Book Award. The cofounder and editor of the *Ontario Review* literary magazine, Ms. Oates teaches creative writing at Princeton University. This is the first time her work has been adapted to comics. *Photo by Marion Ettlinger.*

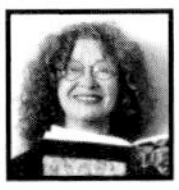

Retired cartoonist and award-winning writer **TRINA ROBBINS** calls herself a feminist pop culture "herstorian." She has produced a dozen books on various aspects of women's history in as many years, writing about dark goddesses, women who kill, women who create comics, and Irish women. She has written comics as diverse as *Wonder Woman* and *The Powerpuff Girls*, as well as her own ongoing graphic novel series *GoGirl!*, drawn by Anne Timmons. *Photo by Steve Leialoha.*

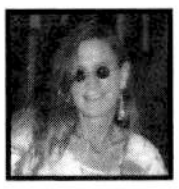

DIANA SCHUTZ iis a former editor-in-chief at Dark Horse Comics and an adjunct instructor of comics history and criticism at Portland Community College. *Photo by Leo Bossy.*

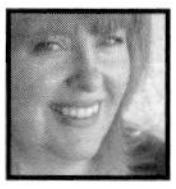

Former hairdresser **GAIL SIMONE** is one of the busiest writers in comics. She's written *Deadpool*, *Agent X*, and *X-Men Unlimited* for Marvel Comics, *Killer Princesses* for Oni Press, *Simpsons* material for Bongo Comics, and *Action*, *Birds of Prey*, *Rose and Thorn*, and *Teen Titans* for DC, among others, as well as an episode of the *Justice League Unlimited* animated series. She lives on the Oregon coast with her husband, son, and two dogs.

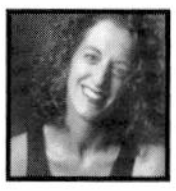

JILL THOMPSON has been drawing comics professionally for a good long time. She really enjoys it and has no plans to stop. Jill is the creator of *Scary Godmother*, published by Sirius Entertainment and seen on Cartoon Network. *Photo by Dano Martin*.

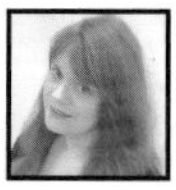

In addition to illustrating the Lulu Award-winning comic *GoGirl!*, Oregon native **ANNE TIMMONS** has done work for *Wired*, GT Labs, *Comic Book Artist*, and Malibu Comics, among others. The titles have ranged from *Star Trek: Deep Space Nine* to the Eisner Award–nominated *Dignifying Science*. She has also worked on the graphic novel *Jane Goodall, Animal Scientist* for Capstone Press. *Photo by Donald Johnson*.

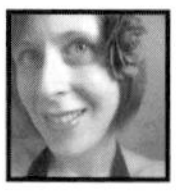

REBECCA WOODS has been involved in the comic book industry in one way or another for the past ten years. She is a member of Mercury Studios and lives with her family in Portland, Oregon.

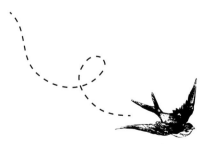

MORE TITLES FROM MULTIPLE EISNER AWARD-WINNING CREATOR

JILL THOMPSON

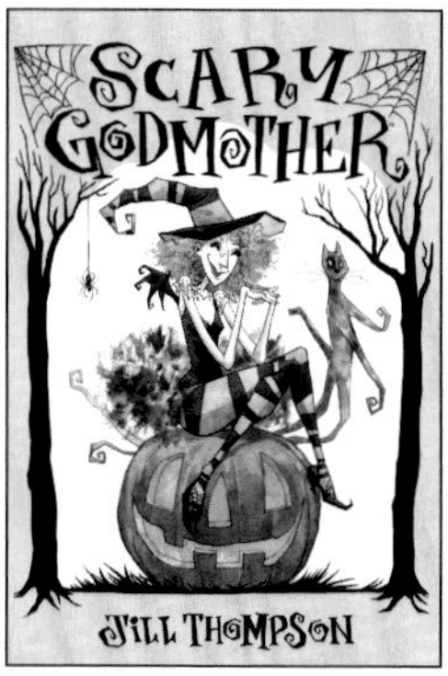
SCARY GODMOTHER
JILL THOMPSON

SCARY GODMOTHER OMNIBUS

By Jill Thompson

The definitive collection of the hit series that has been adapted into two animated specials and a stage show, full of strange happenings, kind monsters, and Halloween adventures sure to delight and spook young and old alike!

ISBN 978-1-50671-620-6 | $29.99

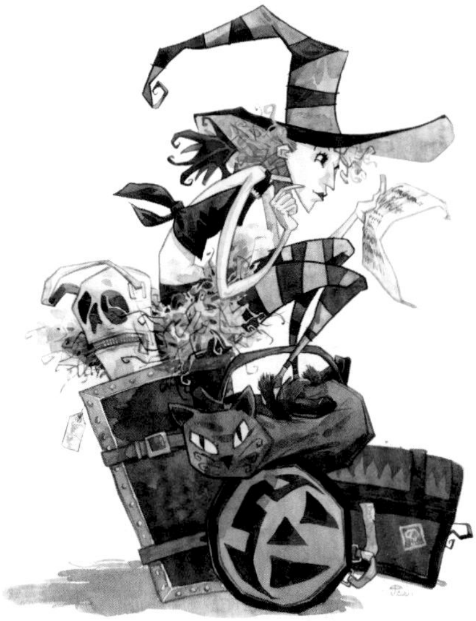

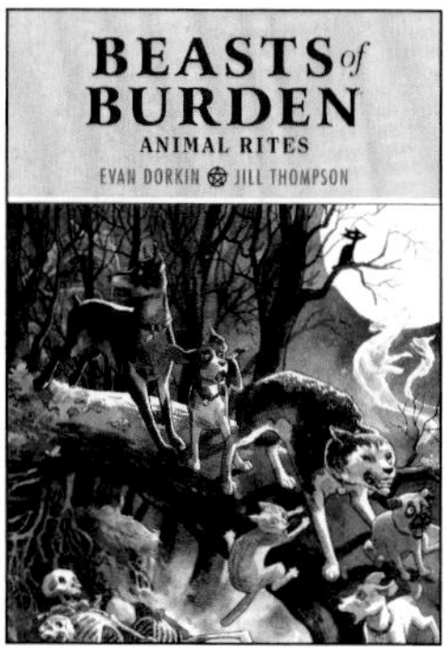
BEASTS of BURDEN
ANIMAL RITES
EVAN DORKIN JILL THOMPSON

BEASTS OF BURDEN: ANIMAL RITES

Written by Evan Dorkin, art by Jill Thompson

Beneath its surface of green lawns and white picket fences, the picturesque little town of Burden Hill harbors dark and sinister secrets. It's up to a heroic gang of dogs—and one cat—to protect the town from the evil forces at work. Adventure, mystery, horror, and humor thrive on every page!

ISBN 978-1-50670-636-8 | $19.99

BEASTS OF BURDEN: NEIGHBORHOOD WATCH

Written by Evan Dorkin, Sara Dyer, and Mike Mignola; art by Jill Thompson and Benjamin Dewey

As a growing evil threatens to overwhelm their town, the animals find themselves some unlikely allies, most notably a seasoned paranormal investigator named . . . Hellboy.

ISBN 978-1-50671-410-3 | $22.99

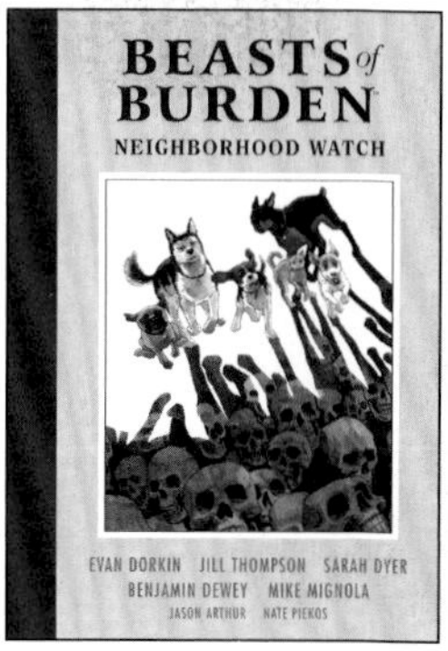
BEASTS of BURDEN
NEIGHBORHOOD WATCH
EVAN DORKIN JILL THOMPSON SARAH DYER
BENJAMIN DEWEY MIKE MIGNOLA
JASON ARTHUR NATE PIEKOS

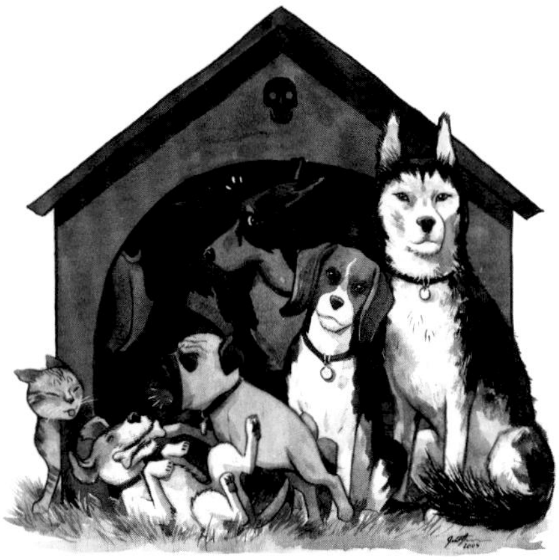

THE DARK HORSE BOOK OF HORROR

Written by Mike Mignola, Paul Chadwick, Kurt Busiek, and others; art by Jill Thompson, P. Craig Russell, Gary Gianni, and others

Mike Mignola, Jill Thompson, and a roster of great creators and characters explore the dark corners of the horror genre in thirty-five stories of witchcraft, ghosts, and the risen dead. Originally published in four award-winning anthologies, these stories featured the debut of Evan Dorkin and Jill Thompson's *Beasts of Burden* series.

ISBN 978-1-50670-372-5 | $19.99

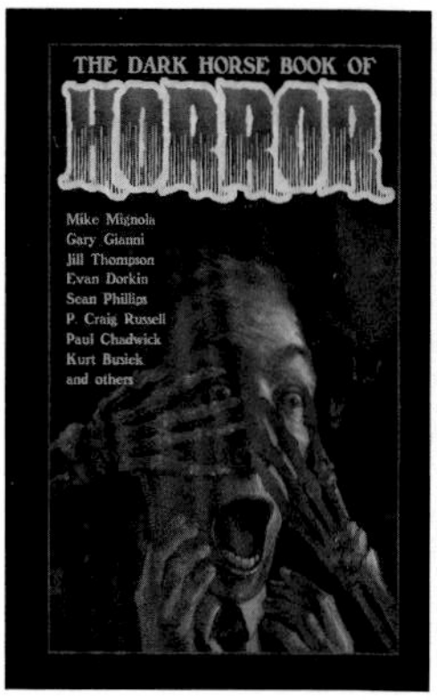
THE DARK HORSE BOOK OF
HORROR
Mike Mignola
Gary Gianni
Jill Thompson
Evan Dorkin
Sean Phillips
P. Craig Russell
Paul Chadwick
Kurt Busiek
and others

www.thescarygodmother.com
thejillthompson thejillthompson

AVAILABLE AT YOUR LOCAL COMICS SHOP OR BOOKSTORE! • To find a comics shop in your area, visit comicshoplocator.com.
For more information or to order direct visit DarkHorse.com